You will say, Christ saith this,

and the apostles say this;

but what canst thou say?

Art thou a child of Light and

hast walked in the Light, and

what thou speakest is it inwardly

from God?

George Fox 1652

ISBN 0-9751579-1-4
This We Can Say: Australian Quaker Life, Faith and Thought

© 2003 Australia Yearly Meeting of the Religious Society of Friends (Quakers) Inc
PO Box 108, Armadale North, Victoria 3143
Website: www.quakers.org.au

Design by Design Edge, Canberra
Printed by New Millenium Print, Canberra

this we can say
AUSTRALIAN QUAKER LIFE, FAITH AND THOUGHT

Australia Yearly Meeting
of The Religious Society
of Friends (Quakers) Inc

Contents

Introduction			**vi**
1	**Inspiration: our faith**		**1**
	1.1	experiences of the Spirit	3
	1.16	images of God in creativity	12
	1.34	in science	20
	1.42	in place	24
	1.64	faith traditions	41
2	**The Religious Society of Friends: our practice**		**65**
	2.5	silence, stillness	70
	2.15	listening, meeting for worship	76
	2.37	meeting for worship for business	86
	2.44	membership	92
	2.49	clearness meetings	94
	2.51	leadings and concerns	96
	2.59	sense of community	104
3	**Living our faith**		**113**
	3.1	faith in action	115
	3.7	prayer	118
	3.16	service, justice	125
	3.31	lives speak	132
	3.45	our testimonies equality	144
	3.53	truthfulness and integrity	148
	3.58	community, caring, healing	151
	3.79	simplicity	162
	3.86	peace	165

4	**Finding our way through life**		**197**
	4.2	life stages	childhood	199
	4.8		youth	202
	4.12		relationships	206
	4.29		death	218
	4.38	life challenges		222
			disability	223
	4.42		illness	226
	4.52		stress	232
5	**Facing the challenges of time and place**		**239**
	5.2	children and young people		241
	5.9	indigenous people		246
	5.37	this land		268
	5.53	our region		277
	5.62	our world		285
6	**Advices and queries** (Britain Yearly Meeting 1994)		**295**
7	**Historical perspective**		**307**

References — 325

- Glossary — 326
- Sources — 329
- Contributors — 341
- Subject index — 344
- Acknowledgments — 351
- James Backhouse Lectures — 352

Introduction

This collection of writings is in the time-honoured tradition of Quaker faith and practice books. It introduces the beliefs and practices of the Religious Society of Friends (Quakers) as they have developed in Australia. The move for this book began in 1993 among Canberra Friends who felt that it was time to collect Quaker writings to reflect Australian experiences and to offer inspiration for the 21st century. Up till now we have relied on faith and practice books published by Britain Yearly Meeting and these are still much loved resources.

Australia Yearly Meeting Faith and Practice Committee began a process of wide consultation in 1994. Through various themes and workshops, Friends from all over Australia contributed items to five working papers, published between 1996 and 2000. Wide discussion of those writings led to the drafting of a first chapter in 2001, accepted at the annual gathering of Australian Friends in January 2002. We completed the remaining chapters during 2002 and reworked the manuscript in 2003.

Undoubtedly this first Australian version will be revised from time to time. Its focus is perhaps more contemporary than we had expected. It includes inspirational writings and personal stories about challenge and opportunity, which reflect on the geography and social history of this land. Nevertheless, traces of the history of Quakerism in Australia are evident in some much older writings, and a special chapter gives a fuller account of this history.

You will notice some shaded paragraphs throughout the book. These are valued quotations from other Quaker writings, which have been included to illuminate the international, historical roots of our beliefs and practices. For the most part, however, the writings are by members and attenders of Australian Quaker meetings. We have edited the items to make their points as concisely as possible, indicating omissions (by '...') only where necessary to preserve meaning. We hope that readers will seek out the original sources. Many items refer to key concepts such as 'the inner light', and 'that of God in everyone'. Words which have particular meaning in the Quaker community are explained in the Glossary. The inspirational work of visual artists and musicians has made an important contribution to the form of this book. These items recognise the importance of creativity in communicating the Spirit's presence.

Our purpose is to introduce the reader to our faith: what inspires us; our images of God; our ways of conducting our work and worship in community, in unity. Quaker practices revolve around the importance of meeting quietly together in worship, waiting for the guidance of the Spirit within each one of us. Sometimes we feel prompted to share how we experience the Spirit working in and through us. This leads Quakers everywhere to strive to live by the principles of equality, truthfulness, integrity, simplicity, and peace. In Australia we are inspired and challenged in special ways by this ancient land and our varied heritages. We sense there is still much to learn, much that will change us.

These writings come together as rays of light from a great variety of individuals. We hope they inspire you to seek the stillness within you, from which loving words and actions grow.

inspiration

1

Susannah Brindle

1 INSPIRATION: OUR FAITH

Experiences of the Spirit

1.1 *'Spirit Now' was the theme of Australia Yearly Meeting's summer school 2001*

We affirm that the Spirit is everywhere and always accessible.

We affirm that the Spirit is shaped by the mysteries and contrasts of the ancient Australian landscape, the climate, our rivers and oceans.

We affirm our need to be open to the Spirit in Indigenous cultures.

We affirm that ordinary experiences of life — imperfections, yearnings, birth, suffering and death, nature, beauty, art and science — are the Spirit.

We affirm that the Spirit is in goodwill, in small acts of kindness and in being utterly truthful.

We affirm that being held in the Spirit is a way through brokenness, darkness and sorrow.

We affirm that the Spirit is breath, hope, light, love, dancing, singing, laughing, creativity, wholeness, connectedness, focus, integration, courage, journeying and leadings.

We affirm that the Spirit is unsettling, paradoxical and doesn't necessarily follow our timing.

We affirm that the Spirit is in all our ways of living and working.

We affirm that the Spirit shines through our connections with, and support for each other, and our community.

We affirm the need for stillness to listen in silence to the Spirit.

We affirm the utter availability of the Spirit of God.

Australia Yearly Meeting 2001

1.2 Quakers don't look to a leader or a book for the answers; we turn to the Spirit. Listening to others who are experienced and reading books where people have explored their experience with the Spirit provide important ground work for all of us, but in the end we come back to George Fox's 'What canst thou say?'

Our authority is the Spirit. This is a huge and exciting challenge for us. We need to practise our faith by learning to let go of our burning passions and our daily concerns; learning to get to that place within us where we are centred, where we listen to the Spirit. This is what we practise in meeting for worship and what we practise in meeting for worship for business. In that centred place our decisions will flow from the Spirit.

Jenny Spinks 1995

1.3 And when all my hopes in them [priests and preachers] and in all men were gone, so that I had nothing outwardly to help me, nor could tell what to do, then, oh then, I heard a voice which said, 'There is one, even Christ Jesus, that can speak to thy condition', and when I heard it my heart did leap for joy.

George Fox 1647

1.4 No matter how immense a concept one can describe, God is bigger. The best I can do is say I believe God is Spirit, way, way, way, beyond male or female. To give any of the attributes of humankind to God is too limiting. God is involved in the entire universe and yet still able to be a personal friend, comforter and help to us individually. God's nature is love and if we can submit our will to God's, many things are accomplished. Not always the way we would expect, or in the time frame we would like. But the solution is always more appropriate than anything we could have dreamed up ourselves.

Elaine Polglase 1997

1.5   Thomas Muntzer (born before 1490, died 1525) described the Holy Spirit in terms of the inner Light, a concept of great comfort to Quakers. Perhaps the illumination is reflected from an external source (that is, a transcendent God, up there away in heaven), but more importantly it is inherent (that is, part of our deepest being, internal, behind even our unconscious selves). Not quite the same as the conscience either, which arises largely from upbringing. Nor the same as ecstasy, which can be induced by drugs, or mania, as well as religious fervour. Two words which better indicate the flavour of the inner Light are 'inspired' and 'connected'.

Most people would modestly deny having been inspired to the degree that Jesus was, say, or even Shakespeare or Beethoven. But it is not uncommon to be able to recall rare peak moments of amazement, of discovery, intuition or creativity, which make you aware of intensities of living beyond the everyday. This is what being inspired means, as though you are infused by the energy of an invisible hypnotist, maybe from within oneself.
A sudden view of sublime beauty, the 'ah-ha' experience of abruptly overcoming a significant problem, examples of extreme self-sacrifice, great danger, death, uplifting oratory, certain music — such awaken responses quite out of the ordinary. There is a profound consciousness of deeper levels to life, which is at the root of the religious quest. All can be negated by preoccupation with the ephemeral, but it often leads to a hunger to live in harmony with almost unknowable, underlying, eternal, powerful forces. A feature of the inner Light which contrasts with the significance of rare peak experiences is the sweetness of lives we see lived quietly in harmony with it.

Edward Linacre 2000

1.6   At last, after all my distresses, wanderings and sore travails, I met with some writings of this people called Quakers, which I cast a slight eye upon and disdained, as falling very short of that wisdom, light, life and power, which I had been longing for and searching after. After a long time, I was invited to hear one of them (as I had been often, they in tender love pitying me and feeling my want of that which they possessed). When I came, I felt the presence and power of the Most High among them, and words of truth from the Spirit of truth reaching to my heart and conscience, opening my state as in the presence of the Lord. Yea, I did not only feel words and demonstrations from without, but I felt the dead quickened, the seed raised; insomuch as my heart, in the certainty of light and clearness of true sense, said: 'This is he; this is he; there is no other; this is he whom I have waited for and sought after from my childhood, who was always near me, and had often begotten life in my heart, but I knew him not distinctly, nor how to receive him or dwell with him.'

What shall I say? I have met with the true peace, the true righteousness, the true holiness, the true rest of the soul, the everlasting habitation which the redeemed dwell in.

Isaac Penington 1667

1.7   My motive for taking the inward journey was not curiosity, nor was it a wish for intellectual enlightenment, nor in order to gain power. Neither was it remedial. It was simply that the world had failed me and, being earth-empty, I longed with my whole strength for the eternal love, the eternal truth that I felt was hidden in God himself.

To long for and listen for the divine spirit may be called prayer, or meditation, or communing with nature. This I did every day for short or long periods until, one evening out of the listening silence a vibrant voice sang: 'Come unto me..... O come unto me.....' and my soul trembled, and my heart melted at the love and truth in the tones.

Ruth Sansom 1971

1.8 I had a very religious boyhood and youth. When I went to university, I studied philosophy, partly because the philosophers were the only ones in the university who spoke about God in a serious way. But they were very strongly atheist. They were good, friendly, highly intelligent, and helpful, but they were unrelenting in their atheism. Moreover, it was often implied that there was something dishonest about religious belief, that it involved deliberate self-deception.

I pursued my religious enquiries in this context for years, and in my seventh or eighth year, when I was well into my Ph.D., studying alone in the library, I felt that I was flooded by God's life, so that it was within and around me, powerful, undeniable, loving, peaceful, and joyful. The experience lasted about twenty minutes. It happened again next day, also for about twenty minutes.

There was a slightly curious aspect of the experience, or rather, my reaction to it. The experience was not overwhelming in the sense that it made me incapable of doing anything else. After I had been wondering at it delightedly for about fifteen minutes, I asked myself what else I should be doing, a question that embarrassed me.

It was only later that I realised that the experience wasn't meant to occupy my whole life, and that it could co-exist simultaneously with ordinary mundane pursuits. Since then, I have sometimes been aware, for days at a time, of God's love and peace within, in a less intense way, as I went about my daily business. This experience was never as engulfing as the ones in the library, and at its strongest, was exactly as Friend Marmaduke Stevenson wrote in 1655:

> I was filled with the love and presence of the living God, which did ravish my heart when I felt it, for it did increase and abound in me like a living stream, so did the life and love of God run through me like a precious ointment giving a pleasant smell.

Reg Naulty 1999

1.9 I was convinced before I ever heard of Friends. I was convinced that I could experience God in my life directly. This happened at a time that I needed a push, a 'prompting', and it came unexpectedly, but in a way that I knew somehow was from God.

Convincement seems such a good way to describe the process. It could be compared with conversion, but to my mind the latter implies that you were turned away from God, and now you are turning back. Friends believe we are always with God, and so we cannot be completely turned away. Convincement is a recognition of something that you may have always suspected was there within you, and outside of you at the same time.

Convincement is not necessarily something that happens in a blinding flash. It can be a slow process, a testing time, but at some point, there is a part of you that says 'I know'. Certainly not 'I know it all', and definitely not 'I know, therefore I am right', but perhaps 'I know enough to keep going'.

It can be a difficult line to tread — assurance in one's belief and a heart that is open to the Light whatever its source.

Michael Jones 2000

1.10   It happened one night in October 1960. I felt I had experienced something very basic and important, something which seemed very real and genuine, personal, liberating, caring, practical, not at all 'airy-fairy' — goodly, godly, God. An experience of what's beyond the cloud of unknowing. What I had read about and not understood, something many people had experienced, in their own existential way, and tried to describe (the indescribable) in their own words which were often off-putting — vision, miracle, voices from heaven, a Damascus Road experience. I was sure that it was what I had searched for, intellectually, and not found. And now, when I was not expecting it, it had found me, hit me on the head, opened my eyes, in a mystical way — almost laughably appropriate for a so-called hard-nosed scientist! Lots of things about my life seemed to fall into place and into perspective. I had to a large extent been trying to live life along Old Testament lines, according to rules, but now it was the New Testament perspective, 'the good news' that I was experiencing. But where, then, did Jesus Christ come into it? I couldn't figure that out; but lots of things about him and about the New Testament seemed to come alive, to be understandable, to be very simple, common sense. I felt that he, or his influence, or shadow, or spirit was definitely involved — so closely that I couldn't see it, like spectacles close up to the eyes.

Malcolm Whyte 1991

1.11   I spent a couple of weeks on the west coast of Scotland roaming the hills and taking photographs. One day I was sitting on top of a small hill, every blade of grass feels clear in my memory. In the far distance are the Scottish islands and down below me is a small bay with cattle wandering around. Below, to the right is a dilapidated wall. The sky is full of puffy summer clouds. I am sitting and feeling warm. Suddenly I feel connected to everything in the universe. The energy of everything in the universe is passing through my body.

This was one of my life's major turning points. After years of rejecting God, because of my experience in the Church and my scientific training, I still recognised this experience as a fundamental recognition of the importance of my spiritual life. It was so overwhelming the only thing to do was cry tears of connectedness.

Drew Lawson 1995

1.12   The phrase 'Spirit of Place' reminds me of my reflections when I sit on the back verandah at home, looking over the gum tree valley behind and below our house. One morning I had a powerful sense of love and tenderness in the air, streaming through the gully and around the suburb and throughout the world. I pictured how it would be if everyone was touched by this spirit and if we all sat silently on our back steps, as a community of neighbours, worshipping this tender goodness together.

As I came out of this meditative moment, my mind put words to it. With great wonder, I thought, 'It's a spirit of holiness.' I thought I'd discovered something. Then I realised that 'the Holy Spirit' is one of those phrases from my Anglican childhood that I had rejected as hackneyed and meaningless. Now my perception of holiness was fresh and personal. I felt God was very lovingly tickling my ribs and laughing at me.

Sue Wilson 1996

1.13   Integrating transcendent experience into ordinary life is a lifelong task. For most of us such experiences are rare, or occur in clusters, and our lives need time to catch up. Unexpected encounters with the divine are apt to take some getting used to. We have to accept the authenticity of the experience, despite its otherness; and then let go as it unsettles our complacency and rearranges our lives.

Ursula Jane O'Shea 1993

1.14   'God' has become the spiritual force it is, through the cumulative strength of the love, courage, wisdom and goodness that has been expressed through all the stages of evolution in however small a degree. The stilling of our spirits in the attitude of mind known as prayer is the switch that tunes us to 'God'. To me 'God' is power, not person. We add to the stature of 'God' by the way we meet adverse circumstances, by the expression of love, unselfishness, service and compassion. Those of us who are weaker can draw the leaven for our spiritual growth from what has been given to us. Thus everyone has a part to play in the ever-continuing creation of that omniscient force to which we give the name 'God'.

Nancie Hewitt 1982

1.15   There is a Divine Center into which your life can slip, a new and absolute orientation in God, a Center where you live with Him and out of which you see all of life through new and radiant vision...

Thomas Kelly 1938

Images of God in creativity, science and place

Creativity

1.16   It seems to me that we are each created for the Spirit to live in and that when we open ourselves to that indwelling, we are the heart and even the mind of God. The Creator and the created become one.

Ruth Sansom 1987

1.17   [Early Friends] made the discovery that silence is one of the best preparations for communion and for the reception of inspiration and guidance. Silence itself, of course, has no magic. It may be just sheer emptiness, absence of words or noise or music. It may be an occasion for slumber, or it may be a dead form. But it may be an intensified pause, a vitalised hush, a creative quiet, an actual moment of mutual and reciprocal correspondence with God.

Rufus Jones 1937

1.18   I have come to realise that this marvellous light is present in speech and in silence. The light dances in both places if we let go enough to see it. As it dances in silence, it dances in the noise of life itself. It is all around, here, now.

Max Raupach 1990

1.19   Spirit of the Cathedral

Whatever is beautiful, whatever rouses
The heart from its complacent sleep, says
'Man, you are more than man, more
Than a repository of birth and death' — such beauty,
Before the creative chisel of the mind
Shaped it in stone or wood, music
Or colour, lay in the Imagination's eye,
The retina of God.

Clive Sansom 1958

1.20   Each of us possesses this 'inward eye' which gives, not merely sight, but in-sight.

Clive Sansom 1965

1.21   When I come into the meeting house and find a pleasant arrangement of flowers on a small table centred in the meeting room or look out through the windows to find the world framed in such a way that I may visually absorb the richness of the flora and fauna before my eyes, I am quietly reminded that these sights create a 'decoration for the soul'.

These words came to me as a gift from my art teacher recently when our painting group sat discussing why we make art and what gives us inspiration. He said, 'Just look around you. Look at the scenery out there! Now look at the fruit on our table. We make art and arrange various things with care because it's how we decorate our souls!' His simple phrase made me pause in silence. I now begin my days by observing better how I may decorate my soul.

Roberta Turner 2003

1.22   Along the paths of the imagination the artist and mystic make contact. The revelations of God are not all of one kind. Always the search in art, as in religion, is for the rhythms of relationships, for the unity, the urge, the mystery, the wonder of life that is presented in great art and true religion.

Horace Pointing 1944

1.23   It isn't just a question of being artistic or not. It is a worshipful activity; it is a way of celebrating beauty. It is a form of ministry given to all of us to offer in one form or another, all valuable; it is a form of ministry which we can all receive with gratitude — be it music, pottery, painting, poetry, knitting or writing. Creativity and spirituality are very close together. Perhaps they are the same.

Frances Parsons 1997

1.24   **Muse frustrated**

A poem trembles on my lips;
It vanishes in air
Because of dirty dishes
And dust upon the stair.

A painting blossoms in my eyes;
It mists and fades away
Because the beds are rumpled
And it is washing day.

A sculpture forms within my hands;
It falls away and goes
To where my other visions lie
Beneath unmended clothes.

Break, break my bonds, unloose me
From guilt of undone chores
And I will be creative
Upon unpolished floors.

Bridget Hodgkin 1966

1.25   Creativity is the gift that we were given on the eighth day of creation. In naming and re-making the world we are co-workers with God, and whether we are making a meal, a painting, a piece of furniture or a computer program, we are sharing in an ongoing act of creation through which the world is constantly re-made.

Jo Farrow 1994

1.26   Garden Ministry

It's early winter and I've been working in the garden. At first, gazing at the carpet of brown from which protruded bare-boughed shrubs and trees, I wondered how much to leave Nature to itself. Was this not the perfect mulch, already in place?

As I started to rake up the leaves I saw the shape of the garden begin to emerge. I felt I was opening the garden up and allowing it to breathe. When I saw how pale the shoots under the sodden mass of leaves were, how bent and crushed the blooms of violets and stems of primulas, I knew it was worth clearing the debris.

Deeply absorbed in my task I found it was a process working through me on many levels. In the house I have been clearing a space. In my life I am sorting through papers and throwing out old letters. It is all a letting go, moving with the season. Like the stark trees there is simplicity and truth in a return to the essence.

I rested on my rake a minute and it was a sheer joy to watch a sleek, strong-billed butcher bird swoop past my shoulder. It had been perched on a low branch in one of the enormous chestnut trees at the bottom of the garden, source of most of the leaves. The bird fed almost at my feet from grubs I had exposed and I realised with a jolt that one's actions are never neutral.

The next day, working under the same trees, I was surrounded by no less than four kookaburras. It was awe-inspiring to pass to and fro within a couple of inches of the nearest one. The bird did not move. I could see every detail of its feathers, their colour and texture. I could feel the kookaburra's strength and power — then, suddenly, also feel the struggle of the spider in its bill. In the garden I was filled with a heightened sense of presence and of large forces at work in the world.

Working in the garden was a gift. At first I wanted to go on raking leaves for ever but after a while all I wanted was to finish! Each moment has its time and I needed to move on. It's mid-winter now and the year is turning. Bright daffodils are in flower and camellia buds are opening. The garden is doing its own work, greening and growing.

Kerstin Reimers 1996

1.27 We must train our minds through creative thought and imagination 'til we can observe ourselves changing what is negative into positive. Creative thought is not an intellectual exercise but a development of awareness, with meditation being the surest way to this awareness.

Dorothy Gibbons 1988

1.28 I believe art is a necessity for everyone, and not a luxury for the few. Art is an essential part of the trinity of life's values. There are three spiritual values and three only: goodness, truth and beauty and these three are interwoven into the fabric of our personalities.

Ernest Unwin 1935

1.29 Most men and women are divided beings — divided in their selves; or separated from God; or apart from other people; or forgetting their connection with the natural world they share with trees and animals and birds. The most potent unifying factor is the creative imagination, which includes the faculty of love. This is the binding, shaping, reconciling influence.

Clive Sansom 1965

1.30   I love music, yet a hundred years ago, and still more in the hundred years before that, Quakers disapproved of music as liable to distract a person's thoughts from God. Yet throughout human history music has always been a means of spiritual uplift and intercession, from the beating of a hollow log to the mystical heights of Palestrina or Handel in *Messiah*. It can sometimes lift me onto a different plane where I feel almost in tune with the universe. I don't think that it is distracting me from God. I think it is a part of God.

Kelsey Aves 1996

1.31   In 1990 I began to see a correlation between my healing process and my artistic process. The symbols I was using reflected my inner state and being. It was in 1995 that I received a book called *Creative Mandalas* by Susanne F. Fincher. I began consciously to use mandala drawing or circle drawings, using colour and form. From this process I became aware that I could express and release feelings and unconscious issues. This would lead to a feeling of resolution.

Before I begin a creative process, I go through what I call the 'birth process'. I feel anxious and restless and usually frustrated. Then I prepare my work space and collect materials. After centring myself I am ready to begin. Afterwards there needs to be a time for reflection.

Leanne Mooney 1997

1.32   I've been learning the discipline of everyday writing and painting (art-making). Not waiting for inspiration to strike: creating the environment, the time, the space for inspiration. I started out stealing half-an-hour each day from the busyness of life. I hid in the spare room refusing to answer the door, the phone. Half-an-hour slipped into two, three, four hours.

Now my art-making process is like a feast. I love the words. I love playing with words. I love experimenting with paint. Firstly, I banish all 'shoulds' and 'nots'. I allow the unexpected; stretching words and paint beyond the usual.

The main course involves crafting the words, honing the text or image into a work that surprises, challenges, supports, excites and catches the reader's breath. It involves waiting — taking breath between bites. I let the work rest for days, sometimes weeks or months. That way when I return to the work I see clearly what needs to change, and have developed the courage to cut out the bits I most loved at the start — all because the integrity of the work comes first.

The art-making process is meditative and uncomfortable; I enter the state of heightened awareness yet I'm resting at the same time. It's exciting. It teaches me wisdom. Emerson said, 'All honest work is prayer.' For me, the process of art-making involves following my leadings: knowing how to wait; trusting I will know the 'when', 'how', 'what'; giving time to the discipline of everyday art-making; holding back from publishing the first draft; and learning to work, wait, work until the work sings.

Deborah Faeyrglenn 2001

1.33 While Friends have been among the pioneers of modern science, they have, until recent years, repressed all taste for the fine arts. These, at their greatest, always contain some revelation of the spirit of God, which is in the fullest harmony with our spiritual faith. In the fields of music, art and literature, as in others, Friends may witness to the glory of God and advance that glory by their service. 'The fulness of the whole earth is his glory', and we mar the beauty of this message by every limitation we set upon it.

William Charles Braithwaite 1895

Science

1.34   After more than three score years and ten I have come to a profound realisation of the interconnectedness of all creation. All creation is in God, God is in all creation.

I commit myself to the Mystery.

Joan Roberts 1995

1.35   The mystery of life is already in evidence. In a sense it does not matter where life originated, for wherever it was the mystery remains: how combinations of carbon, oxygen, hydrogen, nitrogen and sulphur evolve all the way into a brain! Perhaps we are not meant to know the answers to the deepest questions?

Andrew Glikson 2000

1.36   Today science is rediscovering the creative mystery of the universe. The old self-assurance is largely gone. Within the first quarter of the twentieth century a revolution has taken place. The laws of mechanics no longer explain all things. The intellect of man has become aware of something strange and unpredictable at the very heart of existence. Matter and radiation have assumed a complexity which was hardly guessed at in the 1800s. The exploration of the minute structure of matter seems to take us as far into the unknown as does the exploration of the farthest reaches of space.

Howard Brinton 1931

1.37   The more we approach this realm of higher aspirations, the realm where we can doubt even our own reason, the more necessary it will become to use criteria other than those of abstract reasoning. Here the exact equations of science give way to the metaphors of poetry and to the myths and parables of religion. Certainly they are less exact, but they are not indefinite, and are closer to truth in those fields in which another approach to truth is impossible. The conviction that all claims of being in possession of the final truth are unjustified and even dangerous to human brotherhood and humility has made me a Quaker. It may appear paradoxical but nevertheless true that we may be able to approach God in our whole living and being more closely than by rational thinking.

Rudolph Lemberg 1979

1.38   God is the spirit of creation of all things: of good and evil, of past, present and future, and of the earth and the cosmos. It's hard to have a spirit without a face, so for convenience I say God encompasses the he, the she and the it. I do see God in the trees, clouds, earth, stones, stars, and in all the creatures that I cannot see with the naked eye.

To me creation is not based on a hierarchical structure with God on top, and man underneath, with everything else under him. I see a wavy oval shape with humans as part of the ecological chain. I believe it is our responsibility to cherish and nurture the earth and to take that attitude when we go out into space. We have finite resources, and we need to be good stewards for the wellbeing of the earth and our own spirits.

Gabrielle Watt 2000

1.39 Whilst it is not vitally necessary for our survival to have a knowledge of the fact that our planet is hurtling through space at 800,000 kilometres an hour, it is crucial for our survival to realise that we are all part of a greater reality, which unifies us. Seers down the ages have always proclaimed this truth and it is enshrined in the sacred scriptures of the world's religions. Marcus Aurelius wrote (AD 151):

> All things are interwoven with one another; a sacred bond unites them. Everything is co-ordinated, everything works together in giving form to the One Universe. The world order is a unity made up of multiplicity. God is One, pervading all things; all being is one, all truth is one and the path to perfection is reached by myriad ways for beings that are alike in kind and spirit.

There are hopeful signs that we are increasingly recognising the inter-relatedness and unity within the world. How can we live out the reality of this unifying power in our everyday lives?

Leonce Richards 1994

1.40 George Fox saw the ocean of darkness and death, but he also saw an infinite ocean of light and love flow over it. Though he wisely admonished us not to dwell on evil, I believe that had he lived today, he would have understood the importance of what science has contributed to our insight into the nature of evil — avoidable and unavoidable — and to our insight into the ocean of light. For modern science knows that regularity and purpose can grow out of individual chance events and that the whole process of evolution depends on the interplay of chance and purpose.

Rudolph Lemberg 1979

1.41

Can I, imprisoned, body-bounded, touch
The starry robe of God, and from my soul,
My tiny Part, reach forth to his great Whole,
And spread my Little to the infinite Much,
When Truth forever slips from my clutch,
And what I take indeed, I do but dole
In cupfuls from a rimless ocean-bowl
That holds a million, million, million such?

And yet, some Thing that moves among the stars,
And holds the cosmos in a web of law,
Moves too in me: a hunger, a quick thaw
Of soul that liquefies the ancient bars,
As I, a member of creation, sing
The burning oneness binding everything.

Kenneth Boulding 1993

Max Raupach

Place

1.42

Windswept Silence

These words remind me of a place away from civilization,
perhaps a desert or a plain, or even rolling fields of grain
as far as the eye can see, the heavy ears nodding, bending in
one direction at the wind's continual force.

Windswept Silence — I found these words in a Zen book on meditation.
Like the ears of grain they were heavy with meaning for me.
Windswept meant a great open space with no boundaries to block,
divide, or give shelter. And yet the silence is not alien there;
there is no choice but to feel at one
with the landscape and the force of the wind.

The breath of the Spirit blows away all boundaries,
boundaries of self, walls that I have put there and others have imposed.
The wind is free to blow where it wills, unfettered.

In the silence, deep in the silence, the boundaries fall away.
I am neither this nor that; my mind releases the clutter.
Minutes before this impedimenta seemed essential, but now it's gone,
and the calm of the windswept silence blows over me.

I am not lonely. I am beyond loneliness. I am that I am.
I feel the life force within me. I am fully aware,
awake to an inner vitality that connects to the presence of others,
here gathered in company, and reaching back over the ages.

When I return from the silent place, I am not the same,
but renewed, strengthened. I feel the Psalmist say,
'When I awake I am still with Thee'.

I think I understand people who go into desert places to find themselves,
their real selves. I feel at one with them.

Max Raupach 1989

1.43   My mother gave me a tree when I was born. It was the tradition in my moiety. To it I could go to nurture my spirit. My crying times, my happy times. It is a Moreton Bay fig which is now part of a park on Gregory Terrace, not far from the first dump in Brisbane. That is where we murris lived. I still go back to it. It is a spiritual place to visit. Some Sundays I go there and it becomes an extension of Meeting for Worship.

David Carline 1995

1.44   **Meeting at Ewaninga**

Rock before rock. The flat slab on which I kneel, and on which you knelt so many centuries ago, slopes upwards to the rock which you marked with patient striking of stone on stone.

I would know you as a brother, I would sense your continuing presence in this land and its seasons, in this life which abounds in its seeming barrenness, in the interconnectedness which you so respected and which means that nothing is lost or fails to continue. There is oneness here, and you and I are part of it. The roughness of the rock beneath our knees brings us together, the dust and sand between our toes makes us one, the fierce sunlight on our kneeling forms fires our being and our minds to a common awareness of our part in a greater whole. We meet here and this holy ground becomes yet more holy through our meeting.

How shall we talk? How shall we teach each other? The tracks of animal and insect which you read so easily, the stories of the lives of those trackmakers which you know so well, are lost to my people. The new tracks which circle this small rocky hill each day, and the stories of the lives of the trackmakers I know, were never part of your physical life although they are now made part of the experience of your people. How shall we understand each other? How shall we be a means of grace to each other?

And the word comes. Across the separation of times and cultures comes the word. 'If you would understand yourself, look to your dreamings. If you would understand me, look to my dreamings.'

Ken Carroll 1998

1.45 Though I believe as a Quaker that all places, times and seasons *are* equally sacred, I at the same time believe — and no inconsistency in this — that there are places, times and seasons that are specially sacred. I believe that the great cathedrals, Durham and Chartres and St Peters in Rome are specially sacred; that Swarthmore and Jordans are specially sacred; that Ayers Rock [Uluru] and other places of worship of the Australian Aborigines are specially sacred and there is no way in which the desecration of them can be justified. They are sacred only because at these places and these times men have regularly and with sacrifice and devotion penetrated the veil that separates us from the unseen. The veil might have been penetrated anywhere else or at any other time, or on any occasion, but these are the places where it has happened and been marked; these are the places of celebration.

John Ormerod Greenwood 1982

1.46 As I experience the primal life force, expressed in my very heart beat, in the creative mind and exuberant energy of the child, so too in the petals of the evening primrose opening before my eyes, in the unfolding of that palm frond as it reaches for the light, I stand in awe at the wonder of creation. And now I reach into my pocket for the little chip of rock given me by one of the children. She had been enchanted by the light refracted from its many surfaces and wanted to share its beauty. It was the same light I had seen reflected off the leaves of the eucalypt trees overhead during a walking meditation that morning.

God is in all creation. All creation is in God.

Lloyd Williams 1995

1.47 We shall not have to search far and wide for a common language. The voice that sounds in every cell of our human bodies, sounds as well in the rocks, vegetation, and our fellow animals. It is the mother tongue of us all. It is the breath of God, the song of the earth. In listening to this song, we shall recognise that we are never alone, but constantly affirmed as an indispensable part of the community of life. Instead of being enslaved to our culture's paralysing fear of dying, we shall welcome the time for us to become part of the earth's dark fertility and life's continuing creative energy. In learning this song we shall reclaim a religion and a cosmology which will reteach us how to live and how to die.

As we journey into the universal realms of the Spirit to prepare our hearts and minds for worship — heeding the voices and the unseen movements of the ancestors — we shall begin to live the reality of what aboriginal peoples have longed for us to know. All creation is sacred and we humans are an integral part of it.

Susannah Brindle 2000

1.48 Nature is not for humanity. Its purpose is beyond our grasp. Maybe it simply is. But if this is so, that in itself is a reason for awe, for amazement, for wonder and worship.

When I feel the need to get away and replenish my soul, I go to the sea and walk along the shore. Symbolically and literally on the edge. By being safe on the sand, yet so close to a great moving mass whose force would end my life in four quiet minutes if I did not keep watch — for the waves certainly shall not. The sea demands respect, not foolishness.

The noise of the sea hushes my mind into silent contemplation. Its enormousness puts me in my place. Yet I feel a wonderful sense of my own being. Here I know my own life and death is something beyond my understanding, and doubtless of little significance. And it doesn't matter.

For these blessed moments, at least while the water seeps between my toes, I can give myself up to sheer joy and know I am just here, now, purposelessly, but ecstatically aware of the physicality as well as the spirituality, of my 'being on the edge'. In this I realise I am worshipping my God.

Eleanor Morphet 1995

1.49   As I grew up, my most intimate connection with nature was with the ocean. The sound of the waves lulled me to sleep, the north-easterlies whipped up the waves and blew the salt spray high and inland, pruning plants and encrusting the windows. When the southerlies blew, the world was grey and at times it was all I could do to keep my feet. The ocean was a cauldron, with waves smashing and swirling at the base of the cliffs. When the wind abated and the sun shone, light sparkled from the placid surface, and the blues and greens of the sea, merging with the blue of the sky and the curling white of the breaking waves and the warm yellows and browns of the sandstone cliffs delighted the eye. On days such as these time did not matter. The clear rock pools with their many hued seaweeds, their anemones, starfish, periwinkles, limpets, scuttling crabs, tiny darting fish, pebbles, sand and shells of mother of pearl filled our world with wonder. It was an enchanted world. Each morning the sun rose over the horizon, making a golden pathway and sometimes, when I looked out my window at night, there was a silver path from the full moon to the shore.

It was easy to learn stillness, to experience awe, connectedness. As I grew older and came to be at home in the sea, to plunge into the waves was exhilarating. There was the shock of cold water, the taste of salt and then the wonder of being surrounded, upheld, of needing only to move a foot, an arm ever so slightly to be part of the immensity of this cradle of life.

Ruth Haig 1995

1.50 ...an insistent daily hunger to be out near dawn and at dusk to find my leading for the day, to celebrate life, to honour my source in nature, or to wind down and give thanks for the day. And what treats, what feasts along the way! The dolphin shooting the breakers at Cape Paterson, the brilliant orange sun burnishing the trees, the possum scurrying home in the foggy dawn as I did my T'ai Chi before my beloved gnarled gum tree in our local bush reserve.

Valwyn Beggs 1995

1.51

I feel the earth beneath me, ground of my being.
I taste the running water, living water.
I feel the air around me, the breath of God.
I hear the hum of insects, song of creation.
I see the campfire burning, the holy spirit.
I smell the food that's cooking, our daily bread.
I taste my lover's kisses, the love of Goddess.
As darkness falls around me, I know thy presence.
Walking and praying in the bush,
Walking, my soul is lifted up.
Walking and praying in the bush,
I am who I am, I am who I will become.

Helen Gould 1989

Bushwalk

INSPIRATION: OUR FAITH PLACE

1.52   Perhaps 'belonging' is not exclusively the Aboriginal prerogative we have been led to believe. Maybe it was just that those who habitually lived this way became more sensitive to their reciprocal responsibilities in the continuing cycles of nature. It was a fact of life that to ignore the principles of conservation in one season meant empty bellies for the tribe in the next season. But I suspect that a real sense of belonging stems from more than an understanding of the group impact on the surroundings. When one is confronted each night by the vast expanse of planets and stars, it is almost impossible not to be moved to awe and wonder at the mystery of it all. Under the night skies I am made humbly aware of our individual insignificance. To know at one and the same time, one's importance and one's insignificance, is to have entered a spiritual understanding of one's place in the scheme of things. Perhaps all who experience this sense of 'belonging to the land' have touched the sacred Oneness in the nature of existence.

Mary Mathews 1995

1.53   **The Desert**

Warm wind in swirling caress
Flowers covering the earth
Colouring and patterning her skin
In pastels, soft light, mystery
Peace surrounds all

Tenderness, connectedness, joy
I whisper in the wind
I hear antiquity
I have gratitude
I am not alone.

Annabelle Cameron 1999

1.54   Often for me connection with the land means a deep-rooted sense of belonging, being earthed in two places — here particularly in the Whipstick Forest where I live and in Scotland where I was born. In both there is spiritual connection, that came together for me in a creative imagination where I flew from the red earth of the Whipstick to the top of Uluru and sat at the feet of an Aboriginal elder. He accepted me and showed me that if I looked far enough in the distance I could see Iona, my Scottish spiritual home. With that came a sense of unity, of transcendence which confirmed my sense of spiritual connection to the earth and particularly where I live.

Fiona Gardner 1996

1.55   A child of just past four, I discovered the purple of the bougainvillea vine that covered the back fence. The purple flowers radiated against the strong blue of the sky: far above, a single bird flew overhead and I heard the long, mournful cry of the storm bird.

As I stood in silence I felt that time had stood still and the world had ceased to spin. I know now the word for what I felt then — adults call it 'awe'. But then I just knew the world was beautiful, and I was linked to that creation.

Some things you leave behind when you grow up. You forget the games and dreams that held you captivated when you were just a child. But that sense of awe remains. It comes again at unexpected moments — a sense of the Source of All Being.

Judith Aitchison 1999

1.56   Fresh gum tips and the blue-green roundness of new growth. Scent of the leaves crushed between fingers. Childhood walks. The taken-for-grantedness of the environment. I was a farm child, not a 'bush' child. Yet the farm was dotted with, edged by, remnants of bush which were an intrinsic part of our lives.

The big tree that dropped the twigs and bark we collected for kindling. That held the rope-and-plank swing where I learned to swing, and stretched my legs in an effort to touch *that* twiggy bit of branch. Until, one day I could, easily.

Not a wild, free bush tree. A tame, domesticated beside-the-old-chook-shed, next-to-the-drive tree. Our hang-out place, with its low-slung branch we could lean on, bounce on, ride on.

Tree that had been there before the grass, the fence, the sheds. Tree that was once part of a bushland which included that row beside the road, those over the hill in the neighbour's paddock. As far as the eye can see must once have been a forest of eucalypt, wattle, blackwood, native cherry. A sea of tree tops, subtle variations in colour, shape and size hinting at the diversity below.

Our tree. We knew no other time.

Our home, security, playground, provider, landmark of our time and place.

Catherine Heywood 1996

1.57   Most summer holidays as a child were spent, with my family, on my grandparents' beef cattle property in northern NSW. The road to their property passed over a number of high ridges covered by eucalypt forests, predominantly spotted gum, ironbark and stringybark trees. Passing through these particular forests still gives me a strong sense of being 'home', that I'm in familiar territory.

The far corner of the property included the high country of the Richmond Range, in particular Mt. Neville — locally known as 'sugarloaf' due to its distinctive shape. It was here that I first experienced stands of flooded gums, growing majestically straight and tall at the head of the mountain gullies. Their silvery white trunks seem to radiate more than simple beauty and grandeur, for whenever I see a stand of these trees my sense of self seems to fade and merge with the forest. It is difficult to find the right words to describe the experience, but is definitely a spiritual experience, where I find myself standing in silence, my thinking mind emptied to the experience of just being there in awe. On all occasions (less so if I am driving through a forest) I have felt a prolonged sense of lightness even after leaving the trees.

David King 1996

1.58　For me, the spirit of place resides in a particular tree in our garden: not even a native Australian tree, but an English oak. When Norman and I arrived in Australia and in this garden with our one-year-old daughter, the tree was probably not more than three metres high, its trunk just beginning to thicken. Now its long branches lean over and embrace the house, providing shade and coolness in summer, and letting sunlight through its branches in winter. It has grown as our children have grown and have climbed its much-loved branches. Our eldest grandchild has been climbing it for years now, with younger ones following her as they become tall and confident enough.

For the first few years here, we used to look eagerly to the tree to signal the counterparts of the seasonal changes we were used to from England: a touch of 'home'. We still look to it, though becoming used to the more subtle seasonal changes in the native bush.

When I first looked across to our garden from a distance and thought 'that's a foreign tree,' I knew something had changed. Though I am not native to this place any more than the tree is, I am at home. The tree provides shelter, not only to our family but to tree ferns and miniature palms, as well as a variety of birds: rosellas, king parrots, noisy miners, magpies, cockatoos, noisy friar birds, and at night, possums use it as a stairway to the roof. The creatures don't worry about where the tree came from.

For better or worse I am in and part of this place like the tree. The tree eats up our breathed-out carbon dioxide, breathes out the oxygen which we breathe in. I pray that those of my family tree tread lightly on the earth and are beneficial to it. The tree is my focus. Under it I live and breathe. One day my ashes may be buried under it. I am of it and it of me.

Jean Talbot 1996

1.59 [While studying eagles in Africa] at one nest, after years of visiting, I was accepted. The female eagle stayed on the nest with me and continued to incubate her eggs, single chick or brood. I could remove an egg, or a chick from beneath her, measure it and return it; take the temperature of her brood patch with a clinical thermometer. She was wild, not tame, but there was now a relationship of trust between us. Only if I touched her prey was she disturbed.

It was an intensely moving experience to enter so intimately into the life of an eagle. But it had a greater significance in the light of my growing understanding of the inter-relationships between the eagles themselves and between them and their habitat. For example:

- each pair occupies a defined territory and maintains this without combat with its neighbours; common boundaries are respected
- a pair occupies an area that it needs for survival and makes no

> - attempt to command territory beyond its requirements
> - the birds neither pollute nor exhaust their resources
> - if the food diminishes they breed less often

Such characteristics do not indicate that eagles have wisdom, foresight, consideration for others or for their environment. They are simply programmed for harmony, because harmony means survival. This is the natural order and it provides a compelling reason why we must preserve the wilderness. The more we change the face of the earth, the more difficult it becomes to remember how it was meant to be — or what it could yet become if humans used their special faculties to co-operate with the natural world.

Val Gargett 1990

1.60   Christmas Storm, Hunter Valley

Nothing moves that can stay still.
In hot December light nothing
matters. The mind stretches after
noon, making itself a shadow.

We call the shadow up by sunset
up the south face of the round sky
up the copper-cobalt flush
over the hanging bushfire smoke.

The valley throbs open, opens,
becomes a breathless gap waiting
for something cold, pulsing,
blackgreen and furious to rush in.

We can hear the wind before it comes.
A colourless storm. God-coloured?
Then it's tearing at the bangalows, while
leaves whirl up the length of the coast.

Now our parched, cynic, secular valley
flails alive with rain.
We are gasping cold air, a mighty fact
has come back into the world.

The black storm's got in the house!
It reels. In throes we quicken,
grin at each other, born
into a real place again.

The wind rocks the roof. All the lights
flicker and fall and rise.
The yard will be a holy mess,
mudfooted, green and diamond.

Worldround there's a story of steady light
under a stable rooftree.
That story's a shock too, a chill
smack of starting out.

Light without stars? Stormlight.
Light inside and out. The lawn
cries now like a baby
for the lightning of the skidding sky.

A storm is given us, light and dark
at once. Right now. Feel it?
You couldn't catch that wind!
You couldn't crib that child!

Norman Talbot 1969

1.61   The great Australian outback is awesome even to one familiar with the vastness of North America's western deserts. It stretches dark red and implacable as the tiny plane skims along, up through the centre of the continent's 8 million square kilometres. The low grey spinifex bush and a few scattered small trees seem to be the only vegetation. One is filled with wonder that the early peoples who roamed this harsh land for at least 20,000–30,000 years could have survived but so skilled were they and so sensitive their balance with the ecology that until the coming of the white settlers the land supported them. Outback survival was not comparatively easy, as in the south-east coastal areas and the lusher northern and eastern seaboard. But the Aborigines' discipline, ingenuity and respect for the land formed a very special bond with the areas that nourished them. 'The white man says the land belongs to me. We say, the Aborigine belongs to the land.' This I was to hear all over Australia from the Aboriginal people.

Charlotte Meacham 1972

1.62   Aboriginal teaching and learning developed before the last ice age. It has matured generation after generation, always based on the permanence of the land and the cyclic rhythms of nature. Harmony with the land, knowing it, learning from it as mother and teacher, has provided a solid and permanent basis for law and for harmony with one another.

Through art, song, dance, ceremonies, stories we have seen knowledge, identity and community strengthened. The potential of each individual has been developed to the fullest in a non-competitive way, so each person is able to exercise his or her responsibility to the land and the community.

Lilla Watson 1988

1.63   It was about this time that one First-day after Meeting, being retired alone in the mountains, I met wonderfully with the breaking Power and Presence of the Lord, far beyond what I am able to express; it was indeed a time of great love and high favour. After I had been here a little while, it pleased the Lord to draw me with some of my school-fellows into a particular society and nearness of mind and heart together and we were concerned often to walk in the fields together and there to wait upon the Lord who was pleased many times to break in wonderfully upon us and tender our hearts together.

John Kelsall, aged 18 c.1700

Faith traditions

1.64   I kept steady to Meetings, spent first-days in the afternoon chiefly in reading the scriptures and other good Books, and was early convinced in my mind that true Religion consisted in an inward life, wherein the Heart doth Love and Reverence God the creator, and learn to exercise true Justice and Goodness, not only towards all men, but also toward the Brute Creatures... I found no narrowness respecting Sects and Opinions, but believed that sincere upright-hearted people in every society who truly love God were accepted of Him.

John Woolman 1740

1.65   The first question to answer is, 'What do Quakers believe about belief?' Quakers see Christianity not as a collection of doctrines or of traditional observances, but essentially as an experience and as a way of life based on that experience. The main purpose of early Friends in mid-seventeenth century England was to bring the Church back from a Christianity of ideas (which they labelled 'notions') and forms to a living experience expressed in a way of life. They also insisted that the possibility of this experience was open to everyone and not only to an elect, a privileged few. Creeds represent an attempt to formulate and describe experience, while rituals represent an attempt to fix and define the way in which experience is to be communicated. It is easy, fatally easy, to assume that our words are God's Word.

William Oats 1990

1.66   As a Christian organisation we are inspired by the life of Jesus and his teachings and hold that we are doing as he did when we listen to the promptings of the Father — I think he spoke of God in as varied ways as modern Quakers do.

Furthermore, rituals, dogmatic pronouncements and articles of faith, as propounded by the later established churches, actually divert us away from the religious or prayerful life; they take us away from the immediacy and authority of the inner voice. It is in this sense, I think, that religion has become an almost pejorative term, because pseudo-authority or pseudo-religion has replaced or been confused with the essential religious activity of communing with the divine.

Taking up one's cross, or becoming committed to the prayerful life in the face of, or despite, our human frailty is, I think, the Quaker religion. Recognising that people come seeking, finding their own path to the divine is, I think, the Quaker religion. We are united by an overwhelming need to see God in all things; by a drive that is beyond us, in our deepest being.

Chris Castle 1999

1.67 A number of Jews, some of whom practice Judaism, are members and attenders of Quaker meetings, here and elsewhere. Liberal Jews acknowledge Jesus as an important prophet. I am comfortable with this perspective. Jesus was thoroughly Jewish. I do not think Jesus was a Christian; the development of Christian theological thought derives really from the interpretations of Paul and others. Jesus has been the most important teacher in my life. Many Jews have a passion for social justice, which is in keeping with the prophetic tradition. As a Jewish friend said to me, both Quakers and Jews believe we have responsibility to 'tikun olam', repair the world. This links with the liberal Jewish concept of 'messiah', not identified as a person, but as a coming age of peace and equality, when all peoples shall come to the mountain of Yahweh.

Helen Gould 1992

1.68 We remind Quakers that anti-Jewish oppression is real, and ask us all to search our hearts lest we harbour prejudices and stereotypes.

Some Jews see Jesus as a great rabbi. Judaism is central to Christianity and today, as always, has much to offer. For example, it is a Jewish insight that we are co-creators with the Divine. Judaism is rich in ritual, stories, festivals and dance, in rites of passage, and in support for those who mourn.

We call on Quakers to honour all our cultural and religious heritages, Jewish, Catholic, Aboriginal, Muslim etc. We encourage Jewish Quakers to share with other Friends what our Jewish heritage means to us.

Jewish-Quaker group 1996

1.69 Most Friends will know that there is a well-established Friends' School in Ramallah and that there is a Quaker community there. The Meeting is very small, but it was led by local Palestinians and it was very good to be able to share with them their experiences in the present troubles. Theirs was certainly a different story to the official Israeli one and I could only marvel at their calm fortitude as they talked about their young people on the 'front line' who went out to confront heavily armed troops and who knew that they were in for a beating if they got arrested.

Space forbids me to relate the encounters I had with inter-religious groups in Israel who are using silent Quaker worship as the best means of expressing their shared hope and values, or with groups of both Jews and Palestinians who are in dialogue with each other as they seek peace between their peoples.

It was meeting the people involved in struggle, reaching out to each other that made Israel a Holy Land for me.

David Thomas 1989

1.70   When asked for an opinion on church unity, we explained that Friends cooperate whole-heartedly with other churches in many ways in a united witness on social and moral questions; but that our own method of worship and the equality of men and women, without paid ministry, means a great deal to us, that unity with some diversity is a healthy condition.

In the closing session one church leader asked why there was no credal basis in the Australian Council of Churches constitution. The answer given was that the Council values and wishes to retain the membership of the Society of Friends, therefore such a credal basis was not included.

Margaret Watts 1964

NOTE: The National Council of Churches in Australia now has a clear Trinitarian basis, and Section 5.02 of its constitution reads: 'A church or Christian community which does not have credal statements within its tradition, and therefore finds it difficult to subscribe formally to what appears to it to be a written credal statement in the Basis, may apply for, and be elected to membership, provided that the church or Christian community demonstrates by its life and conduct that it upholds the spirit of the Basis.'

1.71   It has always been clear that George Fox was not unique in his spirituality, but an eminent member of a community experiencing an outbreak of mysticism. Some of those who joined George Fox had already experienced a spiritual illumination similar to his. Early followers were never George Fox's 'adherents', but were already spiritual 'finders' in their own right.

Ursula Jane O'Shea 1993

1.72   There seems to be something in common between the vividly described events in part of Acts about Pentecost, and the dramatic and emotional events of early Quaker history. These events changed the early Christians from a frightened band of people huddled behind doors in the upstairs room of an inn to amazingly courageous and confident wise men, able not only to influence public opinion but to heal people.

The early Christians had Pentecost. Their emotionalism at the time made it necessary for it to be pointed out that they were not drunk. The early Quakers had their own highly charged experiences. I smile as I visualise what the reactions would be if, at some Meeting for Worship, a Friend (or could it only be an attender, and a very new one at that) either spoke in tongues or really 'quaked'.

Frank Lindsey 1997

1.73   From our deepest being, using all the forces of creation, the Spirit pushes itself into our awareness and demands our complete attention via a racing pulse, immobility, darkness in our eyes, loss of hearing and waves of emotion. These are whole-of-body recognitions of the Spirit as it breaks into our humanness and takes us wholly in its grip. How else is 'that which is beyond words' to communicate with us? And how else can we reply except through our bodies with laughter, tears, sweat, shivers, knots in the belly, tight throat, dry mouth? When we dismiss these as passing emotions, we deny the Spirit and turn away from God. Indeed they will pass if they are not recognised and so will the light therein. This is the way the Spirit leads, and we must be open to it. We must embrace the Spirit's work within ourselves and others, not try to moderate or control it, and, above all, we must take notice of the messages we receive.

Helen Bayes 2003

1.74 As a child I thought that Jesus was the Son of God and that he was always good and kind. In some way I gained the notion that because he was God's son it was easy for him to be perfect — much easier than for me, a very ordinary human being — and this grudging belief helped me to excuse many of my own shortcomings. But as I grew older I began to be aware that Jesus knew the trials of human existence — hunger and weariness, anger and bitterness, the need for prayer and rest, the need for friends, the need to be alone — and he knew the great temptation to use the special talents God had bestowed on him for his personal power and gain. Throughout these experiences he was confident of God's help and love and so able to live courageously and effectively, and this example helped me to accept his comfort when I too knew the strain of being human. Thus I discovered that the way of life he offers is tried and true, and the realisation that his life was not insulated by his divinity gave me a new respect for him.

It is in the Easter story that I find the final proof of his humanity, and his answers to my ultimate need, for in this tragic situation he faces the supreme test — and knows doubt. A few moments before death releases him from torture he cries, 'My God, my God, why hast thou forsaken me?' At that moment it must have seemed to him that it was all a terrible mistake, as though his acceptance of the cup of bitterness had led him not to triumph but to defeat. I believe that he had to know this final moment of despair — the failure of faith — so that, later, he could help us when we too know failure. But the apparent failure became victory. What joy he must have known on the Easter morn to find his Father's promise fulfilled and his spirit risen, forever able to give himself to those who love him. This is for me the revelation of Easter: we may let God slip from our human heart, but he holds us forever in his. With his help we can rise again from doubt and despair and, our faith redeemed and strengthened, give ourselves anew to those who need our love.

Shay Jones 1966

1.75   Let us take heed of our beginnings, the reliable and original root stock. Here was a society not afraid to talk about Jesus Christ nor to turn to the Bible. It could testify to the personal, immediate, and experimental revelation of God and, above all, it had no compunction about publishing the truth. I wish to stand and be counted but only in the strength and love of the Holy Spirit.

Brigid Walsh 1992

1.76   The human spirit finds its witness in metaphor rather than in definition, in poetry rather than in dissertation, but the clearest evidence for the reality of the human spirit is to be found in the lives of human beings in whom the Spirit has struggled for expression.

Surely this was the source of Socrates' willingness to drink the cup of hemlock rather than betray his 'inner god'. This too was the 'inner voice' which Gandhi said had urged him to lead his people to freedom without recourse to violence. This too was the source of the dream of Martin Luther King which called him to walk up the mountain of his vision even though this meant the assassin's bullet.

But the richest evidence of all is in the person of that intriguing, elusive, yet compelling figure of Jesus of Nazareth. He, like so many other explorers of the potential of the human spirit, suffered not only a death from crucifixion, but another sort of death at the hands of those who would exalt him by enshrining him in an institution and encasing his inspiring life in a mesh of dogma and ritual.

Jesus represents one of those great quantum leaps in the evolution of the human spirit. No distinctive culture, no self-appointed religious cult has proprietary claims of possession, nor exclusive rights of dispensation. There, deep within each one of us, is this evolutionary potential.

It can stand the searching light of reason, but it relies upon its own intuitive powers of imagination to guide it through the surrounding darkness beyond the reach of reason's searchlight.

This too is the source of the promptings of love and truth in every one of us, if we would but heed them and trust them.

William Oats 1990

1.77 As one who sees the Society of Friends as essentially a body of friends of Jesus (along the lines of Jesus' own request, as recorded in John's Gospel, for us to be his friends), I hope and pray that those members and attenders who feel awkward about references to Jesus will be willing to accept that there are many of us for whom our society has Jesus as its cornerstone. That is our experience, not a dogma. Indeed, I suspect that there are as many varying views of Jesus as there are Friends who are committed to his memory and message.

Hector Kinloch 1992

1.78 The Quaker idea of responding to 'that of God in everyone' fits in so well with understanding the New Testament writings; and here I am especially remembering the Gospel stories which continue to shed new light as one's circumstances and experience change. Yet Quakers also join with those who want to share experiences of religious truth, irrespective of their source in terms of race, culture, religious affiliation or philosophy; and feel the common bond of working together for a better world. These ideas, put together, emphasise for me that religion is very much an affair of the present tense.

David Evans 1998

1.79   I consider it borders on arrogance to describe the Bible as 'rubbish'. Whether or not it contains literal and consistent truth, it certainly contains valuable religious and ethical statements in the New Testament — and much that is compelling and meaningful as metaphor, prophecy or statements about life in both Old and New Testaments. For example, one can relate the casting of money changers out of the temple to the commercialisation and trivialisation of religion by tele-evangelists.

As Isaac Penington expressed it,

> the end of words is to bring men to the knowledge of things beyond what words can utter. So, learn of the Lord to make a right use of the Scriptures: which is by esteeming them in their right place, and prizing that which is above them.

Warwick Everson 2000

1.80   When I saw that Matthew Fox was talking about 'original blessing' instead of original sin, it just put a whole new perspective on the creative process and the renewal process and the rebirthing process. We are all blessed creatures, whether we're humans or whether we're part of the animal world or part of the plant world: we have that right to be here. Of course we're all blessed and that's how we begin our life and that's how we should continue to think of ourselves.

Jo Vallentine 1990

1.81   Historically we belong to the 'second wave' of the Reformation, to the century following that of Luther, the Council of Trent, Calvin, and the 'first wave' radicals like the Anabaptist Thomas Muntzer, and Hendrik Niclaes, the founder of the Family of Love. The historian Emile Leonard said that the English seventeenth century is entitled to a place in the forefront of the general history of Protestantism, for elsewhere, Church life was mainly the concern of princes, councils, clergy and theologians, while in England the popular masses played a decisive part.

It is important to remember that George Fox and the first generation of Quakers emerged as a religious force in a turbulent period when the political and social order, as well as 'orthodox' protestantism, were under radical challenge. It has been well said that Puritanism 'implied, rather than a creed, an attitude of mind, a dynamic element in society which belongs to all times'. Early Quakerism was a vital expression of this dynamism.

After the storm, the calm. In the eighteenth century, writes Alec Vidler, the Society of Friends gradually subsided, along with other dissenting bodies, into 'much the same condition as the Established Church — dry, commonsensical, averse to "enthusiasms", acclimatised to the Age of Reason'. After a long interval of quietism and sectarian seclusion, in the early nineteenth century it was aroused by the new and increasingly influential evangelical movement, whose religious tenets and philanthropic fervour profoundly affected Friends. Its influence brought back an intensive life to the Society but it also provoked schism in America, and effected an appreciable shift in the foundations of Quaker belief, both there and in England. The principles of Light and Leading were overborne and pressed into the background and in their place came a new evangelical emphasis on the total depravity of man and his dependence on Christ's sacrifice for his salvation, and on the Scriptures as the final authority for 'making known to us the blessed truths of Christianity' (in the words of the Epistle of London Yearly Meeting of 1856). Friends seemed no longer to be standing by the distinctive witness of their founders of the 'apostolic age'.

It would be wrong to suggest that the evangelical phase in the society's history was all loss and no gain. It was a period that saw effective work by Friends in the anti-slavery cause, in the peace movement, in penal reform, in education, in the initiation of Quaker missions abroad and in efforts to alleviate the miseries of poverty at home.

Otto van der Sprenkel 1973

1.82 The George Fox Song

There's a light that is shining in the heart of a man,
It's the light that was shining when the world began.
There's a light that is shining in the Turk and the Jew
And a light that is shining, friend, in me and in you.

Chorus: *Walk in the light, wherever you may be,*
              Walk in the light, wherever you may be!
              'In my old leather breeches and my shaggy, shaggy locks,
              I am walking in the glory of the light,' said Fox!

With a book and a steeple, with a bell and a key
They would bind it forever but they can't (said he).
Oh, the book it will perish and the steeple it will fall
But the light will be shining at the end of it all.

'If we give you a pistol, will you fight for the Lord?'
'But you can't kill the Devil with a gun or a sword!'
'Will you swear on the Bible?' 'I will not!' said he,
'For the truth is more holy than the book to me.'

'There's an ocean of darkness and I drown in the night
Till I come through the darkness to the ocean of light,
For the light is forever and the light it is free
And I walk in the glory of the light,' said he.

Sydney Carter 1964

1.83   George Fox (1624–1691) was a central figure in the first phases of Quakerism from 1650 until his death. In an age when an exclusively male clergy still held enormous ideological power to maintain the interests of socio-economic, gender and religious privilege, Fox proclaimed the coming of Christ 'to teach and lead his people himself, liberating anyone who comes to the light within'. Fox's writings are therefore of interest to a variety of people. Religious seekers who hunger for a vision that cuts through the deep contradictions of our times may find in Fox's writings a message of liberation, commensurate with the depth of their personal struggles.

The culture of the 1640s, as he was coming of age, was a rich ferment of new ideas, given particular impetus by the suspension of censorship during the Civil War. The Puritan political ideal of a parliamentary monarchy had been frustrated by the absolutist intransigence of Charles I, not only resulting in civil war between King and Parliament but also enabling the outbreak of republican and even communist policies from the Levellers and Diggers. By the end of the 1640s as Fox's ministry began, the confusion of the day led some, such as the Ranters, to nihilistic celebration of chaos in religion and politics. Others like the Seekers retired into quiet waiting for some new revelation equal to the dilemmas of the day. Moving from group to group in his late teens and early twenties, Fox, the radical, imbibed all these ideas, felt the same despair and burden until he began to feel in 1647 a deep integration in the presence of an inward teacher, Christ. He had found the core, which began to grow through the interplay of inward guidance and an evolving set of concrete ethical practices developing among his associates.

One of Fox's great strengths was his ability to win converts through theological debate. As his Journal narrative shows, this was no academic enterprise but a rough and ready spiritual warfare, in which Fox sought to unmask a variety of deceits among the clergy including financial interests, false doctrines and pretended authority. A vanguard of Quaker prophets that came to be called The Valiant Sixty shared in the preaching, debating and writing that made the Quaker movement both a dynamic and controversial phenomenon. Fox remains the crucial figure, first among equals, a catalyst whose integrative preaching and writing most cogently defined the movement. Fox had the vision to transform the volatile revolutionary movement of the 1650s into a viable religious body that became the Religious Society of Friends.

Monika Smith 1996

1.84   After three hundred years we may be justified in taking an optimistic view of the achievements and resilience of the Quaker Way, and the success with which it has lived out its prophetic and conserving roles. However, to live out the Quaker Way faithfully in our own time and land is not to try to repeat what early Friends were called to do, not to cling to whatever Quaker forms we have inherited in this Yearly Meeting. What we share now with Friends who have gone before us is a task and some fine tools. Our task is to inaugurate the Way of God in this time and in this land; our tools are our personal experience of the Light within, and our corporate experience in using collective guidance to discover and enact God's will in the world. To do this we must not become more like early Friends, but more like ourselves as we are in the eye of God.

Ursula Jane O'Shea 1993

1.85   Quakerism is the do-it-yourself religion. It is wholly experimental and depends totally on the revelatory experience that is a gathered Meeting for Worship. We need to talk about and understand as much as we can about it. Its success will depend upon ordinary people like us who try to be worthy of its promise. The event, the experience, is indeed what counts.

Knowing the words of Fox and Penn, of Penington and Woolman as they describe the experience that gave them spiritual power and life is of immense help. In the end, though, it is still 'What canst thou say?'

Kenneth Wright 1992

1.86   Quakerism is far from a comfortable faith. It is full of queries. Are you? Have you? Do you? Then as one grows in the silence and in the development of the craft of Hope, there comes the realisation of another thorny growth — the inability to avoid responsibility for the suffering of others. 'Let your lives speak!' The challenge George Fox threw out three hundred years ago has not lost its barb. Do I? Am I? Should I? There are no easy answers in the Quaker way.

Elizabeth Stevenson 1997

1.87   Friends do not pretend to have all the answers. As wayfarers we are on a journey in search of Truth and on an exploration of the unseen world of spiritual dimension. We have to learn to struggle with doubt. So, Quakerism is not an easy faith. It would be more comfortable to have a ready-made creed, rules and regulations. But perhaps this is the greatest thing about the Religious Society of Friends: it is what we each, individually and personally, have found to be true that matters most, even if what we have found is bewildering and stressful at times. After more than three centuries, the challenge of George Fox still rings true — 'What canst thou say?'

Quaker Ways 1996

1.88 All weekend I felt a deep contentment, a certainty that I was exactly where I should be, and, most exciting of all, that I was not alone. Never have I doubted the existence of God even if my ideas of how, where or why he exists change. For these four days I knew God had been close to me and my joy was unbounded. It was as if I had been lifted to the top of a snow-clad mountain and my whole being filled with the perfect beauty of that view. It filled me so that I might burst. I danced with my children, we skipped and hopped in the garden, played hide and seek with the washing on the line — anything to use up all this energy! I was so excited about discovering I was a Quaker I wanted to tell the world. How surprisingly difficult that was. Most of my close friends were genuinely pleased for me, but could not identify with the feeling of being full to overflowing with the 'problem' of excess energy. Few of them had any real knowledge of Quakers and I found myself mostly trying to explain what was so dynamic and empowering about sitting together in silence, what it is that joins and connects such a diverse group of people. I hardly knew myself. No one really understood what I was trying to describe.

Sarah Hancock 1987

1.89 In spite of my history of evangelical atheism, God had pursued me, ensnared me and broken through to me. I will never forget the day when, alone, and suspended in the ecstasy of a brilliant autumn day, I knew I believed in God and that God was for me the summation of all the goodness, all the truth, all the beauty, all the love that could ever exist. Although my theology has developed since then, this was my Damascus Road experience and my life was not less turned around than Paul's. But I soon knew that I could not spend the rest of my life luxuriating alone in the glory of God's love. I had to discover people who could help me understand what this miracle meant and what to do with it, or I would burst.

Looking back to the time of my entry into Friends, I'm astonished by the amount of loving nurture I expected and received and by the fact that it never entered my head that membership could mean reciprocity because I believed I had nothing to give.

Early Friends did not suffer so that I could worship in untroubled freedom, physical safety and spiritual comfort. For them God wasn't a pleasant extra in their lives, but the very warp and woof of their being — not just high priority, but that without which their true life would cease to exist. That was what Quakerism was in essence — humble, expectant waiting upon God, in the faith that God would speak in their hearts and minds and bodies.

Susannah Brindle 1991

1.90   My fantasy of the churches I lived in is of a number of large walled cities — standing nearby each other — and a little apart also. Nowadays they relate to each other and even send diplomats and hold occasional cultural exchanges and 'show and tells'. People can always come in; but inside, especially for residents and more so for officials, there are rules and a constitution to be followed.

Outside, I found a little village, few inhabitants, no walls and no clearly defined boundary. If you ask where the boundary is, they gesture vaguely, and say 'somewhere about here'. 'How do you know where?' 'Well we have these stories and these bits of writings from the past' — and an elastic piece of string. Everyone is welcome. Quite a number come for a while and leave.

In the middle of the village is a little group who have built more or less permanent houses. Some were born in the village; most come from one of the walled cities, or elsewhere. There are lots of 'elsewheres'. They too just walked through the gate.

The organisation is horizontal, not vertical; the constitution and rules fairly minimal. Many visit the cities occasionally. Many do good things in the world around. They value peace, individual responsibility and equality. They value experience. They like sitting round quietly together before beginning to do anything in a group. They tend to say 'we' after doing this, rather than 'I', even though they don't vote on anything. There are no officials; people just take turns doing things for a while.

I set about to get a block there and build a house — a free form one with large open spaces. Close to some Friends already there, and to contribute to the well-being of the village for a while. I like how they believe and how they live. They imagine there is an inner thing (presence? person?) in everyone, but that we mustn't be too dogmatic about it, just follow where it leads. I think they appreciate that anything more than that is mere words anyway.

John Edwards 1998

1.91 I seem to prefer to adopt provisional positions rather than final ones. I think this must characterise me as a 'seeker'. A seeker is, I think, one who is happier with a spiritual journey in an environment of questions and searching and uncertainty rather than one of answers and findings and dogma.

Peter Wilde 1998

1.92 Quakers sense the sacrament in all of life. Given the meaning of being 'doors to the sacred', sacraments become symbols of unity with the divine in the other and so are inherent in relationship. This causes special problems for the seeker isolated by circumstance or geography. In these situations it is one thing to find the appropriate symbol but quite another to find the meaningful sharing. So, for the isolated Quaker, greater relevance may be found in the divinity of nature than in the company of fellow seekers after truth.

Brian Connor 2000

1.93   There is something about traversing a bush-walking track in Australia that closely resembles exploring spiritual paths in the Quaker sense. While a pedestrian excursion by an individual along well-defined paths presents few problems for a short time, it is essential for serious walkers exploring the depths to have companions. Just the same, as seekers in our Quaker faith, we are not alone. We belong to a group, a society of friends, who willingly accompanies us. Still it is individuals who do the actual walking and seeking, so, as explorers, they must be conscious of their own nature, temperament, constitution, and what really satisfies them.

Sheila Given 1999

1.94   George Fox believed in that of God in everyone, in every person, and that's still the essence of Quakerism. It's the reason Quakers fought against slavery and the reason that there were Quakers in the early feminist movement. For me, that's the constant challenge day by day to see each person I deal with as having that of God in them, as I do in me. I see that God in action here is what moves between those people — the reaching out and touching between those human beings.

There's still an essence of earnest seeking for a new spiritual pathway, of seeking the truth and the light in your life. That is the central point for me: 'What is the Light for my path?' even if I see only one footstep at a time. It's not a Sunday thing, it's an everyday thing: it's everything that you do from the moment you get up to the moment you go to bed and every day of your life.

Judith Aitchison 2000

1.95   The Quakers have been and are some of the gentlest people in the world. They have been people with great compassion. They were the first Christian body to free themselves from complicity with slavery. They became the backbone of the anti-slavery agitation in America and England, and, later on, the anti-opium movement. It is impossible to deny — whatever one's own opinion — that their protest against war has been magnificent. They have taken a leading part in prison reform, in temperance work, in popular education.

But in this gaunt soul of George Fox, who stands at the head of the movement, it is difficult to discover very much of the gentleness and meekness of Christ. He did indeed refuse the use of carnal weapons; more than once he refused to enter the army, but he made vigorous and unsparing use of the tongue.

There must have been some quality in him which bound men's hearts to him in a wonderful way. How else could he have reared Quakerism in England when again and again the ground he had boldly staked out was flooded with the tides of persecution? It was said of him that he had an uncanny gift of turning enemies into friends. Often he won the hearts of his gaolers.

Annie Wilton 1924

1.96   One thing is certain. I am not speaking of a man-centred religion, or even one where God is made in the human image. It is very much a God-centred religion, but centred towards a God not cramped by definitions which will satisfy some but estrange others, towards the God each of us finds in our own experience. It is the same God. It is our approach and our response which differs, just as each of us will respond differently, and perhaps differently on different occasions, to a symphony, to a poem, or a great work of art. We must admit that there are dangers, at least for some, in the freedom of the religion I have sought to outline. People who are emotionally unstable may be swept off their feet, instead of finding surer ground. This danger is probably the main source of criticism of our society by the churches: that there is no objective standard; no rein on the individual's thoughts, whims or even their mental imbalance. A great protection against this danger is the corporate experience of worship together and the loving guidance of fellow members of the society. The exercise of this guidance is certainly demanding, both for those who need to offer, and of those who need to accept it. But the more religiously mature both are, the more likely it is that this speaking of truth in love will enrich and not embitter.

David Hodgkin 1971

1.97 Sunday 4 February 1798

Today much has passed in my mind of a very serious nature. I have had a faint light spread over my mind. At least I believe it is something of that kind, owing to having been much with and heard much excellence from one who appears to me a true Christian. It has caused me to feel a *little* religion. I wish the state of enthusiasm I am now in may last, for today I *felt* there is a God. I have been devotional and my mind has been led away from the follies that it is mostly wrapped up in.

Sunday 17 March 1798

May I never lose the little religion I now have, but if I cannot feel religion and devotion I must not despair, for if I am truly warm and earnest in the cause it will come one day. In my idea true humility and lowness of heart is the *first grand step towards true religion*.

Elizabeth Fry 1798

1.98   By God, what do I mean? My answer is conditioned by the culture into which I happened to be born. Dogmatism so often has a cultural base. We therefore need to beware of those who confidently assert that there is only one path to God and that they hold the franchise to this travel package. One of the greatest obstacles to the acceptance of Christianity has been its proclamation so often that it has an exclusive right of entry in heaven. There are many paths to the one God.

William Oats 1990

our practice

2

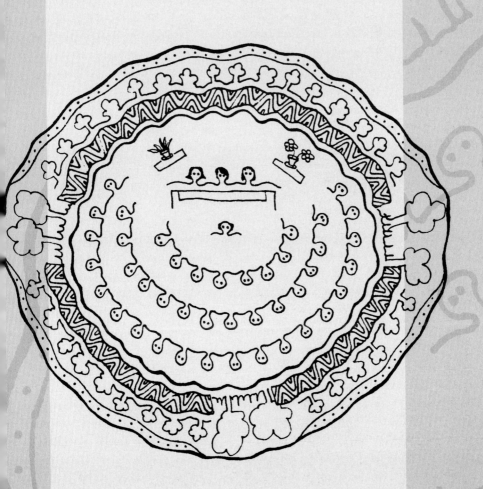

Justine Shelton

2 THE RELIGIOUS SOCIETY OF FRIENDS: OUR PRACTICE

2.1   If Quakers were challenged by the question, 'What do you believe in?' I think it would be safe to say that the majority would reply, 'We believe in the Inner Light.' From this central idea other implications follow: that in silence and meditation (individually or corporately in what Quakers call a Meeting for Worship), the Inner Light can illumine our own spirits, enlighten our conscience and reveal to us what God's will is for us; that this light can illumine every area of life and that therefore there are no such divisions as secular from sacred, Sunday from Monday, human from divine; that we are all bearers of the light which is universal and that therefore we believe in the worthwhileness of each person in the sight of God and of each other.

William Oats 1990

2.2   Ours is essentially a religious society. It is in the inmost depths of our beings that contact with the spirit of God exists and our real attitudes and convictions are born. The life of the spirit is the reality, and no amount of busy involvement in movements or organisations can take the place of that inner commitment.

Eric Pollard 1964

2.3   Look around us Friends. And what do we see? We see Quaker Catholics, Quaker Anglicans, Quaker Methodists, Quaker Buddhists, Quaker Jews, Quaker Universalists, Trinitarians and Unitarians, plenty of Quaker agnostics and even — horror — perhaps some Quaker atheists. We stay together because we are all, or nearly all, Quakers first and the other thing second; we find no conflict between our two personae because the Quaker model ignores doctrinal niceties. By having no credal statement, we sidestep doctrinal conflict. By basing our worship on silence, we allow complete freedom of thought. But at the same time we lose the right to speak of a Quaker religion — at least in the ordinary sense of the word religion.

What then holds us together if it is not our religion?

Our meeting for worship in silence is perhaps the most important single common bond, followed closely by our startlingly successful business method. But there are deeper factors. It is our common attitude to life that really holds us together. Our society has a long history of active concern for the weaker and poorer members of society, for persecuted minorities of all kinds, of support for nonviolence, of regard for the truth, of plain living, and many other principles and causes. If a way of life is a religion, then we have a religion in our way of life.

Christopher Nordin 1999

2.4   It is only through letting God work through my life, by succumbing to the unrelenting prompting, deep, inner voice that I have gained perspective and ultimate peace.

Being someone who has been convinced of 'the truth', I would humbly offer these words: I believe that we are convinced of the presence of God in all things and that the actual mind of God is knowable within our deepest self. This deepest self is not our own self but it is the divine; it is that which is inextricably connected to all things and, through listening closely to the 'still, small voice', we may be guided in our actions. This process of deep listening is tempered by our sharing our concerns with others.

Chris Castle 1999

Roberta Turner

Silence, stillness

2.5   This noisy world needs stillness and serenity nearly as much as it needs hope.

The deepest moments of life are preceded by hush: daybreak, the pauses in music that come before the statement of the greatest themes, the unforgettable moment that follows the travail of birth while one waits for that first haunting cry of life.

Silence of this kind involves anticipation, an eager waiting, a deep listening. This is the silence of the Quaker faith.

Elizabeth Stevenson 1997

2.6
Stillness is the fathomless well
Deep..... deep
Within us;
It is of the Source from which its mercy is born.
Always we may draw upon its bounty.
Stillness is our spring which seeks its opening —
What else can it do?
From small beginnings it flows
Into the Living Water,
The Ocean of God.
Through our stillness God *moves*.

Gerard Guiton 1994

2.7 I pause, reflect in the deepening silence
And feel the warmth of acceptance of myself,
affirmation of my personhood,
flowing through me.
I know it to be the love and acceptance of the Divine Spirit —
And because I feel accepted and affirmed, I can reach out to each of you
with the same acceptance and affirmation and love,
God moving through me to you
And from you to me.

Carol McLean 1976

2.8 Silence and finding space to centre and find 'that of God' is at the heart of my Quaker faith. The environment of Quaker meeting gives me this space and the communion with others that occurs here is spiritual nourishment. I try to have sufficient discipline in my life to find at least a small space each day for silent waiting, but often fail and am overcome by busyness or its by-product, inertia!

Jo Farrow in *World in my Heart* says 'Quaker spirituality is about letting ourselves down into a deep place. It involves us in living from the deepest centre of ourselves where the real prayers of our life are made, and learning to trust our inward knowing. It is not religion that matters so much. It is life.'

Finding my centre involves a deep search for Self, for the knowing of who I am personally; a state of always becoming, an ongoing, ever changing process. This is life with all its many facets. Living my life incorporating my beliefs, that is the challenge.

Anna Bell 1997

2.9   If a Meeting for Worship is held 'in the life', each individual has something to bring to it, first of all ourself and our need, with a deep sense of responsibility and humility. We tend to restrict the meaning of 'ministry' dangerously, when we refer to it as if it were merely the spoken word.

We are engaged in nothing less than being reunited to the ground of our being, where we find our true, integrated self and our neighbour. Our gathered silence can become a great unifying force when our aspirations and strivings are used, our sense of need is uncovered and met, and the gap between what we are and what we were meant to become is highlighted.

Leonce Richards 1993

2.10   Core to my being a Quaker is not silence or ministry. It is waiting in stillness with a people, in a state of receptiveness to God's will and love, 'gathered unto God'.

Annabelle Cameron 1998

2.11   Can we enter a spiritual community not restricted by time or place, where what we want to say is really beyond words? Is this communication to be through prayer, which some say is the deepest form of language? Do we forget linear time in communal awareness of the individual moment? Does silence give us the courage to be intimate?

Brian Connor 1997

2.12   We gather
in the place where words come from,
to find the unity we know at the end of words.

Ursula Jane O'Shea 1995

2.13   In the united stillness of a truly 'gathered' meeting there is a power known only by experience, and mysterious even when most familiar.

Caroline Stephen 1908

2.14   Silence to Friends
Is caught not taught.
Through the silence
Does the self dissolve
To become part
Of a gathered self
Working together within?

Max Raupach 1999

Susannah Brindle

Following Silence to its Source

When we fall into silence, what do we do? What do we experience? And is there a state that can be regarded as something that lies beyond the silence?

In silence we contact the divine or big MIND in the universe. In silence we contact one another as we reach out to share, giving and receiving from one another, as a body of many parts. In silence we contact ourselves, reaching into our minds and sifting to find the things that really matter and leaving the peripheral ones.

The Chinese thought of this in terms of an ox herder (you) looking for an ox (our inner dualistic thought patterns) in a sequence of ten pictures that may help us to follow our mind going into silence and beyond.

1 This ox herder, rope in hand, searches for the ox, which is nowhere to be found. It is a valuable possession, so the search is in earnest.

(The ox (self-mind) is our clue to finding and knowing MIND; we have not found it but strive to see it.)

Why do we search for the ox?

2 Here are the tracks of the ox, going in all directions, stopping and starting. Seeing the tracks gives confidence that the ox exists and can be found.) The mind is wandering and erratic. In trying to clear the mind sometimes we succeed and sometimes we do not. Some are firmly resolved to search; some are not.)

3 Eventually the ox's tail is glimpsed; the whole ox is not seen (seeing our self-nature for the first time is like travelling a long way and seeing a high mountain in the distance, close enough to see but too far off to climb. We were blind, but for a moment we have opened one eye. We have to stick to our task.)

4 The ox herder has now caught the ox, but it is wild and resists. It would rather be off eating grass.

(One continues to search hard after recognising self-nature. At times things are unclear, but the search for MIND continues on afresh.)

5 The ox is now tame enough to be led by the ox herder.

(Knowledge of self is now part of everyday life, although some difficulties remain.)

6 Riding the ox back home. Practice is now effortless and the ox is familiar with the way.

(Events no longer cause feelings of anger or greed, although there is awareness of them. One feels close to all that happens for all contain MIND. Practice continues effortlessly for all is practice.)

7 Now we can only see the ox herder, resting on the grass. The ox too is off sleeping; where, is of no concern.

(In the beginning it was like trying to swim upstream, but now the swimmer has become one with the water. One is still; self-cultivation now ceases.)

8 Now there is no person and no ox.

(There is nothing to say; all is one without duality. There is no them and no us. This doesn't mean doing nothing or not caring about relationships of the family or society.)

9 This is called "returning to the origin".

(The person returns to the world and all is seen as before, but with this difference; previously there was discrimination and attachment, now all is at one, expressing and proclaiming MIND.)

10 The ox herder has now returned to the world with one hand stretched out to help, and on the shoulder there is a bag of all sorts of things to be distributed according to need.

(At all times and in all places the aim is to help other conscious beings to attain this goal.)

Listening, Meeting for Worship

2.15 The timeless hour

Let action go; and with it all the thought
Of action. Even when the world is racked
It may be worthier to refrain from action
Than it is to act.

Forget the world one hour; when you return
Its beauty will be there, its tragedy;
And though the past and future shake their chains,
The now is free.

Think yourself out of thinking; exorcise
Even that ghost of thought, the echoing word —
Till in the haunted chamber of the brain
No sound is heard.

Then, when its windows open on a world
Beyond the world, when all its walls are dumb,
Into the silent room, the wordless mind,
The Word may come.

Clive Sansom 1957

2.16 Long before I became a Quaker, there were Bible passages that stood out for me. One is I Kings 19:11–12: '...but the Lord was not in the wind; and after the wind an earthquake, but the Lord was not in the earthquake; and after the earthquake a fire, but the Lord was not in the fire; and after the fire, a still small voice'. So the Quaker emphasis on listening in the silence to the voice of the Spirit rings very true for me.

Doreen Cope 2000

2.17   I believe that we are asked and expected to do things, to change our direction in life or to help others in certain ways, by listening to that still small voice, the leadings of the Spirit. All sorts of things happen and opportunities arise, directing us in the way we are expected to take; and these coincidences can be quite disconcerting, pushing us forward. I believe we have to be constantly aware of that call of the Inner Light, and be prepared to be under the guidance of the Spirit.

Cathy Davies 1997

2.18   Let us listen. That is the Quaker gift: to listen deeply, beyond listening, to the spirit that guides and is sure to lead us where justice and peace need our witness. This may happen in Meeting for Worship. It may happen amongst friends, family, in workplaces or in the queue for the unemployed. It may lead us away from our home to a new home, the home of the journey, remote and yet secure, while emptying us of our preconceptions and prejudices to make ourselves available to a universe rich in diversity and invitation.

Adrian Glamorgan 1997

2.19   We cannot estimate the influence for good which goes forth into the world from a group gathered in silent worship. It is in these meetings that we gain the strength to carry on our work and that definite guidance which must be behind all effective effort.

If we let the Spirit of Christ take possession of us we will not necessarily follow the same lines as others have done, but will do what He leads us to do and will have His blessing.

In the days of George Fox the conception of the Light within as an authority, greater than the Bible itself, was a wonderful new Gospel. Today it is accepted by a very large number of people outside the Society of Friends. Should we not now get together to seek for ourselves further revelations of truth?

Australia General Meeting 1927

2.20   I look around the room briefly, just to see who is there, the people I know. I give thanks for God in the lives of these people, shut my eyes and go to that place of stillness within me, being thankful for that of God I find there. I wait. I listen. I listen with my internal ears. The sounds from outside fail to register after just a few moments, and I listen to the sounds made by the silence from within. Sometimes, I stay in this stillness as though suspended. I am not aware of the passing of time. The only awareness is of the journey deeper and deeper into the stillness. What peace! I understand 'He restores my soul'. I am not aware of anyone speaking. The depth has a beauty of its own and I want to stay there.

anon. 1996

2.21   About seventh year of my age, it pleased the Lord to reach unto, and secretly incline my mind to love to go to Meetings and at times I would be so tendered in Meetings, and affected with divine goodness (tho' I scarce knew what it was) that desires were raised to feel more. About the ninth year of my age, I was frequently sensible of inward reproof and one time in Meeting I was much broken and tendered, so that many tears ran from my eyes, yet I was sweetly affected with inward comfort.

George Bewley 1748

2.22   If, as occasionally happens, there are quite a number of Friends quietly settled in the Meeting House when we arrive, we feel a sense of joy and thankfulness, and are able to move into a living, welcoming, expectant silence. If, as happens more frequently, the Friends in Meeting are still settling down then we, too, must take our time to rid ourselves of mundane concerns before we can move into the still centre, the gatheredness.

That gatheredness or centering down is a sense of peace within ourselves, a profound sense of the presence of that eternal element of each one of us in the meeting (the corporate nature of the experience is vital), an opening to a loving power that is within each of us and is also beyond us. It is a loving concern for all creation and a readiness to be led.

In all, it is a sense of the oneness of all things. We know that we are part of it, and are aware both of the minute nature of that part and of its importance.

Barbara Wright 1992

2.23   There are times when God seems not to speak to me at all, times when I feel rejected, not worth considering.

People in the meeting help, the ones who are quietly centred down, and the ones who are coping with situations that seem intolerable, old friends to whom one can talk unreservedly, friends with their loving natures and their gift of friendship, all speaking to me of God.

Barbara Wright 1996

2.24   'Waiting on the Spirit' — this is the quietness of the Quaker Meeting for Worship. It is amazing when you are in a room with a group of people, and you sense a gathering in the silence, and it is just that — waiting on the Spirit. Something magical happens, and answers to problems emerge out of the silence. Sometimes if you are wrestling with a problem or an issue in your life, someone else in the meeting will say something that is just right for you at that moment. Yet some meetings are absolutely silent, when nobody says anything for a whole hour, and they can be the most meaningful and deepest of all.

Jo Vallentine 1990

2.25   As members of the Society of Friends, we believe that every individual should be ready to receive messages from the Divine Spirit, and that the message is given in various ways. It does not follow that the person who receives the message must stand up and speak — we may worship in silence, better, perhaps, than in speech. The best messages are not delivered in abundance of words. Let us seek in our meetings that we shall be under the guidance of the Spirit, so that our meetings may be held in the power of God.

The Australian Friend 1903

2.26 Ministry is the contribution made to the gathered meeting by one who has made the journey to the still centre of his being that we call centering down. This condition of mind and spirit — something much more than simple introspection, more akin to contemplation — is still a lonely one. To develop into ministry there must be movement of the spirit towards others in the worshipping group, a movement urged by loving concern. This is the real Meeting for Worship. When it takes place, one is aware of one's own individuality, but also one's awareness of the individuality of others is heightened. Paradoxically, one is also keenly aware of our involvement one with another — our essential unity; and another's still centre, the still centre of the whole meeting, becomes the focal point of our spiritual activity. It is then that we minister — whether by giving way to the insistent demand that we express in words an insight that has come to us, or whether we remain silently upholding to the Light the whole worshipping group.

Kenneth Wright 1980

2.27 Vocal ministry comes to hold a middle place in our worship. It is essentially serving, helping. No matter how simple or faltering the utterance, words help true communion with our Heavenly Father infinitely more than silent worship that is reserved, critical. Silence can be baffling, killing. Probably, on the other hand, there is an awful silence to which no words reach and which no highest eloquence could surpass for bringing us a true revelation of God in the soul.

L V Hodgkin 1909

2.28   Towards the end of the discussion one question made us sit up. The Friend at whom the question was directed is much-loved and not many years short of celebrating her centenary. She is confined to a wheelchair yet she does not seem restricted in her mobility as one would expect. The question was, 'You never give spoken ministry in meeting, yet, your silent ministry is so powerful that the whole meeting knows when you are missing. Could you give us the secret of your influence? What makes you so serene and at peace always?'

She replied with only a few words: 'I am aware of God's presence.'

Leonce Richards 1992

2.29   In worship we enter with reverence into communion with God and respond to the promptings of the Holy Spirit. Come to meeting for worship with heart and mind prepared. Yield yourself and all your outward concerns to God's guidance so that you may find 'the evil weakening in you and the good raised up'.

Britain Yearly Meeting Advices & Queries 1995

2.30   A prepared mind is not a mind made up as to what it is going to share with others, but it is a receptive mind, prepared to receive rather than to give, but also capable of reflecting.

Dorothy Gregory 1963

2.31 Words must be purified in a redemptive silence if they are to bear the message of peace.

The right to speak is a call to the duty of listening.
Speech has no meaning unless there are attentive minds and silent hearts.
Silence is the welcoming acceptance of the other.
The word born of silence must be received in silence.

Pierre Lacout 1969

2.32 Does the spirit of our worship, the very spring and source of dynamic living, flow into our listening, really listening, to that of God in others as we share hurt and pain, joy and thankfulness, anger and frustration? Are we always sensitively aware of the tender feelings of those friends on the fringe?

Australia Yearly Meeting Epistle 1975

2.33 Ministry which seems out of place is hard to deal with but I think that if, as we claim, we are truly trying to place ourselves individually and corporately in the presence of God and to be receptive to His leadings, then we cannot reject an offering. Nothing in a gathered meeting can be seen as a purely individual outburst. This person is standing before God and has been prompted to minister in this way; the whole meeting is also standing before God and has a responsibility to accept the ministry in that spirit and hold it before God. So our understanding grows, so we reach out to others in the love of God. This seems to me to be true worship.

Frances Parsons 1990

2.34   I sometimes think of a Meeting for Worship as a time when nobody speaks, but everybody listens. Sometimes a person is moved to listen aloud, and this transforms itself into spoken ministry.

anon. 1995

2.35   New Forest worship

We exchange warm smiles
settle ourselves on dry leaves
lower closed eyes to the forest floor.

Soft breezes whisper through ferns
high above our heads a green canopy
dances in afternoon sunshine.

Inhaling deeply we drink silk air
each breath drawing in silence
easing us down into prayer.

The Spirit weaves between branches
springs from moist moss at our feet
feather-light brushes our skin.

Time moves forward with tiny steps
we surface slowly without ripples
join hands as silence lingers long.

Where two or three are gathered
I say softly and your smile
affirms our worship is blessed.

Sue Parritt 1993

2.36   Morning. Rising. Feeling fractured.
In anticipation I arrive.....
The peace and silence come.
A sense of glowing grace.
I am blessed and I belong,
I am accepted.
I am made whole.

Jan de Voogd 1996

The silence of religious experience is never a silence in which the soul shuts itself up in isolation. It is a silence which opens out on to the Infinite in a true communion of minds and hearts, in real unity founded on respect for diversity.

Pierre Lacout — God is Silence

Meeting for Worship for Business

2.37   A Quaker Meeting for Worship for Business is a meeting for worship in which decisions about the life of the community are made. The process of searching for decisions can be a transforming experience both for the meeting and its individual Friends. To have that experience we need to be clear about the distinction between finding the best solution and coming to unity in the Spirit about a matter of business. The 'best solution' is obtained by canvassing the opinions and ideas of individuals followed by decision-making processes that may include debate, negotiation, compromise, general agreement, consensus or voting. Those are secular processes. Traditional Quaker decision-making in meeting for business, on the other hand, is a Spirit-led process in which we seek to learn the will of God for the meeting in the matter at hand. This difference has profound implications for what it means to be a member of a Quaker faith community.

To discern the leading of the Spirit we listen for promptings within ourselves and in the ministry of others. This does not mean that we don't use our brains or think. It does mean, however, that we try to open ourselves to an awareness of the working of the Spirit both within ourselves and within the meeting as a whole. It is this experience of being gathered in the Spirit that is the unity we seek in making decisions. We share our knowledge, opinions, and insights as we feel led, but in the end we release them as we discern the leadings of the Spirit in the gathered meeting.

Once the clerk or a member of the meeting senses that the meeting is united on the matter at hand, a verbal expression of this sense is tried. When shaped to the satisfaction of the meeting, the expression may or may not be recorded, and, if recorded, it may or may not take the form of a minute. Committees, for example, may choose to keep written notes of the decisions made, but not to adopt formal minutes. Writing a minute is not the focus of meetings for worship for business. That is a technical exercise. The focus, rather, is to achieve unity in the Spirit.

Occasionally a Friend may feel strongly that the discernment of the meeting in a particular matter is not Spirit-led and that she or he is not in unity with it. Since there is that of God in each of us, the meeting listens deeply to that Friend in its search for the truth, both within and behind the words spoken. If more time is needed, the matter may be carried forward to another meeting for business after further listening to and discussion with the dissenting Friend. Out of this effort on the part of both the meeting and the dissenting Friend may come a new proposal that provides a way forward to reach unity. Alternatively, the meeting may retain its original sense of unity and make its decision accordingly. There is no such thing as 'blocking' the working of the Spirit within the meeting. It is incumbent upon all members of the meeting to support the decisions of the meeting that have been made in right ordering, even if their personal discernment is different. In either case, both the meeting and the dissenting Friend accept in humility that their grasp of the truth is never complete.

Meeting for worship for business is a central part of the life of a Quaker meeting, for it is here that we experience the corporate gift of God: love in action.

Roger Walmsley 2003

2.38   All meetings for church affairs and all committees arrive at their decisions in a way which has stood the test for well-nigh 300 years. In a strict sense there is no chairman, but his place is supplied by the clerk, who brings before the meeting the various subjects to be considered, and when a subject has been considered sufficiently the clerk embodies 'the sense of the meeting' in a minute which he reads to the gathering, and this minute, with any suggested modification, is accepted by all. Under no circumstances does any vote take place, and the view may not represent the views of a numerical majority. The clerk who is a Friend of discernment, clear judgment and a knowledge of character, has to decide the value of the opinions expressed. It is obvious that rhetorical skill or argumentative subtlety, applause, or noise of dissent are out of place, where men are conscious of the unseen presence of the Head of the Church.

Ernest Unwin 1933

2.39   The failure of the potato crops in mid-nineteenth century Ireland not only led to starvation and the deaths of a million people, but it also left a devastated economy long after the food supply had recovered.

Since Quakers are ordinary people, answering to that of God is not always easy. As the extent of the disaster in 1846 became evident, Dublin Quakers must have struggled to decide what, if anything, they could do. I have no idea what was said in those meetings, but if they resembled us it might have gone something like this:

> Silence..... Friend Joseph rises and says, 'I have a concern. I feel called to organise a committee to import thousands of tons of corn and distribute it to the hungry. To answer this call I need the support of Friends in this meeting.' Silence..... Another person rises and says, 'We have not yet found a way to pay for cushions

to cover these hard benches.' Silence..... A third rises and says,
'And we adopted a minute to do that three years ago.' Silence.....
A fourth and very experienced Friend rises and says, 'We were not
even able to pay our quota to Yearly Meeting last year. The notion
that we can feed a million people, dear Friends, is misguided.'
A very long and prayerful silence ensues. Some heads bow.
Others turn to gaze out the windows. An occasional sigh stirs
the air. Then, a feeling of conviction begins to gather in the room
until, at long last, the clerk speaks and says, 'I offer you a minute,
which I hope captures the sense of the meeting. It reads as follows:
"The meeting supports the concern brought by Friend Joseph
to constitute a Central Relief Committee. Its membership shall
be open and it will convene at the rise of this meeting." Do Friends
agree?' Slowly, wearily, around the room heads begin to nod assent
and murmurs are heard saying, 'I hope it will be done.'

Roger Walmsley 1996

2.40 Different ways of understanding the divine life may occur among us. These differences should not be ignored for the sake of superficial unity. They should be recognised and understood so that deeper and more vital unity can be reached. Convictions which might divide and disrupt a meeting can, through God's grace, help to make it creative and strong. Friends should keep their faith and fellowship with each other, waiting in the Light for that unity which draws them together in the love and power of God.

Editor, The Australian Friend 1981

2.41 Threshing meetings

This term currently denotes a meeting at which a variety of different, and sometimes controversial, opinions can be openly, and sometimes forcefully, expressed, often in order to defuse a situation before a later meeting for worship for business.

Britain Yearly Meeting Quaker Faith and Practice 1995

2.42   Humans are social beings and the wellbeing of society is as crucial as the wellbeing of individuals. Central in the wellbeing of society is the health of institutions. Strong institutions mean a strong society.
But institutions become strong only because people make them strong by committing themselves to them.

Reg Naulty 1986

2.43   Do we enter into Meeting for Worship for Business in a spirit of worship and inward peace?

Do we feel gathered in the presence of God in meeting for business and trust our corporate guidance?

Do we listen and share in a spirit of forbearance and charity toward others?

Are we sensitive in pressing our views?

Are we mindful of seeking the corporate sense of the meeting?

Are we able to feel in unity with the spirit of the meeting even when our own opinions and ideas differ from the opinions and ideas of others?

Are we patient when the process of discernment by the meeting seems slow or stalled?

Are we able to open ourselves in prayer to the promptings of the Spirit and to follow a new path in search of unity?

Do we experience a sense of inner peace when the meeting has concluded its consideration of a matter and has made a decision?

Roger Walmsley 2003

Membership

2.44   What 'vows' would a new member make to God and to the prayer community and what vows would the community make to the new member? Vows of commitment to the journey, of obedience to the call of the Holy Spirit, and to nourish one another?

Drew Lawson 1996

2.45   Being a member of the Society means on the one hand that you can rely on Friends, and on the other hand that they can rely on you. It involves a sharing of loving care, and a sharing of responsibility.

Before applying for membership, you could ask yourself these questions:

Has the Meeting for Worship based on silence become an essential part of my life?

Have I discovered the variety of Friends by going to Meetings for Worship other than my own?

How do I respond to the *Advices and Queries*?

Have I read the anthology of Quaker writings, *Christian Faith and Practice in the Experience of the Religious Society of Friends*, describing the Christian roots of the Society? Am I aware of what Friends have stood for in the 300 years of their existence, and of the close association between Quaker faith and practice?

Am I prepared to take on one of the jobs which are essential in a group which has no leaders or paid helpers? Am I willing to contribute financially to the extent to which I am able?

Am I willing to be a friend, in the broadest sense of that word, to the other people in my Meeting?

Quaker Home Service, London 1993

2.46   Let our meetings for discipline be open to our children and young people... that they may have every facility for learning the methods, principles, and traditions of the Society, and find a share in simple appointments for service, as doorkeepers, librarians, etc. But their names should only appear as attenders in our registers until the time comes for them seriously to accept the responsibilities and privileges of membership. Let us not attempt to fix any time or age for this step.

The Australian Friend 1896

2.47   *The gold rush decade*

Allow us to express the desire which arises in our hearts that, in the exercise of the discipline, whether it has regard to the admission of members or to deliberating upon the acts of those who have departed from the right way of the Lord, there may be a care to proceed with impartiality, with caution, with tenderness and love, but with firmness and integrity of purpose, ever remembering that a principal end of all Christian discipline is to watch over one another for good, and to seek the restoration of those who may be overtaken with a fault.

Epistle to Hobart Town, Adelaide, Melbourne and Sydney from a Committee of a Meeting for Sufferings, London, 1855

2.48   Our membership is never based upon worthiness. We none of us are members because we have attained a certain standard of goodness, but rather because, in this matter, we still are all humble learners.

Edgar G Dunstan 1956

Clearness meetings

2.49 [Clearness meetings] may be called to prepare a couple for marriage, to test a concern, to make decisions about membership, to consider new forms of service or to seek guidance at times of change or difficulty. Such meetings may sometimes be of help and comfort to the dying.

Sometimes individuals or a family will need help when confronted by difficult choices at turning points in their lives. There may be interpersonal differences that sour relationships, or a meeting may have identified a particularly fraught area of divergence of opinion or belief in its membership. Any of these and similar situations, if they are faced openly and with love, may be tested in an atmosphere of worship. So those concerned may find a way forward.

Britain Yearly Meeting Quaker Faith and Practice 1995

2.50 A clearness committee meets with a person who is unclear on how to proceed in a keenly felt concern or dilemma, hoping that it can help this person reach clarity. It assumes that each of us has an Inner Teacher who can guide us and therefore that the answers sought are within the person seeking clearness. It also assumes that a group of caring friends can serve as channels of divine guidance in drawing out that Inner Teacher.

The purpose of committee members is not to give advice or to 'fix' the situation; they are there to listen without prejudice or judgment, to help clarify alternatives, to help communication if necessary, and to provide emotional support as an individual seeks to find 'truth and the right course of action'. The committee must remember that people are capable of growth and change. They must not become absorbed with historical excuses or reasons for present problems, but rather focus on what is happening now and explore what could be done to resolve it.

Jan Hoffman 1996

Leadings and concerns

2.51   When we talk about service being grounded in worship, we mean that the constant practice of turning towards the Light, of abandoning preconceptions and allowing ourselves to be led, inclines us, when called, to respond without apparently thinking; we make the choice without it seeming to be a choice at all.

Mark Deasey 2002

2.52   My sense of being led seemed to be renewed by vivid images, powerful dreams and plunging emotions. They were like electric life-giving moments of connection. It was as if I was being made alive again and again to the deepest meaning of my being — my life — each time experiencing it as new. I still feel in awe of this mysterious experience. Nevertheless, my certainty of being led was accompanied by chronic doubts about the details of what to actually *do*, and whether I was able really to do it. I felt weak. I knew I must trust the process because it would, if I remained in a continuous attitude of listening and waiting, give me inward guidance at each step.

People commented on my dogged persistence. I think now that this is probably *the* defining symptom of being led — a seemingly extraordinary persistence, which pays no regard to human measures of achievement and is not shaken by the non-appearance of outcomes in the world.

Helen Bayes 2003

2.53   James Backhouse was born in 1794 in Darlington, County Durham, into a well-established Quaker family. He was only 18 when, in response to the ministry of Stephen Grellett, he first sensed a call to service in far-off countries. Three years later the focus of vision sharpened to identify the far-off country as Australia.

> I was first impressed with the belief that it was the will of the Lord that at a future time I should go on a gospel errand in to Australia. The impression was sudden but very clear. It occurred as I was standing in the nursery ground at Norwich, not thinking on such subjects. I felt as though I could have sunk under it, but I dared not to oppose it and I prayed in spirit that if it were indeed the will of God, He would be pleased to prepare me for it, and to open the way for it, both in my own mind and in the minds of my Friends.

Another fifteen years were to pass before vision was translated into opportunity. Backhouse chose as his companion George Washington Walker. The thought of Walker came to him in a dream. In the half-waking hours of early morning he seemed to hear a voice say, 'Now look northward'. Thereupon, not wanting to use a form of heavenly blackmail to persuade Walker of his duty to offer himself, Backhouse wrote, simply asking him to consider whether he felt any urge towards accompanying him. The offer came at a time when Walker needed such a challenge. The way was open for Backhouse as a travelling minister, and his companion-secretary, Walker, to enter upon a remarkable partnership.

William Oats 1981

2.54   It appears to me that there is a range of divine communications which we are able to receive individually, when we are open enough:

- *light* which is always there, giving us insights into what is right and true

- *moments of connectedness* which happen involuntarily giving an experience of love and personal validation

- *promptings* which niggle away within our conscience (associated with guilt and shame) or within our hearts (associated with longings and inspiration)

- *leadings* which are quite specific, personal and painful to deny

- *concerns* which have an enduring certainty of rightness as a broad and long-term field of witness, individually or corporately.

Discernment is the conscious, prayerful discipline we can (must, in fact) follow to find clarity about openings, different paths or timing, and to guard against self-interest on the one hand and human scepticism on the other. It is about paying attention to God's guidance, not about taking control ourselves.

Helen Bayes 2003

2.55   Here is a story just as it was given to me by a Quaker Friend of ninety, Dick Propsting, as he remembered it from his boyhood.

> I have never forgotten a talk I heard given by Joseph Neave of Sydney, after his return from Russia in 1894. He went to the Annual Meeting one year, and towards the end of it he said that for a considerable time he had had a weight on his mind. He said 'I am convinced that I have a call. There is something I have to do concerning Russia. I have prayed and prayed but I can find no further guidance. I feel it right for me to go to England, and there the way may open up. But,' he said, 'I have not the means to do this, or for whatever further I may be called on to do. Friends, I lay this matter before you, knowing that only in doing this, can the load be taken from my mind.'
>
> After a long period of silence, and much weighty and prayerful consideration, these old Quakers said they would provide the money to send him. He went to London and contacted Friends there. He said the curious thing was, that every time he felt up against a blank wall, something happened to open the way. He was told there was a group of people in Russia called the Doukhobors, who were being persecuted, and many of them were being exiled for their religious convictions. Then a short time afterwards, something like 50 Doukhobors were liberated. Friends provided money and they emigrated to Canada where their descendants still live.

Nancie Hewitt 1971

I realize now that I have always had leadings - a little wave breaks across my face and I think 'of course.' Generally, however, the little waves need to come a number of times before I understand and sometimes they become very big. Sometimes I feel I am drowning, yet I have learned that I cannot drown even in the Ocean of Darkness.

2.56   Historically important Friends such as Lucretia Mott or John Woolman sought a consistent pattern of truth in their lives, a 'dynamic web of truth' as it were. This web found expression in the belief that God would give immediate, practical guidance on day-to-day issues, that this guidance could then be checked against the collective wisdom of the gathered meeting, the history of God's past revelations, and the direction of their own lives. They used the Advices and Queries to check themselves, but also looked to whether their deeds bore the fruits of the spirit: love, joy, peace, patience, kindness, goodness, faithfulness, gentleness and self-control (Galatians 5:22).

Ron Frey 1990

2.57   When Friends lay down a concern or committee the work may not stop, but go underground and struggle in the darkness. Often what happens in the wider world provides new openings and this can enable some corporate unity to be found again.

Thus Friends corporately are slow and moderate in action, but individually are more radical and more what the world might see as impulsive. Thus the amazing mosaic of individual witnessing is the story of Friends' action in the world, while the corporate responses are the story of how we respond, nurture and learn from each other.

It tends to be seen the other way round, but Friends are a bottom up organisation, not top down. We do things, not because the Yearly Meeting or Regional Meeting says we should but the Yearly Meeting or Regional Meeting does things because one or more individuals present it with God's light.

Helen Bayes 2003

2.58   Leadings are intensely private business in our personal relationship with God. Being led does not confer any authority in the world — or in the meeting! It cannot be interpreted as a divine direction to require anything of anyone else. In particular it should not give rise to expectations of support and cooperation.

However, it is clearly important, especially in the early stages, to share the experiences with trusted Friends, who will be most helpful if they respond with acceptance, trust, and respect whether they feel personally touched by the leading or not. If we truly believe that leadings come from beyond us — from a mysterious connectedness with the inexpressible power we call God — we will also know that we are carrying a message which must not be hidden. The meeting is accountable to us in this and we are accountable to the meeting.

As the inward guidance becomes more specific, the led individual will invariably need to turn to the meeting for some sort of affirmation and more formal support. Based on my own experience, I suggest that this first appearance of the leading in business meeting is best preceded by two or more clearness meetings, held in the usual manner.

In some situations, the meeting may not need to do much more than give continuing love and interest; in others, it may extend to adopting the leading formally as a meeting concern, setting up a longer term way of working on it, and raising the matter with other meetings and with Yearly Meeting.

Helen Bayes 2003

Sense of community

2.59   Individual experience can be enriched, intensified and augmented in the setting of the spiritual community. Balanced by corporate discernment, it can completely transform that community. The life and concern of John Woolman are a classic example of this reciprocal process. A spiritual community strengthens and steadies its members, nurturing them as they gain experience, and passing on a communal wisdom which a lifetime of individual searching may never uncover.

Ursula Jane O'Shea 1993

2.60   The influence of London Yearly Meeting on the embryo of Australian Meeting was considerable. Not one nineteenth century Meeting House was built without liberal financial assistance from England. All new emphases in Quaker thought emanated from London. Indeed the migrating Friends themselves, educated in Friends schools, brought with them strong English or Irish traditions. In the sessions of London Yearly Meeting reports were received annually from the colonial meetings.

The Colonial Committee of London Yearly Meeting was supplied with the most intimate intelligence of the colonial meetings through local correspondents who were encouraged to be open and frank in their reports. One important power of the colonial committee was to select Friends to visit Australia.

Most prominent of these was Joseph James Neave who first visited Australia in 1867 and later married and made his home in Sydney, although he continually travelled among Friends. In order to visit a Friend in Omeo he crossed the Bogong High Plains in the depth of winter, on foot and without matches. Lost one night he 'found a comfortable seat in the arms of a gum tree'.

Charles Stevenson 1973

2.61 *Friends in country areas without meeting houses were sometimes reluctant to meet in another's home because of the social obligations involved.*

His own family live so far off, that unless all had horses, where milking, etc., must be done, they could not possibly get to our house by 11 o'clock, and as W^m [a brother] observed, it was too far for them to walk back again before dinner and he was sure they would not like to come regularly, even if they could, if obliged always to dine with us, which most Friends do when they come to Meeting. Then, if ours was made a public Meeting, and the worthy members could not, or did not like to, come regularly, it would make them delinquents, and their non-attendance must be noticed — whereas, as no public Meeting is held at Mt. Barker now, no notice will be taken of their remaining at home.

We do sadly want a Meeting house midway between G.S.'s and our house, but there appears no probability of our being able to build one, for it cannot rise without money, which we find as difficult to catch as a pig with a soaped tail.

Margaret May 1844

Susannah Brindle

2.62   We are sensible of the difficulties which some of you are under, in residing at remote distances from any of our meetings for divine worship, now established amongst you; but whenever practicable, we would earnestly and affectionately urge upon you, the importance of making the effort to attend those meetings; and although they may be at times held in silence, and often under a sense of much weakness, yet how mercifully does the Great Master of all rightly gathered assemblies sometimes condescend to our condition, and thus lead us availingly to seek our strength and comfort in Him.

And if there should be any quite unable to reach a meeting, even the sitting down in quiet reverent waiting upon Him who seeth in secret (if only the one or the two in a family in your various solitudes) we believe that such an offering will not be in vain. The tendency of divine worship, when rightly engaged in, is to direct the mind unto God, and if it be pursued with sincerity and earnestness, our hopes will be fixed on God, the unfailing source of help. The sacred truths of the Holy Scriptures are often at such times brought to remembrance with consolation and strength.

Devonshire House (London) Monthly Meeting, to members resident in the Southern Hemisphere 1855

2.63   As we have contemplated you in your far off isle, your little meetings so widely separated from each other, and thought of lone individuals seldom meeting with any large body of Friends, the prayer has arisen that you may in your several localities indeed be germs of good that shall expand into comely and beautiful branches in the garden of the Lord.

Epistle of Iowa Women Friends to Australia 1873

2.64   *New Zealand and Australia both separated from the care of Meeting for Sufferings of London Yearly Meeting in 1902.*

This General Meeting of Friends for Australia now holding its first Annual session, in a glad consciousness of the sense of strength and mutual helpfulness that springs from Union, desires to send a word of cheer to all who are struggling to uphold and increase the scattered gatherings which meet under the name of the Society of Friends throughout New Zealand.

Australia General Meeting, Epistle to New Zealand 1902

2.65   In Australia she crossed the continent many times by car, sometimes alone, a journey of over 2,500 miles. Margaret's deep sense of the need for pastoral care led her to visit widely among Friends. When travelling in the outback she often felt it laid upon her to make a deviation to include a family miles off the main route.

Testimony to Margaret Roberts 1979

2.66   *On travelling in ministry in 1985.*

One of the biggest advantages of our visits was that it brought Friends together — shared meals (an 'eating Meeting') — and we watched the pleasure Friends had in meeting each other. In one Meeting Friends included those unable to come by arranging 'phone conversations — a slightly daunting prospect that proved most valuable.

Everywhere we sensed an aliveness, an eager seeking, whatever the varied interests of Friends or the difficulties that were being encountered, the main difficulties being isolated friends and huge geographical distances. Starting a new meeting, perhaps with only one family, hundreds of miles from the next, the likelihood of being able to know and experience only one Quaker meeting, and the difficulty expressed that only the wealthy could get to Yearly Meeting and thus meet a wider number of Friends, are all part of the same problem.

Annette Wallis 1985

2.67   Very slowly, new attitudes reached Friends in Australia, in much the same way that Australian Friends have always been influenced by the theological thinking of English Friends, by correspondence, periodicals and literature as well as being conveyed by visiting Friends. As was the case in the 1860s, younger Friends were the first to imbibe the new beliefs. These young people at the 1907 General Meeting in Sydney had inaugurated the Australian Friends Fellowship Union which in most meetings became the nucleus for Young Friends activities.

The first interstate camp of Australian Young Friends was held at Healesville in Victoria immediately after the 1910 General Meeting. These camps cemented young Friends in deep comradeship.
This organisation was more than a coincidence for it bound young Friends together in time for the severe trials which compulsory military training (prior to World War I) demanded. Popular radical trends of Australian youth have influenced young Friends, and tempered by a strong sense of fellowship at their annual camps, Young Friends have often sparked a spiritual stimulus in the society by their frank and sincere questioning.

Charles Stevenson 1973

2.68   As I settled into meeting, aware of all the people in the room already and sensing those who entered after me, I had a wonderful feeling of coming home. I knew that this was a place where I was valued, and could be nurtured. This is very important to me as I do work in connection with other churches where I sometimes have to struggle. I had recently returned from five weeks in Indonesia, where I attended the Christian Conference of Asia General Assembly and Youth Forum. During my time away I realised that in being a Quaker there were many things I had taken for granted, like that young people are seen as valid contributors, are listened to, and that there is a desire for dialogue between younger and older members of the meetings. I expected the same would be the case elsewhere. I learned the hard way that this was not so!

All I know is that I felt very isolated in the work I was trying to do — simply striving to have young adults included as important people in the ecumenical movement.

Anna Wilkinson 2000

2.69   Do you value the children in your meeting and help make them feel they are welcome?

Do you seek opportunities to involve children actively in every aspect of the life of the meeting?

Are you open to the ministry of children of all ages, however it may be expressed?

Children's Committee, Australia Yearly Meeting 1996

2.70   Australia and New Zealand took on more autonomous roles in 1902. This involved appointing representatives from their General Meetings to London Yearly Meeting. Thomas Hodgkin was a visitor to Australia from London Yearly Meeting.

I can truthfully say that I went out believing in the school [Friends School, Hobart], I came back believing in it far more. And less than ever am I disposed to regret that some non-members' children get their education there, for I think one thing that we want to cultivate in Australia is that kind of general knowledge of 'the ways of Friends' and respect for their character as a religious body, which is generally diffused in this country [England], but which through their ignorance seems to be wanting in many parts of Australia.

Thomas Hodgkin 1909

2.71   Janey O'Shea sees the society as being at the crossroads and in serious need of spiritual renewal from the grassroots upwards; that is, beginning in the heart and will of each individual. The dissatisfaction and unease that are currently felt need not be cause for despair because we do have the remedy at the centre of our heritage, if we will only claim it. Central to the teaching of George Fox was that there is a spiritual process that will lead us to truth for our own time. We are to live out in our own time the unique Quaker Way or talent that God has entrusted to us through generations of faithful Friends.

It is still all there and available — the discipline of waiting on the Spirit to lead us in the Light, and to empower us to transform our lives, the life of our community and the world.

Joan Humphreys 1993

2.72   Dwell in the love of God, for that will unite you together, and make you kind and gentle towards one another, and to seek one another's good and welfare. (George Fox)

Communities must have peace within themselves if they are to survive, and the shared experience of God's love provides the foundation of peace.

Reg Naulty 1990

2.73   To listen, as Woolman observed, is to act 'like dew on tender plants'. Judgmentalism is contrary to faith and forgiveness and has no place in the act of true listening.

Let us live in the knowledge that we are wholly unique, that we are loved. Let us be tolerant of each other, being mindful that, despite everything, the other has equal access to God's delight. Let us understand that our personal testimonies are inextricably bound together, one in the One. In our meetings let us 'live adventurously', let us risk. Let us treasure our gifts, knowing they are just that — gifts. Let our creativity burn brightly remembering what the orthodox tradition teaches:

I said to the almond tree,
'Sister, speak to me of God'
And the almond tree blossomed.

Gerard Guiton 1991

3

living our faith

Erica Fisher

3 LIVING OUR FAITH

Faith in action

3.1 The spirituality that is real to us finds its inner strength in the mystical experience of connectedness with each other and with the whole of creation. This is the deep, still and vibrant centre that transcends time. From that dynamic place it is possible to turn outwards and work in one's own available and chosen action spaces to help make manifest the harmony that is already known. This radical mysticism is the mainstream of Quaker tradition.

At the very centre we are indeed one, but as we turn outward for action our differences of tradition and experience distinguish us and enable us to partner each other in the dialogue and the dance. The harmony is possible only because of the difference, the distances between.

David James and Jillian Wychel 1991

3.2 If our concern is with the love of a creating, sustaining, sanctifying, indwelling Spirit for the life and wholeness of the world, we will be caught up and enlivened by images of the Spirit, desiring to break through in reconciling, whole-making love between all people, all beings and all things in the universe. This God is within us, empowering us, flowing out from, to, between us and all things — both immanent and transcendent.

To live in the Spirit is to act in the belief that love is stronger than death; in the belief that if we act in goodwill toward another we overcome our fear of them and their fear of us. And in such action is the proclamation of peace.

To live in the Spirit will mean moving towards being open to those modes of being, thinking, deciding and acting that are empowering from within rather than controlling from without for ourselves and for our neighbours.

Margaret Bearlin 1984

3.3   Our spontaneous reactions under unexpected crises provide the crucial test of what it is we value. Jesus reacted unerringly from his concern with the person involved. Thus to the 'righteous' who accused him of breaking Mosaic law by healing on the Sabbath, he reacted with 'The Sabbath was made for man, not man for the Sabbath', and without hesitation, to the ill man himself, he said, 'Stretch out your hand'.

Similarly, in another incident of confusion between the claims of the individual and the demands of the community as embodied then in Mosaic law, Jesus reacted immediately on the level of the personal. He confronted the would-be upholders of the law with a personal decision: 'Let him amongst you who is himself not personally guilty cast the first stone.' He met the woman accused of adultery on the personal level of forgiveness, that both lifted the intolerable burden of lonely guilt, and reassured her by awakening in her a sense of what she herself might become.

William Oats 1990

3.4   To love God with your whole heart and mind and strength, and your neighbour as yourself brings a peace and sense of unity with all creation, and as a result you seek to relieve suffering — not to cause it.

Don Pescod 1960

3.5   Our relationships with other people are the real expression of our concern for them. The love which Jesus demonstrates, and to which he calls us, is an all-embracing love which allows no discrimination between those who are pleasing to us and those who are not; no discrimination between those whose customs and morals we find laudable and those whose ways are an offence to us.

This was Jesus' answer to the question, 'How can war be prevented?' By contacting the people who appear to be on the other side, by love and understanding, by patient humility, by realising that at least fifty per cent of the cause of disharmony lies with us, and by winning them and ourselves to a new way of life.

Jean Richards 1962

3.6   The effects of our actions are largely beyond our control. Any happening they may influence has multiple causes that can never be unravelled; the contribution of what we did is as hard to assess as that of a single strand in a rope. We must have faith that if we purify our hearts making our motives more compassionate, what we do will strengthen unimaginably the great forces that can save humanity.

Adam Curle 1990

Prayer

3.7   To pray is to enter the presence of the Eternal. As a weak magnet strengthens when placed in a strong magnetic field, so we are strengthened. Our discord becomes order, our own field of energy is enhanced. Prayer strengthens, heals, renews, extends. By remembering and holding others in the presence of the Lord, we strengthen them also through the empathy and telepathy of prayer.

Margaret Olesen 1981

Leanne Mooney

3.8 Although I am a great talker who needs somehow to articulate my experience, I find that my prayer life consists of listening rather than talking to God. By listening, I mean exploring the world so that through my five senses I come deep into the sixth sense of the interiority of things. This feels like what George Fox referred to as a 'sinking down to the Seed'. I know that if I listened and attended more in this way I could be at prayer all the time — in the world, but not of it (and its reasonings and values), so to speak.

Increasingly God is everything I encounter, the actuality and the potential. God is neither good nor bad, but a power, an energy, a force for Life and for transformation. I am often sensible of living and moving within an infinity of time and space with the certainty that my decisions (made with the guidance of the Light I currently have) somehow contribute to the development of love and justice and healing. I don't feel insignificant at all but rather part of that power for life and transformation. Prayer, therefore, feels like listening and responding with appropriate action.

In recent years my close association with Aboriginal Peoples has verified my relationship with the Spirit. It seems to me that their experience of the manifold aspects of the Spirit, connected with every aspect of life in the universe, transcends dichotomies and makes sense of the paradoxes that tantalise, perplex and stress those who try to separate spirit and matter in their lives.

I see the task of prayer as bringing awareness of the life of the Spirit into what we call the physical world. Prayer is the action that unleashes divine will and creates heaven on earth.

Susannah Brindle 2001

3.9   Consider the prayer-life of Jesus. It comes out most clearly in the record of St Luke, who leaves us with the impression that prayer was the most vital element in our Lord's life. He rises a great while before day that he may have some hours alone with His Father. He continues all night in prayer to God. Incident after incident is introduced by the statement that Jesus was praying. Are we so much nearer God that we can afford to dispense with that which to Him was of such vital moment? But apart from this, it seems to me that this prayer-habit of Jesus throws light upon the purpose of prayer.

I think of those long hours alone with God. Quite obviously petition can have had a very small place in our Lord's thoughts. There must have been a sacred interchange far deeper than this.

God is not always interfering with the working of the natural order. But indirectly, by the working of mind upon mind, great changes may be wrought. We live and move and have our being in God; we are bound up in the bundle of life in Him, and it is reasonable to believe that prayer may often find its answer, even in outward things, by the reaction of mind upon mind. Prayer is not given us to make life easy for us, or to coddle us, but to make us strong.

William Littleboy 1937

3.10   Prayer is such a reversal of all that our intellect is trained to do. Prayer is not a laboratory experience, you cannot take the attitude: 'prove it — then I will believe'. It calls for such humility that we can, or at least are willing to, sense beyond ourselves something greater which will establish communication with us — in quite unexpected and infinitely varied forms — on just one condition (and here I must speak in terms of personal experience): on faith and trust; not faith in something, but wide faith — wide enough to accept that maybe there is more than I can, now or ever, encompass with finite, conditioned logic of thought.

Frank Lindsey 1981

3.11   The insistent unceasing calls for help — and little whispers
The prayer of gratitude and joy for unasked gifts and mercies.
The silent listening prayer of waiting to hear, not to be heard.
My prayer is a form of noticing — the beauties of light and shade
— hard dry winds and soft animals and bugs.
The not usually seen
The hardly noticed
The huge and ungainly
The quick and the very slow
The every detail
The tragic and miraculous
The gift of prayer like this touches and saddens my soul.

Rowe Morrow 2001

3.12   For me it is logical and reasonable to believe that when I listen attentively and deeply, I will connect. But there are times when I do not feel as if I do, even though in my heart of hearts, my faith tells me that something has been set in motion — transmission of sorts is under way. The void I experience can seem somewhat arid and I have felt the need for some structure.

So I decided to practise regularly the Benedictine form of prayer. It has been traditionally divided into three parts: *lectio* or sacred reading, meditation, and *oratio* or spoken prayer. You read a passage until you are gripped by some words. At this time the meditation begins. Repeat the words again and again as if soaking them into your being. The aim is not to reflect on the meaning or intellectualise. Once you have relished the words sufficiently you can begin the prayer.

What has been my experience of this? I read passages from the Psalms, Ecclesiastes, Isaiah, Jeremiah, the Gospel of John, and find much to activate and nurture my inner life. Attaining stillness is a pick-me-up in itself. Reflecting on particular words or phrases that stand out for me is grounding and revitalising. I have gone beyond the temporal and felt connected with the eternal, a void bestowing peace, calm and quiet. What I have found particularly compelling and moving is spontaneously speaking aloud after the reflection. Speaking aloud makes a presence come to life as if really there, an awareness I can liken to that of the presence of a loving friend.

I can see it is providential that I have experimented with this Benedictine form of prayer which has provided a way for me to focus on the Spirit — inner simplicity.

Doreen Cope 2000

3.13   In a recent radio broadcast an Islamic theologian said that in the view of Islam 'the practice of medicine is an act of worship, a manifestation of the principle of unity (of body, mind and spirit)'. My mind turned to a moment in my life not long past.

I was sitting at the bedside of our granddaughter, who had hovered for 48 hours between life and death with meningitis and was now lying apparently unseeing, unhearing, shallowly breathing. I sang to her one of her favourite nursery songs and, as always, I got a particular word wrong. She opened her eyes, corrected me (as always), gave me a beautiful smile and relapsed to her former state.

Hilary, at two and a half years of age, was a child of exhilarating vitality, full of dance and song, living life as it were on tiptoe and loving everyone. The threat of death was succeeded by statistical probabilities: damage to brain, sight, hearing and/or mobility. Ultimately she left hospital with just a limp, which slowly disappeared, restoring her former exuberance to the full.

I do not understand the nature of spiritual healing. What words can convey a mystery? What heart can deny it, once experienced? I had no evidence that Hilary would not have recovered, or not so well, in the absence of prayer. I do not picture a God who is deciding who shall live, who shall die and when, and who is influenced in this task by our entreaties. But the experience with Hilary has strengthened my belief that the healing acts of Jesus were not a demonstration of special status, but an illustration of the working of the Spirit through ordinary people. There is a strength, an empowerment, to be channelled through prayer.

Eric Gargett 1991

3.14 In the Meeting for Worship for Healing we have the privilege of specifically focusing on individuals requiring wholeness and healing through upholding them in the silence — in light and love.

In silent worship we make ourselves available to the healing power of the Spirit, to be used on behalf of those in need, whether it be in body, mind or spirit. Not to persuade God, nor to in any way deny the work of those in the healing professions: simply seeking the upholding of God's love in the wholeness we recognise as health of spirit, the basis of healing.

To be effective it is essential that we do not dwell on the negative conditions of illness. Our prayerful upholding must be full of positive expectancy, imagination and thanksgiving. Our groups are meetings, not for sickness, but for health and for healing.

anon.

3.15 As we open ourselves to become the channel of God's healing grace we shall find that healing is given to those who pray as well as to those for whom we are praying.

Jack Dobbs 1984

Service, justice

3.16 Are we aware of oppression and injustice that denies the full glow of the inner light to so many? Do we feel their hurt within ourselves and our own Light diminish until we take action?

Do we sufficiently trust the leadings of the Spirit as it moves through us into our Yearly Meeting, to the community, and to the world?

Australia Yearly Meeting Epistle 1975

3.17 The whole essence of the New Testament is that Jesus came to proclaim that change is possible (Luke 4, taking up from Isaiah 61), and as Friends historically we belong to that radical tradition which seeks not only to care for the victims of oppression (which the Church is quite good at) but also to change those conditions which produce oppression (which on the whole the Church has not been good at). Or in the words of Luke 9:2, Jesus sent out his disciples to heal the sick *and* to proclaim the Kingdom. From both the Old Testament and the New Testament we know that his Kingdom is based on justice and righteousness.

Peter Jones 1979

3.18 When a need exists, or when a process is victimising people, our place is to be with the victims, and to deal with them not with condescension but as children of the light. It is as simple and as complex as that.

John Woolman lived at a time when the American Indians were being driven out of their lands and being slaughtered. He went and lived amongst them seeking that 'I might learn something from them and that the leading of love and truth in me might be of some service to them.'

Stewart and Charlotte Meacham 1976

3.19 Our view of tolerance makes it possible for us — even incumbent upon us — to engage in relationships that are neglected or shunned by others. It finds expression not just in a commitment to ecumenism and interfaith dialogue, but also to many areas of deep social division, wherever people are regarded and treated as less than human.

Eric Gargett 1997

3.20 Perhaps service is gratitude in action and faith in action. It is having something extra to offer back, based on the immense and insupportable inequities and injustices which are the causes of violence.

Service is born of the conviction that the human spirit can witness to 'that of God in everyone', and that inequities such as hunger are intolerable.

Rowe Morrow 1998

3.21 I left India carrying a sense of sadness and despair for much that I saw on a daily basis; yet also strengthened by a sense of hope instilled in me by the many activists I had met who were devoting their lives to social change. On the journey home to Australia I was deeply confronted by my own knowledge that I have the choice to continue working for social justice and change, whilst those most adversely affected by global inequities do not.

Penny Duckworth 1991

3.22   If there is an identifiable Quaker approach to service, we could hope that it is embodied in this: that as in worship we follow the leadings of the Spirit and the Light faithfully, we are prepared to be led where it takes us — to let go of comfortable certainties and be taken into new knowledge, and also into painful and difficult experiences. The journey is not a comfortable one for the most part — it can be terrifying at times, and often leads close to despair. If we accept that there is that of God in everyone, others cannot be objects of charity. We go prepared to encounter their full reality, and to be taught and changed by it.

Mark Deasey 2002

3.23   The Quakers have been and are some of the gentlest people in the world — they have been people with great compassion. They were the first Christian body to free themselves from complicity with slavery. They became the backbone of the anti-slavery agitation in America and England and, later on, the anti-opium movement. It is impossible to deny — whatever one's own opinion — that their protest against war has been magnificent. They have taken a leading part in prison reform, in temperance work, and in popular education.

Annie Wilton 1924

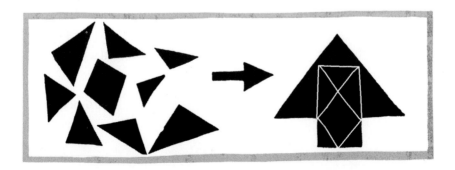

Max Raupach

3.24   I do feel that finding and being found by that of God within me releases me from the dilemma of 'Should I? Is it worth it? What good can I do?' The answers to these questions are no longer important.
What matters is that I *must* act, and that the task will be given to me. In my school motto was my answer — *Servite in caritate* — service with love.

The concept of service had never been clear to me and now it became so. I serve because I love God. My service — my work — is an expression of my love for everything that is of God. So while the work I am asked to do may be difficult and may demand a great deal of me, I know I have been given another opportunity to love. And although loving is sometimes also difficult and demanding, it is, in the end, the most joyous and wondrous thing we can do.

Sarah Briggs 1992

3.25   I have been pondering on the order of greatness given by Paul in his exhortation on 'faith, hope and charity' (1 Corinthians 13). It has struck me vividly that Paul was right and for too long the Church has put faith as the prime necessity. Charity *never* faileth. Faith may, hope may, but we can recognise God in the neighbour in need, the refugee, the outcast, the criminal, the underprivileged, the bodily and mentally sick.

No matter how aged, faithless, weak, sick or busy a person is, God has acts of love at hand for them to do. It may be to join in physical campaigns for the work of peace, alleviating race tensions, improving our legal and social laws, cleansing our TV programs, writing a letter to the prime minister or the press, or just thinking up a kind word to heal a breach. Thus we find God.

Cyril Gare 1961

3.26   I find human rights treaties inspiring and useful, firstly because they present a vision for humanity which is inclusive, peaceful, just and caring, and secondly because they weigh what is necessary for each person to have a whole and normal life and for communities to nurture and support the rich potential of each member. They are shaped so as to transcend human differences in the spirit of equality and, at the same time, underpin differences in the spirit of tolerance and freedom. Importantly, in relation to activism, they carry the weight of agreement between nations of all cultures, religions and economic conditions. They offer a holistic description of how to work for heaven on earth.

Helen Bayes 2003

3.27   Doing bush regeneration gives me hope. There was joy at seeing some eucalyptus, wattles and other natives freed from the burden of lantana, much more likely to survive now, and the pleasure (and tiredness) of physical labour. I was delighted at the thoughtful insights of the regenerators: minimal disturbance. Start from the healthy bush and move outwards. Be caring, compassionate. Watch where you put your feet. Focus. A very small focus: is this a cassia (weed) or the very similar native? Either leave the weeds where they cannot re-establish and will provide nutrients (e.g. by putting them in the forks of trees), or take them away to put in the council tip: nothing just vanishes.

Helen Gould 1995

3.28   [Our guide] described in graphic terms the dust-filled atmosphere of Broken Hill before this regeneration took effect: of the respiratory sicknesses, the dust inside and outside homes and gardens, and the lack of greenery in the town. Now we were able to admire tree-lined streets and refreshing parklands.

Albert and Margaret Morris could be described as among Australia's first 'Greenies' but I would prefer to consider them as having continued a long Quaker tradition of care for, and interest in, the world of nature as part of God's handiwork.

Bronwen Meredith 1993

3.29   I was depressed by the impotence of a peace testimony in a world which seemed to be constantly at war. The arms trade was abhorrent and diverted much-needed Third World funds from services like health and education. The Quaker emphasis quite rightly was on exposing these horrors.

However, I was more deeply concerned at the wider implication of the peace testimony in a world where the environment was being threatened at every level. The war on nature and our fellow creatures just had to stop. The tragedy was not so much that we were destroying life for future generations but that we had not even seriously started to do anything about it. I sensed that, if indeed we had been allowed free will by an all-loving rather than all-powerful Being, the responsibilities placed upon us to do something about saving our planet were awesome.

Brian Connor 1994

3.30 The great opportunities and responsibilities in this vast continent are apparent to us: service to our Aborigines, appreciation of our Asian neighbours, answering to the needs of our children, preserving the records of the lives and faith of our early Friends, and searching for clarity as to our proper place as a member of the world community of Friends.

In all our thought and prayer we must seek first that which needs to be done, then work whole-heartedly for it, believing that, through dependence on God, His will can be achieved. Let us accept Christ's invitation and work with Him daily, remembering that 'they that wait upon the Lord shall renew their strength; they shall mount up with wings as eagles; they shall run and not be weary; they shall walk and not faint'.

Australia General Meeting 1956

Max Raupach

Lives speak

3.31 Love was the first motion, and then a concern arose to spend some time with the Indians, that I might feel and understand their life, and the Spirit they live in, if haply I might receive some instruction from them, or they be in any degree helped forward by my following the leadings of Truth amongst them. And as it pleased the Lord to make way for my going at a time when the troubles of war were increasing and when by reason of much wet weather travelling was more difficult than usual at that season, I looked upon it as a more favourable opportunity to season my mind, and bring me into a nearer sympathy with them. And as mine eye was to the great Father of Mercies, humbly desiring to learn what his will was concerning me, I was made quiet and content.

John Woolman 1763

Deborah Faeyrglenn

3.32   *James Backhouse and George Washington Walker visited Australia between 1832 and 1838.*

What an indefatigable pair they were. Their concern for the convicts, for settler both bond and free, and for the Aborigines, never faltered; and overall they discharged with devotion their 'duty of Christian love'.

Ships of all sizes and conditions, weather so fierce on the west coast of Van Diemen's Land that they were given up for lost, they took in their stride. Off to Flinders Island to visit an Aboriginal settlement, nine days on the voyage from Hobart to Sydney, on to Norfolk Island, back to Sydney then north to Moreton Bay: 'the utmost verge of that part of the British dominions inhabited by white settlers', south again with a stopover at Newcastle to visit the Hunter Valley, and later a visit to the Port Macquarie penal settlement — everywhere inspecting and reporting conditions to the authorities, and always meticulously writing up their diaries. Finally on their way back to England, they visited Port Phillip, Port Adelaide and Swan River.

Florence James 1982

3.33   Charles Wheeler accompanied his father Daniel on a voyage around the Pacific Islands, including Australia, New Zealand and Hawaii, from 1833 to 1838. This voyage arose from a concern of Daniel Wheeler for the post-contact indigenous populations. British Friends provided and equipped a boat, the *Henry Freeling*, for the journey, which was both a fact-finding exercise, especially in regard to the effects of alcohol on the island communities, and a Christian mission — 'gospel labours'.

In Hawaii they held an unprogrammed meeting attended by 3000 people who had to be asked more than twice to rise and depart at the conclusion, 'such precious solemnity prevailed'.

Daniel Wheeler is one of our 'Great Friends', a complex, strong-willed and inspirational figure, whose supervision of the draining of the swamps near St Petersburg is a well-known story. He came to Friends after some years of life at sea and in the army, exposed to many dramatic dangers and disasters. During this time he sowed some very wild oats; his exemplary life after convincement was an expiation of these youthful sins.
The Christian mission of the voyage was of immense importance to him, and description of this aspect, together with accounts of his own devotions and spiritual development, form a large part of his daily accounts.

Maureen Powles 1985

3.34 There was one settler, Robert Cock [who attended Friends' meetings in Adelaide and Mount Barker] whom Backhouse met with on his brief visit to South Australia. He had sought Cock's support in the forming of the committee to assist the Protector of Aborigines. On 15 September 1838 a letter from Cock appeared in *The Southern Australian* under the nom-de-plume of A. Tenant. Enclosed with the letter was a sum of money and the following explanatory note:

> £3.16.6, being the interest at the rate of 10 per cent on one-fifth of the purchase money of the town land purchased by me on 27th March 1837. This sum, in accordance with the pledge given by the Colonization Commissioners for this province, and in accordance with the principle therein signified in their first annual report, wherein it is stated that they were to receive one-fifth of the lands to constitute a permanent fund for the support and advancement of the natives; I beg leave to pay the above sum for that purpose, seeing the Commissioners as yet have neither fulfilled their pledge in this respect, to the public, or carried out the moral principle signified. Under these circumstances, it is impossible to let the question rest, and until that be done, I feel it my duty to pay the proper authorities, for the use of the natives, this yearly rent — the above sum being one and a half year's rent, viz. from 27th March 1837 to 27th instant.
>
> I disclaim this to be either donation, grant or gift, but a just claim the natives of this district have on me as an occupier of those lands.

William Oats 1985

3.35 In 1915 Charles Francis Fryer went to France as one of the Friends' War-Victims-Relief workers, and for about three years shared the labours, dangers, and strain of that body of Quaker youth. His familiarity with motor cars had plenty of scope, as for instance when the French military authorities requested him to evacuate civilians under fire at Rheims.
At Bar-le-duc he would go as one of a batch of relief workers to gather up babies, pack them in straw, label them, and bring them to safety.
Later in the war, when near St Menehould, while acting as chauffeur he helped nurses with patients, and on one occasion when it was bitter cold, gave most of the clothes from his own body to wrap helpless human suffering. At the same time he surreptitiously took photographs of the battle field which, as lantern slides, were used to illustrate his many addresses on peace in Adelaide. His slide of piles of dead soldiers as far as the eye could see was one of the most clinching arguments for peace.

Returning to Australia, Frank Fryer became an ardent supporter of the League of Nations, on many occasions speaking on its behalf at big open-air meetings in Adelaide Botanic Park. The cause of civil liberty interested him, and likewise, radical reform of the social-economic order, along the lines of Christian Socialism.

anon. 1942

3.36   Herbert Crosland gave the perfect friendship. At times he may have appeared to run from contact, but at meeting when one or another spoke haltingly he took the meaning and clarified the message in simple words. When our members were troubled and went to him he never ran from them, but enfolded them in understanding, giving them confidence, faith, hope.

Did he know what he had to face when he elected to come to Australia as Clerk to husband the Society of Friends? Did he know of the miles and miles of arid country he would have to traverse to reach the isolated members? He was an Englishman, and if he was disappointed he never said so because he was a Friend and he knew that God was with him in all his concerns. He, like the Master, did not seek to be consoled but to console; nor to be understood, but to understand. He was the perfect friend.

Mollie Skinner 1947

3.37   The documentary *When Friends were Enemies* (1991) was of special interest to Friends. It arose out of the fiftieth anniversary of the arrival in Australia in 1940 of the ship the *Dunera*, a notorious voyage. In the film there is a moving account about a simple Australian guard who puts his rifle up on the luggage rack of the train taking these men to the Hay internment camp. 'I thought all you men were enemies, but you are friends', he exclaimed as he handed around tobacco and cigarette papers. Indeed, there were a few Quakers amongst them — about 25 of these men attended Meetings for Worship on board the ship and later at Hay.

Charles Stevenson 1991

3.38   To conquer by belief, to vanquish by hope, to overcome by love, is the most important contribution towards the establishment of a better world to come and to be enjoyed by all humanity.

> *Message to the 1942 General Meeting of Australia,*
> *signed by 19 German men, members of the Quaker Group*
> *in the No 2 Internment Camp, Tatura Victoria*

3.39   Because I feel it to be an immoral and unjust law I am a conscientious non-complier with the National Service Act. Non-compliance with this Act means for me a denial of the military machine and the right of the government to use men's lives as tools of its policies, and an affirmation of the right and responsibility of every Christian to take his life into his own hands and use it as Jesus taught he should. I reject the Act in all its forms, whether it be registering, paying fines, attending a medical examination or obeying a call-up notice — in fact, I have a criminal record as a result of refusing to do these things — and of particular relevance to today's case I refuse to exempt myself as a conscientious objector under the terms of this Act. To do so would be to acknowledge the authorities' right to use this law to conscript other men for military training, and to exempt me from not only my obligation to bear effective witness to my faith, but also my responsibility towards those who are serving prison sentences imposed under the military conscription laws.

> *David Martin 1972*

3.40 Kenneth Boulding was fond of saying: 'Anything that is thinkable is possible.' Since he had a formidable intellect and highly idiosyncratic and original thought processes, Kenneth's personal possibility boundaries were vast.

Everything within him and around him produced intense curiosity and delight. He was fascinated by weather systems, economic and social systems, landscapes, and architecture. But most of all he was fascinated by the heights and depths of the human condition and how human beings might realise their full potential. He had an infinite faith in the learning and communicative ability of people and was enormously interested in and invigorated by cross cultural experiences and encounters with people from all nations and all walks of life. He had an ability (shared and shaped by Elise) to endow everyone and everything with significance. This gift has meant that Kenneth and Elise have been richly blessed with friends from all over the world.

Kenneth embodied and epitomised that wonderful Quaker principle of 'walking cheerfully over the world answering that of God in everyone'. Kenneth understood better than most of us the realities that lie behind the limits of our own self-imposed horizons. His mind was constantly searching for new vantage points from which to look at old problems and he also understood that underlying everything was a reality that we only dimly fathom.

Kevin Clements 1993

3.41   In my experience as an anti-Vietnam War worker, and at Greenham Common with the peace women, I learned the power of nonviolent opposition to violence or potential violence. How extraordinary it was to feel so strong, by myself sometimes, in the face of military and police resistance. I put it down to the power of the Spirit. I felt much more powerful, and much less afraid than those who offered violence to violence. When we blockaded the missile carriers we lay on the ground linked only by thin threads of wool. We made a web. The police were baffled and did not offer any violence to us. We were totally still and totally powerful in our convictions. I am convinced from my experience that nonviolence can and does work even to the point of death. For if we ever adopt the way of the opposition, the powerful over us, then we have truly lost.

Sabine Erika 1997

3.42   I was introduced to prison visiting in 1962 by a fellow Quaker who was a member of the Civil Rehabilitation Committee which organised visits to prisoners and also cared for their families in practical ways.

My object was to befriend the prisoner, to listen but not to give advice, to be sensitive that prison is an isolating place and to keep in touch with the prisoner's family. I also made it a point to write regularly and usually received answering letters.

One of the few rights the prisoner retains is to refuse to see a visitor and I learned not be offended when this occasionally happened.

The belief that 'there is that of God in everyone' helped when I had to visit someone convicted of an horrific crime.

Over the years I have learnt that human beings usually respond to kindness and genuine interest in their welfare.

Leslie Storey 1997

3.43 Getting arrested is a spiritual experience for me. Civil disobedience, or holy obedience, is an important tool in my work for social change. It is an opportunity to make a sacred witness for what I perceive as truth, in the struggle for justice, for peace, for care of our precious planet.

It is not something I do lightly, or without a great deal of prayerful preparation. Nonviolence is always paramount, including respect for the arresting officers and potential adversaries who might be present, disagreeing with my point of view. Many times I've been in a position to remind fellow protesters that our argument is not with the officials present, but with the law, and those who make decisions.

I've had some interesting conversations with arresting officers by being courteous, cooperative, and by being open to the goodness abiding in them. It's important to know that we are they, and they are us. Mentally removing the separation, the duality, helps enormously with coping positively with what for some people might be a negative experience.

My more recent arrests have had an added dimension: singing and dancing — songs and dances for the earth. Moving meditations, they engender calmness all round — or is it just confusion for the officials? It's true that it is difficult for arresting officers to be menacing or rough when they are faced with people who are singing or dancing. In fact they're reluctant to interfere with what's going on, perhaps recognising that they are witnessing something deep and meaningful.

Jo Vallentine 1999

3.44 A woman's story

A woman sat, one winter's day, at a bus stop. A man who was warmly dressed but dirty, battered and drunk sat next to her.

Man: It's a cold day.
Woman: Yes and it seems to be getting colder.

Man: I hate murderers, do you?
Woman: I hate what they do.

Man: My sister was murdered. Have any of your family been murdered?
Woman: No. I pray to God that it never happens.

Man: I want to go back up north to my people. They look after each other up there.
Woman: I hope you can do that.

Man: You are a good woman.
Woman: And you are a good man.

Man: Do you go to church?
Woman: Yes.

Man: I used to go to church and pray but I haven't been for a long time.
Woman: You don't have to go to church to pray.

Man: I used to pray for food.

Woman: I most often say, 'God help me — I don't know what to do.' What bus do you want to catch?

Man: It doesn't matter. They all go somewhere.

Woman: Here's the bus to Redhead.

Man: I'll catch that.

The man staggered across to the bus but stopped and turned back to the woman. He came over to her and put his hands on her shoulders and kissed her on the cheek. He left without another word.

Pat Firkin 2000

Our testimonies

We try to live according to basic principles that we call 'testimonies'. They have evolved over time. The chief among these testimonies now are equality, integrity, community, simplicity and peace.

Equality

3.45   There is a principle which is pure, placed in the human mind, which in different places and ages hath different names; it is, however, pure and proceeds from God. It is deep and inward, confined to no forms of religion nor excluded from any where the heart stands in perfect sincerity. In whomsoever this takes root and grows, of what nation soever, they become brethren.

John Woolman 1762

3.46   Early Quakers often referred to the inward light as the 'seed'. Their view was not that it grew gradually through learning (into wisdom), but that it was a divine potential, which could burst forth at any time. For them, and for us today, the seed or the Light is the source of inward guidance, which connects us with the whole of creation and draws us into a total commitment to love and truth. Its power is entirely of God and it has nothing to do with human maturity, education or experience.

Helen Bayes 2003

3.47   After having seen something of the natives of Van Diemen's Land, the conviction was forced upon my mind that they exceeded the Europeans in those things to which their attention had been directed from childhood, just as much as the Europeans exceeded them in the points to which attention of the former had been turned under the culture of civilization.

There is a similar variety of talent and of temper among the Tasmanian Aborigines to what is to be found among other branches of the human family; and it would not be more erroneous in one of these people to look upon an English woman as defective in capacity, because she could neither dive into the deep and bring up a crayfish, nor ascend the lofty gumtrees to catch opossums for her family, than it would be for an English woman to look upon the Tasmanian as defective in capacity, because she could neither sew, nor read, nor perform the duties of civil, domestic life.

James Backhouse 1833

3.48 The basis of our membership is equality: we all have equal rights in meetings for business and worship, and also equal responsibility for the position in which we allow the society to remain.

Charles Howie 1910

3.49 'It is not womanly to be angry! Only frustrated women reject men!' But who has defined womanly? Who has defined frustration? Who said that when a woman of the nineteenth century took to her bed after her seventh and stillborn child that she was hysterical rather than sane? The early Friends knew about defining their own world, rejecting in anger the ways of church and king, and they were made to suffer for it by those who had power, just as the wise women called witches suffered at the hands of those in power. Friends defied the law as fast as those in power defined it. Once Penn asked a woman on trial for witchcraft if she had ridden through the air on a broomstick: when she replied in the affirmative he said he knew of no law against riding on a broomstick and ordered her discharge.

Sabine Erika 1983

3.50   I've been intrigued by the role of women in the history of Quakers: in particular how they were able to minister in the beginning; their extensive travels in the Ministry across the Atlantic, into Europe and West Africa; and the terrifically enlightening statements Margaret Fell made, long before their time. And in truth, there was also much that was unequal in their treatment in the early history of Quakers: the division in the meeting houses, their non-participation in meetings for business, often a distrust of their motives. It is hard to remain free of what happens in the wider society. I was still inspired by the wonderful stories of those women ministers though, struck by the fact most of them were servants or without much 'standing' and by their tremendous courage and faith to follow God's will. Good faith models for both women and men to examine.

Annabelle Cameron 2000

3.51   As a man I am aware that I have benefited from being part of a dominant group, even though I have endeavoured to identify with those outside that group. Growing up in our culture I inevitably enjoyed the advantage of being encouraged to initiate, and to see myself as being capable of changing things. I expected to do well at school and university, to get a good job, to head a family, and to contribute to the community. I learned to define myself in terms of outward roles and not to look at my emotional and spiritual needs.

To a large extent I have created the kind of life I wanted. Yet in recent years I have become more aware of my needs and have heard the anguish of people who have suffered from the social system. I have realised my responsibility for helping myself and other men to change the beliefs and practices that cause so much oppression.

From my experience, until a man is ready to look within and acknowledge his need for help, he is unlikely to benefit from a men's group. A group of men who are resentful and bitter about life may end up as a mutual protection society bolstering each other to reassert dominant values, and this is hardly likely to reduce stress or build new values.

What emerges in the men's groups I know is a shared feeling of concern about how to redefine male identity, how to support each other in a nurturing way, how to be friends, how to challenge each other about sexist language and behaviour, and how to support women and others who are victims of oppression.

David Purnell 1988

3.52   At the centre of Friends' religious experience is the consistently expressed belief in the equal worth of all people. Our common humanity transcends our differences. We aspire not to say or do anything nor to condone any statements, actions, or situations, which imply a lack of respect of the humanity or human rights of any person or people.

The Religious Society of Friends has always recognised that the Spirit of God dwells in every person and we believe that this is regardless of gender or sexual orientation. Committed, same-sex relationships are as valuable as other committed and loving relationships.

Quakers would prayerfully consider celebrations of commitment between gays or lesbians, who are already participants in Quaker Meetings.

Australia Yearly Meeting 1996

Truthfulness and integrity

3.53   I have long believed that speaking truth is both the simplest way of living your life and one of the most difficult to achieve.

Speaking truth with love seems the essence of the teachings of Jesus Christ — and I suspect of all great religions.

Judith Aitchison 1996

3.54   *Margaret Fell was imprisoned and was made liable to lose all her property for her refusal to take an oath of loyalty to the king.*

The same justices sent for me to Ulverston, where they were sitting, and when I came there they asked me several questions, and seemed to be offended at me for keeping a meeting at my house, and said, They would tender me the oath of allegiance. I answered, They knew I could not swear, and why should they send for me from my own house, when I was about my lawful occasions, to ensnare me, what had I done? They said, If I would not keep meetings at my house, they would not tender me the oath. I told them I should not deny my faith and principles for any thing they could do against me, and while it pleaseth the Lord to let me have an house, I would endeavour to worship him in it. So they caused the oath to be read, and tendered it to me, and when I refused it, telling them, I could not swear for conscience-sake, Christ Jesus having forbid it, they made a mittimus, and committed me prisoner to Lancaster Castle, and there George Fox and I remained prisoners until next assizes, and they indicted us upon the statute for denying the oath of allegiance, for they tendered it to both of us again at the assizes, and the indictments were found against us.

> So they passed sentence of Praemunire upon me which was that I should be out of the King's protection and forfeit all my estate, real and personal, to the King and imprisonment during life. But the great God of heaven and earth supported my spirit under this severe sentence, that I was not terrified but gave this answer to Judge Turner, who gave the sentence, 'Although I am out of the King's protection, I am not out of the protection of the Almighty God'.
>
> Margaret Fell 1664

3.55   This General Meeting reaffirms its strong objection to the use of the oath in courts of law and on other occasions, not only because swearing is forbidden by Jesus Christ, but also because it sets up a double standard of truth. By implication it suggests that a person is not bound to speak the truth unless he is under oath. We urge all our monthly meetings to endeavour to get legislation introduced to the various State parliaments to abolish the oath in courts of law and in connection with other legal transactions.

Australia General Meeting 1929

3.56   Source of all Truth
help us to be true to our true self;
let each encounter be face to face
with the essential person
in whom we meet
each other and Thee.

Whatever is false or base,
let it be purged away.
Whatever is artificial,
let it wither.
Whatever is crooked,
may it grow straight,
to reach up closer to the image
dwelling in Thee eternally
of our true Self
contained in Thee.

Leonce Richards 1989

3.57   I'd like to include in 'plain speaking' the difficult and joyful 'speaking of love'. Growing up in a family that loved each other without direct words, I would have said that it was unnecessary to state the obvious. Why then did my heart do a little dance when a close friend, in adulthood, looked me in the eye and said, 'I really do love you, Sue.' And many years later, when my mother was dying, why was it so important for me to say and hear words of love that had already been proved in deed for 45 years?

The power of words cannot be denied. As another friend said, 'When it seems difficult to express our deepest feelings, remember that the difficulty only lasts a few minutes, but regret at not speaking can last a lifetime.'

Sue Wilson 1999

Community, caring, healing

3.58   Our life is love, and peace, and tenderness; and bearing one with another, and forgiving one another, and not laying accusations one against another; but praying one for another, and helping one another up with a tender hand.

Isaac Penington 1667

3.59   To love one's neighbour is not simply a matter of understanding. Awareness is more than this. It is a compound of sensitivity and imagination. To be sensitive implies a readiness and an alertness to receive impressions as a photographic plate is quick to receive impressions of light. It means being quick (in the original sense of 'alive', as in 'the quick and the dead') to feel another's pain, as well as to understand another's point of view. But it also means being responsive to impressions that come from within as well as from without. This is well expressed in the Advice of Friends: 'Take heed, dear Friends, to the promptings of Love and Truth in your own hearts.'

William Oats 1990

3.60   When we take the risk of sharing our inward spiritual lives, it is an affirmation of the seeking process and a gesture of respect and trust in others. It enriches the faith and understanding of our community and helps to strengthen our service and outreach in the world. We truly need to talk to each other about who and where God is for us, what we hear in our inward ear, how we are being drawn, prompted and pushed in action. What we are sensing is our small place in creation. And when confronted with the symptoms of a leading, in ourselves or in someone else, let us rejoice at the nearness of God, let us share it with awe, and seek an adventurous unity in following it.

Helen Bayes 2003

3.61   Look at another in awe for he or she is a child of a loving, freeing God. A child like you, who has equal access to God's delight.
Be still in yourself as you search for the stillness in the other.
Don't judge, or gossip or recriminate but face the darkness in yourself as you face the darkness in the other and Light will be yours together.
And together you will join hands and incarnate God anew.
Know that you are precious, that you are Gift for if God loves your nearness dearly, should you not love yourself? Treasure your gifts knowing they are gifts.
And don't take yourself too seriously.

Gerard Guiton 1991

3.62   Men are learning that we must accept responsibility for what is happening in our lives and in the world. We must liberate ourselves from old ways of thinking. We must be part of the community debate about domestic violence and rape, the deeds of minorities, and conflict resolution. We can begin to see more clearly *who* rather than *what* we are as human beings. We can look beyond our roles to our individuality and our capacity to share power and support others. We can recognise our fears and our insecurities, our need to express feelings better, and to take from women the responsibility for our actions and emotions.

David Purnell 1994

3.63   Jesus left the old ways and brought light into the world, and having found the richness for himself he offered it, the 'abundant' life he had found. It is ours for the taking. Have we the courage to accept, to become aware of the vastness, the magnificence that is in the here and now? Or are we paralysed by doubts, hobbled by fears? New ways are uneasy bedfellows and birth is painful!

Life is an adventure when one feels free to follow new paths that can lead to Love, Joy and Peace.

Irene Speight 1991

3.64   **On the road from hurt to peace**

When I know
    I am fully heard
        Ah then!
            The invisible happenings!
                Expansive joy?
                    Weak coming strong?
                        Walls evaporating .....

Katherine McNamara 1997

3.65 Evening prayer

In the loneliness of the evening I pray:
for comfort at the heart
for the bereft, still bewildered, bereaved,
for the sick, who search for hope in the desolate sky,
for the forlorn, unexpected losers;

may you whisper within them, O God,
to all without companions at the darkening of the day;
may you who brings the morning
breathe within them that they are not forgotten,
that there is a love close to them.

Reg Naulty 2000

3.66 True freedom is experienced in that rare and blessed gift of friendship with one whose mind and heart jump with one's own, who receives the halting expression of one's half-formed thought with understanding sympathy and fills it out, returning it with added content, and who at times responds to the unspoken thought. And freedom in its deepest meaning is freedom for the whole personality to grow, to expand in the presence of God, a freedom in which we make use to the full of our essentially human heritage, our spiritual environment.

Raymond Wilton 1940

3.67 To open the hands and let the love flow through; to realise, no matter what age or stage, there is a skill to learning to live. Always something to learn; and the joy, through persevering to get it right, to know in our most precious and peaceful moments that we can and we did do it.

Joyce Hudson 1991

3.68   Relationships

Frail threads,
meaningless alone,
make up the patterned beauty of life.

Malcolm Whyte 1999

3.69   It is often rewarding if a large proportion of a meeting can come together for a common purpose, whether it be in a silent vigil for peace, or in a working bee to spring clean the meeting house. Such unity in actions is very good. Most worthwhile objectives need this constant and continuing effort. The occasional demonstration, or letter to the Prime Minister, or statement to the press, can be important and can arise 'in the life', but they will not often miraculously and immediately achieve the change in the situation which they seek. There is the need for the concerned individual or small group to give this purpose a high priority in their lives, to be the conscience of the Society on this matter, and to tell the rest of us when we can do something to help.

David Hodgkin 1971

3.70   It is fortunate that we had a reminder, at Yearly Meeting, that the Quaker way is not to sweep difficulties under the carpet; that coming to terms with difference can make us all more loving and effective; because last Sunday was a case in point. When two Friends spoke from their experiences of the difficulties of single parenting and being the children of lone parents they touched vulnerable emotions for any number of Friends present. In trying to come to terms with this sudden burst of energy, I acknowledge to myself the appropriateness of Friends raising, in a spirit of worship, social issues which exercise them, while at the same time recognising the hurt that will be opened for those who have suffered from discrimination and prejudice when they were involved with those issues at the coal face.

We often hang in with Quakers because we identify passionately with issues and want to change the world; sometimes we are frustrated because of the need to talk everything through before embarking on reform. When we hear of other's life experiences we realise the complexity of even the simplest social change.

Another individual characteristic I notice among Friends is to rebel against authority — even our low-grade, revolving-turnstile type of Quaker non-hierarchy. Ministry, notices, clerking, anything spoken, assumes a public face and is so easily partly-heard or heard differently from what the speaker was intending.

Here I must take my own advice about making generalisations and accept responsibility for those times I have allowed myself to be hurt by an unintended slight; for those times when I reacted against another for exposing to myself a flaw in me; for those times when I spoke thoughtlessly and again when I have carried around a wall of silence thinking the tension in me would go away. I ask you to forgive my blunderings and ask you to talk with me about any thing I have done to hurt you. I will try to hear what you are saying from your point of view. When things like this come up for me I will try to trust us both enough to open the issue of sensitivity with you and hope it won't add to your pain.

Katherine Purnell 1996

3.71   I believe that regularly practising being open to the Light can lead on (or back) to living in the Light. I think it is important to explain to little children that adults are limited by that which is not God within them. We can afford to be humble and give to children the practical information that will help them to stay in the Light. We can say that sometimes we make mistakes, sometimes we do and say things that are not of God and that it is not because the child is bad — it is not the child's fault. We love them and are sorry that they get hurt by that which is not God in us. Perhaps we can ask the child to help us notice when we are slipping away from the Light.

Jenny Spinks 1996

3.72   Living within the peace testimony daily is not about an absence of conflict in the external world. Peace, reconciliation, how do I attain inner peace — reconciling with myself and with others, doing God's work in recognising the truth of my behaviour, acknowledging to myself and to God and then to make amends where it is possible. I have thought a lot about George Fox's statement and the denial of fighting and taking up of arms:

> We have wronged no man's person or possessions; we have used no force or violence about any man; when we have been wronged, we have not sought to revenge ourselves, we have not made resistance against authority.

It seems to me that anger and conflict need to be dealt with consciously if there is to be a healthy way forward.

Annabelle Cameron 1999

3.73   Like other individuals and groups, Friends experience conflict as part of life. In *Christian Faith and Practice* (20:70) we find the following statement by Yearly Meeting in 1692:

> Where any have received offence from any other, first to speak privately to the party concerned, and endeavour reconciliation between themselves; and not to whisper or aggravate matters against them behind their backs, to the making parties, and the breach wider. Even though efforts for agreement by private conference should fail, Friends should avoid engaging one another in legal disputes.

This approach reflected several features of Friends' beliefs: the value placed on integrity, the need for direct communication and negotiation, and the danger of using the adversarial court system. The basis of the approach was the strong awareness of God's presence among Friends and the view of the group as a caring fellowship of people admonishing and upholding each other in their search for truth.

As Friends we inherit a commitment to dealing with conflict openly and constructively. The ideal has been set before us and it can be a significant inspiration and challenge. Our failure to reach the ideal should not lead us to abandon it. We can look for better ways to achieve it and to counteract the prevailing assumption that conflict must be controlled, if necessary by violence.

David Purnell 1992

3.74   Conflict generally has a negative connotation, but is this right? It is my belief that early Friends throve on conflict; it brought out the best in them. I have had personal experience of conflict from youth onwards and for the past 25 years it has had a Quaker context.

In my adolescence I loved Whittier's hymn 'Dear Lord and Father of Mankind' and especially the lines 'take from our souls the strain and stress and let our ordered lives confess the beauty of thy peace'. On the other hand, because by genetic inheritance and childhood conditioning I am a thinker and doer, another hymn appealed to me. This prays 'not for ever by still waters would we idly rest and stay, but would strike the living fountains from the rocks along our way'. Conflict indeed, but a healthy diversity of ideas which challenge me to find the balanced path.

Ruth Watson 1997

3.75   During a meeting for worship my thoughts were taken up with how important it is to reach out to those who have hurt us and to seek forgiveness from those to whom we have caused distress. The words of Jesus came to me clearly, almost as if part of the vocal ministry: 'Forgive us our trespasses as we forgive those who trespass against us'. It was a clear statement of fact. We receive forgiveness in the same measure as we are prepared to extend it to others. No ifs or buts — no exceptions.

Like many things, forgiveness is easier said than done. I wriggled and squirmed and tried to avoid the one thing I knew would help me. But eventually I made an opportunity to meet with God in a quiet place and asked to be shown how to forgive, and to be shown how to ask for forgiveness from others. It was a simple act but one of the hardest things I had ever done. As I confessed those against whom I had held a grudge I was then led to ask to be able to forgive them — saying the name and the circumstance.

A sense of peace descended on me and I thanked God for answered prayer. Within the next few days I felt a melting away of my hurt and after a while I couldn't even remember what had caused my animosity in the first place. The other part of the forgiveness act had to be tackled now; this time it occurred in meeting for worship. As I opened my spirit to be receptive to the Inner Light I was shown several people whom I needed to contact and ask their forgiveness. It seemed the best way to do this was by letter and within the next week I wrote three letters which expressed my regret for the pain I had caused and asked for forgiveness.

I had only one reply to those three letters but I knew I had done the right thing. My spirit felt lighter and as time went by I was happier and knew a great burden had rolled away. Now I go forward in the life of the Spirit, which is what living is all about anyway.

Joy Storey 1996

3.76   We had some lads that were very disturbing to the meeting; not that they meant to annoy, but they came for fun and meant to have it. I spoke three times to them about their conduct; the ringleader is a son of a leading man, who with several others is an avowed unbeliever, so the poor boys are to be pitied. I was amused and surprised next morning to find how tried the people of the place were at our treatment. The printer was going to give them a dressing in the next issue of the local paper; a gentleman who had just looked in said, 'Yes, give it them sharp, their conduct was disgraceful.' I turned to both and said, 'What these lads want is to see their elders live Christ among them'; the gentleman walked away, the printer looked thoughtful.

Joseph James Neave 1879

3.77   Forgiveness is a process and decision. It is a decision about how I live, how I treat myself, especially the little girl in me, and how I relate to people who have hurt me. Forgiveness is something I do for myself. It is part of my healing. In forgiving, I experience and let go of the shame and the pain and the bitterness. In working through and letting go of these emotions and expression in my body, I free myself from the power I have let these people have in my life. I am free. I am clear eyed and light hearted. I am walking my own path.

Quakers helped me to realise that I could trust God, other people and myself. Without that trust I could not have healed.

Helen Gould 1990

3.78   One of the few things that gives more joy than finding resolutions of our differences is the discovery that our arms and our hearts can be large enough, like those of our Creator, simply to embrace.

Jean Harkins 1997

Simplicity

3.79 It is our tender and Christian advice that Friends take care to keep to truth and plainness, in language, habit, deportment and behaviour; that the simplicity of truth in these things may not wear out nor be lost in our days, nor in our posterity's; and to avoid pride and immodesty in apparel, and all vain and superfluous fashions of the world.

Yearly Meeting in London 1691

3.80 William Penn set forth the economic reason for simplicity when he said that 'the very trimming of the vain world would clothe all the naked one'. Even more fundamental, however was the Quakers' belief that emphasis on things of the exterior world would distract Friends from their concentration on the interior life of the spirit and take time which belonged to communion with God.

Royal Buscombe 1987

3.81 Simplicity finds primary expression within the meeting for worship in the simple manner of waiting upon the Lord in surroundings unadorned in respect of furnishings and architecture. In the eighteenth century simplicity was insisted upon. The meeting houses of that period exhibit not only plainness but fitness, beauty and proportion. In the nineteenth century this good norm was departed from, but recent structures show a return to functional simplicity. While the concern for simplicity was fresh and living, its expression showed good taste, but when it became largely traditional, Quaker meeting houses as well as Quaker homes and furniture degenerated in form and style.

Howard Brinton 1931

3.82   I understand that living the simplicity testimony means to choose to walk in the light — to make this a constant priority — a simple (though hard) priority:

> Is this going to improve my connection with my inner self — help me to be centred?
>
> Is this going to enhance my connection with Godde?
>
> Is this going to improve my connection with others?
>
> Is this going to help me be connected with the earth?

I came to these guidelines by approaching the simplicity testimony from the angle of outer simplicity. I was asking Aziz Pabeny, an elderly Indian Friend, how we would decide what to do with the resources that would be liberated if we could convince people living in western society to live more simply and stop hogging the earth's resources. He said that I needed to understand that we in western society don't need to be living simply in order to help the third world; we need to be doing it for ourselves — we need to reclaim our connections with each other, the earth and Godde.

Jenny Spinks 1999

3.83   Our use of the word 'profit' usually only includes a material or financial profit, when in fact the word also has a meaning which includes spiritual benefit. How many people have accounting systems for the spiritual gain or loss in their business or enterprise? One can start by setting up spiritual objectives alongside the enterprise's financial objectives. In many organisations the spiritual objective is to 'provide services which assist customers and staff to achieve a balance between the mental, physical and spiritual aspects of their lives'. Because we go into enterprises with only the financial goals clearly defined, we sometimes forget the major importance of our spiritual, physical or environmental goals.

You can look at the spiritual poverty of our lifestyle and deplore its pathetic condition, or you can see the immense opportunities for change and improvement, and rejoice.

Roxanne Hendry 1989

3.84   Individually and as a group we are seeking to let go of internal and external clutter and be open to the light.

Jenny Spinks 2002

3.85   I ask for daily bread, but not for wealth, lest I forget the poor.
I ask for strength, but not for power, lest I despise the meek.
I ask for wisdom, but not for learning, lest I scorn the simple.
I ask for a clean name, but not for fame, lest I condemn the lowly.
I ask for peace of mind, but not for idle hours, lest I fail to hearken to the call of duty.

Inazo Nitobe 1909

Peace

3.86 Peace is the central theme of Christianity — peace within ourselves, peace within the family and peace between nations and groups. This is the most revolutionary challenge that has ever confronted human beings.

Christ introduced a new concept — love is more powerful than fear — and he further emphasised this by asking us to love not only people we liked and those who agreed with us, but also our enemies, those who obstruct us, humiliate us and 'spitefully use us'.

It is when respect, understanding and empathy have been expressed that the miracle of love will transform the communication. Then each participant feels warmth, fellowship and trust for each other and the defensive barriers that block communication are lowered. No longer is each side attempting to find ways to win points to defeat the other. Instead each is striving to reach a settlement that will be meaningful both to themselves and the other side.

Richard Griffith 1992

3.87 Quakers emerged from the turmoil of seventeenth century England with a clear philosophy which asserted that there was 'that of God in everyone'. The consequences of this was that killing or doing violence to others was seen as attacking part of God. The complement to this 'negative' was the commitment to 'removing the causes of war' by working for justice, equity and truth.

The result of this approach was that Quakers underwent repression, torture, imprisonment, and ill treatment of all kinds. Quakers bore this by refusing to be intimidated, and continued to witness. As one said, 'Be willing that self shall suffer for the Truth and not the Truth for self'.

Martyrdom was not uncommon, in both England and the North American colonies.

Other elements of Quaker approaches included refusal to fight in wars, giving help to victims of wars (all sides), and delegations to political and military leaders to seek peace — 'speaking truth to power'.

Quakers were heavily involved in the campaign to end slavery, in working for the right of conscientious objection, in pressing for religious and other freedoms, and in testifying to equality between men and women, and among races.

In all these things Quakers saw a continuity between means and ends. They considered that peace could not be achieved by violence, but only by winning hearts and minds to a peaceful way, and by example. Hence in their corporate life, they made decisions not by voting but after considering all views and seeking Divine guidance.

Nonviolence has the capacity to achieve long-term change, whereas violence may have temporary success but breeds enormous resistance and resentment.

Those of us who are committed to nonviolence face a solid task ahead. We have to devise better models of nonviolence in conflict situations, so that individuals and governments will see alternatives to the use of violence. We have to maintain pressure on power groups to modify their assumptions that violence needs to be used to contain dissident groups. We need to develop more democratic processes for community decision-making.

David Purnell 1992

3.88   *From Friends who witnessed the Eureka Stockade on the Victorian goldfields.*

Leaving the Resident Commissioner's camp we took a number of tracts among the diggers and they were most eagerly received. There was a good deal of excitement in this, many supposing they had reference to the present crisis. They began running towards us from all quarters, which excited such little alarm in us and we found it needful to pocket our tracts and walk off in another direction. However, by many they were most gratefully received, knowing the subject of them. One said, 'We should have had these a fortnight ago'. Another, observing the title of one, 'Unlawfulness of wars and fightings', seemed much interested. At length when our tracts were finished, one disappointed man said, 'You should have brought a thousand'.

Frederick Mackie 1854

3.89   *On the Protocol for the Pacific Settlement of International Disputes, put forward by the League of Nations*

As an attempt to provide for conciliatory and judicial settlement of disputes by arbitration, and so far as it secures a measure of disarmament, we approve the protocol. We believe in the pacific settlement of international disputes by conciliation or arbitration. The only true sanction for international justice is moral consent, and the only security is trust in the spirit of goodwill in all men.

Australia General Meeting 1925

3.90   This general meeting is deeply moved by the prospect of imminent war between Italy and Abyssinia, and implores the churches, statesmen, leaders and peoples of the world to strain every nerve before it is too late to avert threatened slaughter, with all its terrible repercussions upon mankind.

Australia General Meeting 1935

3.91   I was first drawn towards Friends by the consistency of their witness in peace and war. Perhaps you may remember that it was at the invitation of Friends in 1934 that I first made a public declaration of my personal pacifism. Since then my ideas have been tempered by experience of what has been happening in Europe during the last six years. I have had continually to search the grounds for my pacifism and to rethink my position. I have come to the conclusion that all I have the right to claim is that for me, it is the only way, but that for others there may be the equally sincere feeling that the cause of peace can best be served by some other means. I believe that in times such as the present it is not enough to say simply we have nothing to do with war. Granted that the war is the outcome of wrong policies pursued by our own and other nations — policies against which peace groups have again and again protested — I do not feel that we can simply regard war as the vindication of the truth of what we have been saying and leave it at that. There seems to be a great need for some form of community service which would provide group witness to the truth of pacifism as a way of life.

I feel that while my initial contact with Friends was on the pacifist issue, my real reason is something deeper. I can see that the attitude of Friends to peace is the result of their religious position, that they are pacifists because they are Friends and not vice-versa.

I appreciate also the stress which Friends place upon the value of group experience in stimulating this inner experience of the individual and in limiting any of its extravagances. It is through the fellowship of the group that strength can be found to live by that which one feels to be significant. I hope to be able to attend regularly the Sunday morning meeting for worship, not only because I see that it is an integral part of the Friends' way, but because I know what a help it can be to us all personally, and as a group in these times of testing.

William Oats 1939

3.92 *To Members of the Religious Society of Friends in Japan*

Dear Friends in Christ,

We want at this time to send to you a message of loving sympathy and deep regret for the suffering and devastation which have come to you as a result of war.

We have been reminded that we are members one of another, and that in a very real sense the world is one.

We long to be able to share and to lighten the burden which is yours, and we look forward to a time when we can once more find joy and inspiration in fellowship with you.

Here in Australia, after one of our forest fires, the tree trunks stand gaunt and blackened, with leafless boughs held up to heaven. In time, new leaves appear and the trees once more are green and beautiful. We have the promise, 'Behold I make all things new'. May you find courage and strength to build once more on the firm foundations laid in the past, and be sustained by the knowledge that Friends the world over, feel at one with you and are holding you in their thoughts and prayers.

Australia General Meeting 1947

3.93 *In 1964 the Australian Government introduced conscription for overseas military service and the next year began sending Australian soldiers to Vietnam.*

My objections to military service of any kind were — and still are — to the taking of human life for any reason, and to the use of war as a solution to misunderstanding and conflict between nations, or groups within nations.

These objections stem from a belief both in the uniqueness of every individual, and in a spirit or inner self which is a part of every person — often spoken of by Quakers as 'that of God in everyone'. To take the life of another person denies the existence of this common spirit and prevents any possibility of creating understanding, through this spirit, between persons on opposing sides of the conflict. Yet this understanding is vital to the attainment of a mutually acceptable and lasting solution to the conflicts. By its very nature war prevents this understanding both between individuals and between nations.

I now find myself in a position where I conscientiously object not only to war and the taking of human life but, as a consequence, to any law which compels people to take part in these activities.

David Jones 1970

3.94 I am charged under the National Service Act with failing to register for military conscription. I am guilty under this man-made law but I believe that I am obeying the higher law of God in refusing to comply with the Act.

My upbringing as a Quaker has played a major part in formulating my beliefs. Through this upbringing I have come to believe that the essential core of the Christian message lies not in the institutionalised and impersonalised religion woven around it, but in the way of life Jesus spoke of when he told us to love our enemies. As a consequence of this belief I totally reject war as a means of solving problems between opposing factions and ideologies. Jesus' words and example teach me that all men are my brothers and that what I do to the least of them I do to Jesus himself. In trying to force me to kill, the government is guilty of disobeying a basic tenet of the Christian faith.

David Martin 1971

3.95   Something of Friends' view that all war is immoral can be seen in their opposition to the war in Vietnam. In a press statement in 1968 Australia Yearly Meeting wrote, 'We feel a sense of shame that we and our fellow Christians have so failed to stir the conscience of the Australian people that our young men are still being compelled by law to train to kill other human beings'. In 1967 the yearly meeting peace committee joined the Federal Pacifist Council in a deputation to the Minister for Labor and National Service seeking amendments to the National Service Act. An outcome of their representations was that conscientious objectors were imprisoned in civil jails where conditions would be less harsh than in military detention.

Quaker Service Australia has consistently divided earmarked funds for Vietnam equally to both north and south for civilian drug supplies in the Quaker tradition of recognising the human needs of the enemy.

Charles Stevenson 1973

3.96   Interviewer: *Some of the experiences that you go through when you're demonstrating, for peace and anti-nuclear causes, must be frightening at times, I think. I wondered about you when you were in jail in Alice Springs after presenting yourself at Pine Gap; what was that experience like?*

I thought that I'd have quite a nice time in there, and catch up on some correspondence and do some reading and some writing; but, in fact, I didn't even have my glasses with me. I mean, everything is taken from you. And, I suppose, even though you know a little bit about what prison life might be like, when you're actually faced with it yourself, it's still a pretty shattering and dehumanising experience.

What did you call on when you were locked up on your own?

Well, I meditated a lot, which was really very useful. And then I went through a stage of being very angry about the government. I know why I was there and I had chosen to be there — there's no doubt about that, it was my choice — but I felt really angry that our government was allowing Australian soil to be used to further the nuclear war fighting plans of another nation.

And then, I think about the other message, that was Gandhi's very strong message, which is the transforming power of love. And that has to come through in a public sense, because if you're involved in working for peace, there's no point in looking really angry about it, even though the anger might be part of your motivating force. But you really do need also to think about why other people have a very different view from yours. You have to try and understand it and, really, think very much as you do with a child: 'I don't like your behaviour, but I can still love your being.' I constantly remind myself that our call is to passion and action — you see, the two things are close together, but they've got to be underpinned by love. Otherwise, you're really not making any sense at all. Unless that spiritual and loving element is there, what are you doing it for?

Jo Vallentine 1991

3.97   As a foreigner coming into Brummana [high school in Lebanon], I realised that I would have little credibility if I tried preaching love and peace: I was constantly reminded that I had not been through the war, I had not suffered or feared as the local people had. Amongst some local Friends there was a feeling that perhaps violence had been justified in the face of an apparent threat of extermination and, however much we, with hindsight, can point at the propaganda of the time, at the atrocities committed on all sides, I found it impossible to say with certainty that I, in that situation, would have reacted any differently. Certainly we from the West cannot walk in with any notion of moral superiority and consider ourselves bearers of sweetness and light.

The connection between the way we teach our classes, or even arrange sporting fixtures fairly, and our pacifism may seem tenuous, but it is with such mundane things that a witness to nonviolence — respect for others as equally children of God — must begin. While remaining non-judgmental in the face of the bitterness and hatred which so many feel, we must not be seduced into participating in the hatreds of others as a cheap form of solidarity. We can still point to the obvious fallacies in propaganda and lend all our support to those who see the need for reconciliation — no longer a matter of idealism or sentiment, but sheer survival. My experience in Lebanon has been in many ways a humbling one, not only in coming face to face with my own limitations, but also in meeting several people whose unfaltering and clear-sighted witness to peace and the power of God's love is equal to the best our Quaker tradition has shown.

Mark Deasey 1982

3.98   After the senseless bloodshed, destruction, reprisals, government intimidation, after all this hate and fury, the government will do precisely what those it contemptuously categorised as 'mindless peace people' call for — negotiation. The cross is a symbol of great allegory: what was scorned and rejected becomes, in time, established conviction. Immediate results may not be heartening but the work has greater value for the ages, for no more war is the cornerstone of international relations.

Editorial, The Australian Friend 1991

3.99   It has been a thoroughly valuable experience to see first hand how Quakers perform their international work. The Quaker United Nations Offices (QUNOs) do very little lobbying. Rather, they encourage dialogue by holding congenial, informal discussions on pertinent topics so that diplomats can discuss issues as people, instead of as political representatives. In addition, the QUNOs' staff make it a point to take something to diplomats rather than simply asking questions or presenting positions. A further input is our consistent Quaker stand that a more peaceful and just world is possible and is worth striving for. Many of the diplomats and secretariat staff work at the UN because they share its vision, and they seem to appreciate support for their ideals.

Throughout its history the UN has consistently provided a beacon for humans to live up to, even when it has been most conflict-ridden and ineffective. With the advent of the UN, humanity has designed and accepted a conscience for its international affairs. The operation of this conscience reminds me very much of the inner light working on an international scale. It provides a constant reminder of the way to greater harmony, but is utterly powerless unless people choose to follow it. Nevertheless, just like the inner light, you ignore it at your peril.

Andrew Wells 1989

3.100   Although the stall we had inside the AIDEX arms sales exhibition was in a corner at the end of the last hall of exhibits, we still had a constant stream of visitors. Many took our literature and watched the slides and videos constantly showing, and many stopped and talked. I was surprised by the number of people who said to me, 'I think it's great that you are here!' and surprised, too, by long conversations about, 'If conflicts could be solved without violence', about who Australia's enemies were — whether we, in fact, had any — and about Quakers in general. One conversation I remember clearly was with a man who had worked for defence for 30 years, who thought Australia should have a larger aid budget, yet had never previously thought that development issues were linked with defence issues.

Ronis Chapman 1990

3.101   We know that violence is not a solution to anything yet we are all caught inextricably, it sometimes seems, in the mesh of a world where violence is a multi-billion dollar industry and the greatest spectator sport. In our attempts to 'live in the virtue of that life and power that takes away the occasion of all wars', we acknowledge how often we turn to the violent expedient. We recognise that we are part of the world's violence and must ask ourselves if we are prepared to pay the price of our convictions and to recognise 'the enemy within' as a priority to be dealt with.

From a peace retreat 1991

3.102 **'Peace is a Verb' (song)**

Refrain: Peace on earth, peace on earth,
that's the hope that inspires this song.
Everyone says they want peace on earth
and everybody can't be wrong.

What on earth is peace on earth?
Don't conceive it as absence of war.
Not if injustice, oppression and greed
are just as present as before. Peace means:

Co-operate, let others live,
let go of hate, dare to forgive.
It means befriend, open your eyes,
perhaps amend, apologise.
It means take risks, sometimes accept,
sometimes resist, always respect. *Refrain*

Take time to learn, open your ears,
forgo your turn, let go your fears.
Negotiate, straighten things out.
It could mean wait, or do without.
It could mean share your food and drink,
maybe compare, maybe rethink. *Refrain*

Set people free, give them a hand,
try to agree and understand.
It means don't harm. It means don't fight.
It means disarm. It means put right.
It means don't fuss. It means don't shove.
It might mean trust, or even love. *Refrain to 'can't be wrong'*

Peter Low 1996

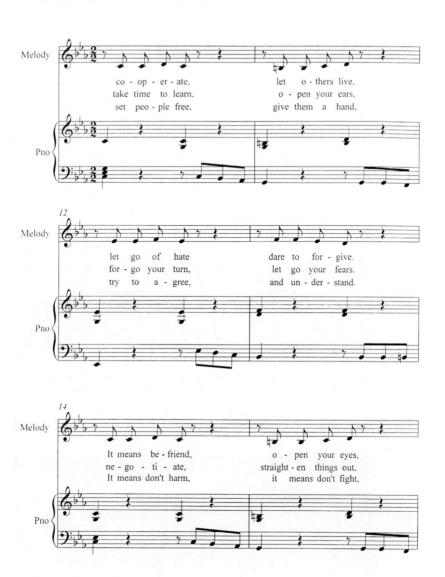

3.103 My involvement with road safety over the years had been a tentative response to a commitment to peace, as I saw road trauma as the most common cause of violent death in our society and with similar psychological effects as those of war. From the start of my medical career I had considered road crash deaths as nothing more than a legalised form of murder and certainly road trauma generally was a cause of untold suffering across all sections and classes of our community. As time went by, however, I increasingly appreciated that road safety was about power, the right to use our transport and the control over those decisions. It seemed that the ordinary Australian really had very little influence over a system which was potentially more dangerous to him and the environment than any other. There was a link between the prevention of trauma on our roads and a gentler treatment of our planet.

Brian Connor 1994

3.104 The start along the path of nonviolence is often an act of faith. But it is a reasonable faith in that it is based upon a belief in the responsiveness of man who has a unique sensitivity to moral, spiritual and what one might call 'higher' feelings which often find expression in poetry, music, drama, dance, art.

War and preparation for war brutalise all that are involved.

The power of nonviolence rests largely on the reality of the unity of the human family — that there is an essential identity between men of all races, nations, religions.

Donald Groom 1971

3.105 We need to have a much deeper concept of peace than the negative assumption that it is simply the absence of war. Peace is an organic concept, living and creative, and concerned with the relationships between people and between groups of people. Peace is the state of health of the body politic, but more fundamentally peace is a matter of the spiritual, mental and emotional health of individual bodies. Peace is concerned not only with the harmonious question of law, order and justice. It is also concerned with the nature of the human beings who will determine the future of that society and it is with this nature that we must concern ourselves if we are to educate for peace.

The biggest threat to the future of humanity is not the atomic bomb, but the provincial mind, the limited outlook, the myopia which prevents us from seeing beyond our own immediate interests. We can be provincial and myopic, especially in our attitudes to people who are different from ourselves in colour, in religious creed, in political affiliation, in educational opportunities, in abilities. Acceptance of others is not merely tolerating others. It is an affirmation of the importance of variety and difference. The most primitive reaction to the fact of difference is one of fear — the other is different and therefore is a threat, a danger.

William Oats 1990

3.106 Speak peace

Speak peace. Hear the half-hearted
anxiety in the threat, the questioning word.
Stretch your sympathy, understand
hate of the heart, anger of hand.

Speak peace, for speech is act,
fastening fact.

Act peace. Encompass strife
with insight for the intricate needs of life,
Not to oppose, protect, contend.
Wait. Wait the occasion to befriend,

to act where act may reach
deeper than speech.

Tom Silcock 1987

3.107 I believe that violence is used at many levels to control other people. For many years Quakers have held that international violence is to be avoided at all costs. I believe that violence in relationships is the ground in which other violence grows and that, if we are to develop a just and peaceful society, we must look to reducing the violence within our families. Thus, for me, working towards a reduction in domestic violence is very much part of my belief that peace is an essential component of life as it should be.

Topsy Evans 1990

3.108   Mothers and Others for Peace (begun by English Quakers) was the inspiration for some Canberra women to mix mothering of their babies with their peace concerns in the 1980s. For many years we focused on war toys. We did not come up with any answers and our children maintained their fascination for military toys but our children certainly knew that we thought that violence and hurting other people was not OK. We passed on very clear messages about our desire to live in a peaceful world and that we thought it was important to look for nonviolent solutions in every aspect of our lives.

The Gulf War of 1991 brought war and violence and destruction into our living rooms. It was a worrying time for all of us and especially our children. During this time my children were exposed to a message of peace through the work of Mothers and Others and through our Quaker meeting. They experienced the power of a small group of committed people, learnt that the victims of this war were our neighbours as much as the people in the house next door, looked to crusaders of peace for inspiration, listened to their inner light for direction and felt the support of a loving, caring spiritual community who were all concerned about war.

Ronis Chapman 1997

3.109   If we would know peace, it is clear that our thinking has to change. For we have had set before us life and good, and death and evil, and people have constantly chosen evil and given its fruits status in our nations. This has inevitably been accompanied by those companions: deceit, distrust, despair, with their associates fear and hatred, insecurity and helplessness. Evil brings with it death in all its forms. However, we have failed to realise that the power of evil is nothing more than the power of our cooperation with it.

If, then, we would have peace, we must turn our lives around, and alter that fundamental choice:

Peace requires embracing life — in all its forms, in all its aspects.

Peace means casting out fear with love, and through love, finding our way to other hearts at a point in them beyond weakness and strength.
Peace is loving our enemies, and thereby changing the relationship.

Peace is honouring truth, upholding it, speaking it.
Peacemakers use truth to overcome lies, and love to overcome hatred — even to the point of sacrifice and suffering.
Peace involves love and care of the earth, its waters, its atmosphere.
Peacemakers stand in the authority of the Spirit and dare to think with one another in terms of the whole planet.
They know that each of us is diminished by another's death, and will risk their part of the world that another might live.

They understand the difference between insecurity and vulnerability — the one with its roots in fear and distrust, the other a condition of life and growth.

They trust and build trust; they risk that faith in the other, both friend and adversary.

Peacemaking is listening — above the noise of our own thoughts.
It is being accountable for how our wealth is spent — remembering that wanting understanding also contributes to oppression.
Peace is living simply, that others may simply live.

Peacemakers will work to set at liberty the captive, to feed the hungry and relieve the oppressed.

They have knowingly chosen, that they and their children may live. Peacemaking is a way of life: living in the Spirit, walking in the Spirit, and endeavouring to keep the unity of the Spirit.

I have set before you this day: Life and Death, and Peace is choosing Life.

Nancy Shelley 1986

the Spirit of Christ by which we are guided is not changeable so as once to command us from a thing as evil, and again to move unto it, and we certainly know, & testify to the world, that the Spirit of Christ which leads into all truth, will never move us to fight and war against any man with outward weapons, neither for the Kingdom of Christ, nor for the kingdoms of the world.

Patricia Wood

The Alternatives to Violence Project (AVP) in Australia has involved people in prisons and local communities since 1991. It has three levels of training for nonviolence. It began in New York in 1975 when a group of Greenhaven Prison inmates asked Quakers to help develop a program to prevent youth from drifting into crime.

AVP's features are: learning through experience; looking for good in all; participants and team members are all volunteers; it acknowledges a spiritual base.

The following three items arise from AVP experience:

3.110 The participants were drawn from all categories of prisoners — from high to low security. Many would be natural enemies in prison. They told us that normally they would not be allowed to mix.

After day one the participants were becoming a team and by the day's end people were smiling and becoming themselves by letting drop the guard all prisoners need for survival in jail.

And it was on the third day that the transformation really showed. At lunchtime they asked to have their own meeting and they decided they would shower early (at dinner time) so the course could run to 9pm.

The reason was that they wanted to do their own presentation to us. We were all given a certificate by the prisoners as well as some design ideas for the Alternatives to Violence Project logo.

It was an emotional ending to the course. It would be difficult to explain the feeling of emotion that flowed on the final day but it was something I have never felt before. It was the feeling of understanding, mutual love, giving, sharing, of being a team.

Terry Pinnell 1992

3.111 Prison may not seem a likely place to meet great men. But facilitating AVP workshops in jails has brought me into contact with amazing wisdom, incredible patience, deep compassion and startling perception. I have learnt from, and journeyed with, the prisoner participants, and together we have rejoiced over wonderful discoveries. Chief among these is that people who are affirmed and valued can radiate goodness in the most unpromising surroundings. Their inner light can shine with astonishing brightness. Affirmation is magic. But the reverse is also true. Abuse and rape can undermine a person consistently, and you have a blueprint for a life of crime. When I hear of a shocking crime I now ask myself where in the past is the injury for which this is the payback?

The central philosophy of AVP is that in all people there is something called Transforming Power which can be called on at any time to change destructive and violent situations into constructive and peaceful ones. Some of the ingredients are respect for self, caring for others, thinking before reacting, and expecting the best. One of my peak moments came when a murderer, halfway through his sentence, suddenly smiled and said, 'I've been thinking this for a long time, but now I have words to express it.'

Laurel Thomas 1997

3.112 I was asked by a parole officer, 'What's this AVP?' He then explained that an ex-inmate who was supposed to report to him each Monday as a condition of parole had failed to report until Wednesday. When he enquired the reason, the man said he'd got drunk. The parolee explained that on Sunday he had come home earlier than expected and found his wife in bed with his friend. He was a man who had been to prison for violent crimes, and in his anger he went to his shed to get an axe.

As he got to the shed he remembered what he'd learned in an AVP workshop in prison two years earlier; about thinking before reacting. His legs carried him past the shed, he went and bought some beer and 'went bush'. 'And,' he said, 'if it wasn't for AVP three lives would have been lost.'

I thought how often when we do something we believe to be for the good, we hope for or expect instant results. But God knows better, and the seed we plant will blossom in His good time. We need to be patient, to persevere, and to trust.

Wilhelmina Walker 1999

3.113 Shakuhachi, Didgeridoo

In the dark before first light
The musicians gather and are placed.
On the harbour foreshores, quietly
Groups with instruments, singers
Take up positions, waiting
For the light. And on the peaks
Of Utzon's mighty sails, three more:
Shakuhachi, didgeridoo
And a child with a voice
As pure as first light itself.

Millennial dawn is flowing
Round the world in a making tide.

We are waiting, breathing softly
And over the ocean, gently
The first dim sheen appears
Floating towards us, quiet as a dream.
In through the Heads the grey light trickles
And slowly the reaches of the harbour
Detach themselves with a pearly dimness
From the dark outlines of the land.
Softly, as gentle as this light
The music begins to flow,
As a spirit breathing.
With shakuhachi, didgeridoo
And a child's pure voice
The music takes wing on wide-sending waves
Around the whole of the turning world
And the light grows.

Shakuhachi, didgeridoo
And a child's pure voice.
From a mighty building, by the gardens
On a headland, in a harbour
The still and poised notes of the flute
Flow out around the world, mending sorrow
Bringing comfort to suffering people. Everywhere.
Asking and offering
Forgiveness. So let us cherish
The makers, the healers
And the bringers of peace
As the music flows, and the light
Grows.

Max Raupach

Shakuhachi, didgeridoo
And a child's pure voice.
From a mighty building, by the gardens
On a headland, in a harbour
The pulsing music of an ancient land
Is throbbing in the bone
Behind our ears. Possessing
Soul and body, magical,
And saying: *We are still here*
Your First Nation, custodians
For solemn ages before you began.
We are here, and the spirits
Of those who went before, they are clustering
On these dark foreshores, here among us now,
Our fathers, mothers, sisters, brothers.
Reach out to us your hands, to them
In spirit. Then we shall all be whole.
So let us cherish through the world
All the First Peoples, and all peoples,
As the music flows, and the light
Grows.

Shakuhachi, Didgeridoo
And a child's pure voice.
From a mighty building, by the gardens
On a headland, in a harbour
The voice soars like the dove
Which they sent out from the ark
Across a dark and flooded world.

The bird rose high, so high
In upper reaches, it left the darkness
Of repressed and stormy air
And the rolling wastes of water
Till its wings glinted, white and silver
For it reached the airy heights
Where it caught the sun. Then a long
Day later, safely flew back home
With a green frond in its beak.
It's the child's voice which teaches us
This hope. So let us cherish,
Above all, children. In all lands.
As the music flows, and the light
Grows.

Shakuhachi, didgeridoo
And a child's pure voice
From a mighty building, by the gardens,
On a headland, in a harbour
The song soars round the world
To people in all nations and all climes.
Saying with joy, we are all
One people, and our world is one, and beautiful.
So let us cherish each other and the world
As the music rises in benediction
And the light
Shines.

Jane Vaughan Donnelly 2000

3.114   When the demonstration was planned, the call went out to women all over the world to 'embrace the base' at Greenham Common, the ultimate symbol of death, with the power of life, with the power of positive energy of women practised in the preserving of life and nurturing of its growth.

And so they came: 30,000 women, on a freezing cold day in December and encircled the 15km perimeter of cyclone fencing topped with barbed wire. They decorated the fence with toys; children's clothes; posters; poems; photographs of families, of babies, of children's pets; children's drawings; flowers; locks of hair; balloons; messages and greetings to other women all around the world in Italy, Denmark, Russia, Norway, America, Australia. (A woman near me put a tiny white dress on the fence. It was her daughter Anna's, she said. Anna had been four weeks premature and this was the dress she had worn in the prem. ward. 'I brought it,' she said, 'as a symbol of Anna's struggle for life.') Symbols of life, of the uniqueness and sacredness and creativity of the human spirit; in stark contrast to the base inside the fence, the symbol of death, of massification, regimentation and control, of the possibility of destruction of all life.

We lit candles as it grew dark, and planted bulbs through the fence — tulips and daffodils in the shape of peace symbols to come up, after the darkness of winter, in the spring.

Margaret Bearlin 1984

3.115   During war people are sad, angry and scared.
When war is over people are still sad, angry and scared
And they want to rebuild.
But it's hard to make houses all by yourself
And it's nice if people help.
It's one way to make a good world.

Rose Dryzek (aged 8) 2003

The Hiroshima Rally

I went to the rally. The kids got to go on stage. They asked the kids to say something. I said that I did not think that bombs were good at all and I did not think that bombs should be used. I was nervous but I managed to do it.

Justine Mobey (aged 8) 1995

3.116   In India there is a tradition in which the word for peace is uttered three times at the beginning of a sacramental rite: Shanti, shanti, shanti. That triple utterance signifies that the power of peace is generated if the will, the means and the end are each of them grounded in peace.

A reporter spoke of two factors which emanated from the Greenham Common women and marked their presence and message: their confidence and complete faith.

Many women around the world are no longer abashed at the size of the stand we must take in face of the obscenity of the arms race. They are undaunted by the action their knowledge of life leads them into taking. Their feet are grounded in the reality of the real world with its suffering, poverty and violence. Their morality stems not from absolutes but from compassion. Their impetus is not bloodletting, but life. Their strength is based on trust, their affirmation is truth. Their goal is a nonviolent world.

> The winds of time are changing now
> As woman grasps each woman's hand
> Encircling earth, embracing LIFE
> Weaving webs of hope across the land.

Confidence; complete faith. It is urgent. You can't expect to be led, you must take personal responsibility.

Look long and deeply into the blue of an autumn sky and feel the gentleness and fragility of the eternal as the balmy air fills your lungs. Stand in the golden light of a tree as it catches and gives out the sun's glow, and respond to the warmth of its ripeness. Listen to the full-throated song of a magpie, and wonder at the power of sound to move you to rejoicing. Hold the eye of another with your own in a moment of unspoken unity, and know the exquisite tenderness within you.

Take a very young baby into your hands, and experience the miracle and vulnerability of human life.

If we ponder these miniatures and distil from them their verities, we may come to understand what is involved as we set ourselves the task of preventing war. Certainly, unless we keep them in view, even in recall, we shall be in danger of losing our way in a labyrinth of death-proclaiming doctrine whose purpose and end are devastation and destruction.

Our task, in contrast, if we would work for peace, is to be life-affirming and the affirmation of life carries with it — robustness in the face of wrong-headedness and evil, tenderness in the presence of fragility, and joy in the business of living. Shanti, shanti, shanti.

Nancy Shelley 1983

3.117 Meditation

Taste peace in your own mouth.
Feel the touch of peace on your own skin.
Let your ears fill with the sounds of peace.
Feel the longings for peace that fill your own heart.
Let your mind rest on the word peace.
Open to what peace would give you and others.

Send peace out unreservedly to all living beings.
To those you know and those you don't know.
To those whom you would call your brothers and sisters and those you would not.

Without unconditional respect and care for all, there can be no peace.
Know that.

Know that when you evoke peace within your own mind and heart,
it moves through you, lifting you, and lifting whatever you touch with your thoughts.
Without taking a single step from this place, your thoughts can encircle the world.
Calling upon the known, you are joined to the unknown.
Calling upon love, you become love.

May we and all who share our planet know hope.

May we and all who share our planet know peace.

Stephanie Dowrick 2003

finding our way

4

Deborah Faeyrglenn

4 FINDING OUR WAY THROUGH LIFE

4.1   We need to know each other. We need to tell the stories. We need to have opportunities where we can talk about our spiritual journeys not only to this point in time but to go on sharing in the future.

Trish Roberts 1996

Life stages
Childhood

4.2   The most serious disadvantage suffered by children and young people is their invisibility to adults. When this remains unrectified, we are not only failing the children and depriving ourselves of learning from their light, but also keeping ourselves out of hearing distance from God's message through them.

Helen Bayes 2003

4.3   Before and during the Gulf War we all went regularly to the vigil our meeting organised but after the fighting broke out I realised that I was not making time for our children to talk about the events. So we began our own vigil — a time for them to ask questions and generally talk about where things were up to. The consequences of these times were amazing — we turned it into a Quakerly event by having silence and having some readings from Quaker books. We drew pictures together and talked about our fears and hopes. Hannah was always involved but did not have as many questions as her older siblings.

One of the most memorable times was when we started talking about our inner light and about looking to this light to help us find a direction — in this instance a direction we may take to express our concern about the war. We had a time of silence to think about this and when we came out of the silence Hannah said, 'I saw it! I saw my light'. Then one of the others suggested we draw our inner light and off we went and my children led me into one of the most moving times I have ever had of discovering the inner light.

Ronis Chapman 1991

4.4   Children are vulnerable in many ways — the same ways — everywhere. Their instinct and need is to trust, to believe, and to attach emotionally to the adults around them. If they are suffering, they accept it as normal, or blame themselves. Their small, growing bodies are easily disabled by malnutrition, disease and injuries. Their emotional capacities are easily disabled by verbal and physical abuse and relationship deprivation. Their learning and memory are easily disabled by oppressive discipline and absence of choice. Their self-confidence and creativity simply wither away unless they receive encouragement and opportunity. All forms of ill-treatment have a numbing effect on their spirit.

Helen Bayes 2003

4.5   I was three-and-a-half, the tree was about 70. The world war was in its first year, and even little boys expected fiendish Germans to invade Suffolk.

My father had a lurcher bitch called Guess, whose litter of pups had been born dead. She was miserable and neurotic, snapping at everyone, and had to be kept on a chain in the yard till her grieving had abated. I was fond of her, and early Sunday morning, forgetting that it was forbidden, I ran to cuddle her. She bit me on the forehead, and of course the blood poured.

It was said in Suffolk in those days that once a dog had tasted human blood it could not be trusted again. That one bite was death to her. I ran away, weeping bitterly, and climbed my beloved horse-chestnut tree at the top of Slushy Lane just outside our orchard. The flowers were still out, and the tree stirred with a strongish breeze. The nearest birdsong was blackbirds, and a cock chaffinch. Further, a cuckoo.

Meanwhile my father had loaded his gun and taken Guess off the chain for her last hunt; she loved putting up game (rabbits and hares) for him. She followed some scent or other along the ditch to the spring-hole under my chestnut, and he stepped to the edge (all the birds stopped their song) and he shot her through the head. He never knew I was six metres above him, to watch, and to feel the shock of the shot. Did the tree withdraw a little from human contact? I know I did, clutching that cool dispassionate bark and witnessing the proof that my blood, given domination over all the earth, was lethal. Still flowering trees and birdsong offer me God's fearless unconditional beauty and individuated love, more clearly than any aspect of our wronged, subject world.

Norman Talbot 1995

4.6 There was a great outcry and search for Frank, who was not used to stray away like me; and on his not turning up, and my being absent also, it was set down that I had taken him with me. On reaching home, my mother scolded me severely for taking this little brother out on such a ramble and with nothing to eat for the greater part of the day, and for once she resolved to chastise me. She took me into a chamber and with a riding whip began flogging away. My indignation was so much excited, that I turned and fought, and I called her 'a fine thing!' At this she could not help smiling, and so the flogging ended in nothing, but this: it stirred in me the very worst passions and in after life, remembering it, I resolved never to chastise my children corporally.

William Howitt 1870

4.7   Children are our tangible link today with eternity. They are the gift of ongoing life to mortal humanity. They renew and refresh the human species with God-given gifts of love, truth, simplicity, beauty and health. They are God's restoration of the human creation, the very reincarnation of what God wants for human life on Earth. They bring us back to basics, both personally and as a species. They are the forward-carriers of faith, hope and love.

Caring for our children, fostering their growth and development, protecting them from harm, is therefore the most sacred thing — the most worshipful thing — that we as human beings can do. To neglect, injure or exploit children is the greatest dereliction of our part, humanity's place, in creation.

Children are not our property. Kahlil Gibran says we own none of them, not even 'our own', for they are 'life's longing for itself'. But Jesus said, 'Let the children come to me and forbid them not'. Perhaps he might have said 'exclude them not'. Though we do not own our children, we owe all of them sacred care, respect and protection.

Helen Bayes 1994

Youth

4.8   The young not only have their own keen powers of observation, they respond to what they see and help change their environment, deal with problems, in ways adults rarely notice. They are in fact co-shapers of their families and of their society, noticed or not.

Elise Boulding 1996

4.9 The Death of a Friend

I saw him the night before
I thought he wouldn't die
But the sight of him made me so sad
His treatment had made him look so different.

His hair had fallen out
And his face had swollen up, I hardly recognised him.
He lay there uneasy as I looked at him with disbelief
This was not the friendly and energetic boy that I loved so passionately
He had changed so much
I hated God for that.

I walked in and picked up a book
It was sitting on a bedside table
I began to read
I had to hold back the flood of emotion.
It was all I could do, read him a book
A friend to a friend who was nearly lost.

I didn't realise it was so close
I thought it would never happen.
Not to him.

That morning after I heard the news
The shock hit me in such a crashing and overwhelming wave.
The tears came flooding.
I couldn't hold back.

I tried to carry on as normal
I went to school, to find kids that were in his year, crying.
I couldn't believe it was true.

Seeing his sisters and parents was the worst.
I then knew what it was like to have your heart break.
To have your heart shatter.

I was asked to read his epilogue.
It was an honour.
It was so hard.
His life seemed too short
As I read it was all too real
I started to cry
But I kept on reading
This was too important.

He has touched so many lives
And he touched mine in a strong way
I thank god for letting me have that last night by his side.

'Sometimes I can even see the kind of friend I'd like to be.'

Suzi Bayes-Morton (aged 15) 1998

4.10   I recalled that at age 19 I struggled with both depression and despair brought on by existential questioning. So I resolved to explore the matter further among Young Friends. I wondered whether it is inevitably a lonely experience that has to be gone through, or if the Quaker community could do more in understanding and supporting Young Friends and other young people.

Several Young Friends encouraged me to persist with this interest in supporting Young Friends to reflect on the more spiritual aspects of their lives. I was hopeful that this could include some discussion amongst them. Almost all the young people said they experienced despair and/or depression.

Often, it seems, people turn to spirituality in times of despair. I believe people should constantly be in touch with a deep conscious knowledge of, and connection to, the goodness of all things. It's a shame that it often takes despair to force them there.

Christine Larkin 1999

4.11   There are turning points, major shapers in my life. Being born a boy certainly had a major impact on all that was to come. Then learning to fear masculinity, and seeing it almost synonymous with barbarity and violence. Later, unlearning that — seeing strength as different from violence. My cultural heritage was important, too. Being born working class, studying law in an owning class context, and now, if I choose, being able to pass myself off as middle class.

Emigrating — crossing cultures, comparing both, belonging in neither. Later, learning to find myself a place of belonging, sexually separating myself from intense and accumulating social expectations to find my authentic self. Spiritually, answering the call and dealing with doubts, learning not to be reactive to opportunity. Career-wise, realising I didn't 'have' a career. Then in 1994, three major turning points were getting married, taking up writing as my vocation, and becoming a Quaker. They each involved a coming home, making a commitment, and surrendering my need to thrash about with choices.

Adrian Glamorgan 1996

Relationships

4.12   I was single until I was 36. It is all too easy to fall for the claims that people in committed relationships are more psychologically mature than those of us living without a partner. Even in some Quaker writings, I've seen self-centredness hinted at in descriptions of living alone.

The result of this interpretation was that I set about proving how mature and selfless I could be. Looking back, I'm glad of the work I did for causes I believed in, but I'm sorry for that part of the motivation. It was wonderful when a perceptive friend pointed out that I kept taking on obligations 'to apologise for having a partner-free, child-free time'.

I began to embrace my singleness without fear of appearing selfish, odd, unchosen. I realised this was the life that I had chosen, in a series of conscious or unconscious decisions, because it suited me.

So I was able to laugh when an acquaintance greeted the news of my newly-partnered state with words: 'It's nice to have someone to care for, isn't it?' As if I'd cared for nobody before! In that one sentence, she dismissed intimate friendship, extended family, good-neighbourliness, passionate social action, and spiritual and personal development. A full life can be deemed empty if one is not caring for one's own partner or family.

When I compare myself then and now, I know that I'm much more selfish in my partnered state than I ever was when single. My partner can be my excuse for all sorts of laziness and insularity, which people are happy to make allowances for. I even give more selfishly — in the sense that I get back all I give and more. This newer life is far more self-indulgent than the old — and respected more by society.

Sue Wilson 1999

4.13 Are we to be so heartless as to require gay and lesbian people to forgo the potential for growth that loving relationships provide, and shoulder a burden of sinfulness and prejudice imposed by 'straight' society?

Personally, I feel joy that Quakers have placed themselves at the forefront of social change, as they did when the ownership of slaves by Friends was eliminated several generations before the rest of the community. Perhaps, then, some of the older Friends grumbled and would have preferred to have remained with what had always been rather than to implement what should be.

John Olive 1982

4.14 As a young woman I learnt that I was a carrier of muscular dystrophy.

In late 1993 my partner and I decided to get married, and soon after I began sensing the presence of a soul wanting to be born. The experience of something of this nature was new to me, and yet I had no doubts as to what was being communicated. My partner too was aware of this invitation from the divine — I remember the sense as being fully inside and all around us — and after a few months of soul-searching we decided to go ahead with trying to conceive a child.

The form of muscular dystrophy in our family appeared to be a recessive one with no real risk of passing it on to our child. This information wasn't a surprise to me but confirmed the inner sense I had had for more than a year that muscular dystrophy was no longer an issue.

Our child, Daniel, was born in November 1996 and of the many adjustments required of new parents, the one I was least prepared for was the shift I needed to connect with Daniel's physical self. I had to keep reminding myself that as well as the spiritual being I had been in close connection with for more than two years, he was also a tiny, fragile human who needed my total attention and support. I remember vividly an experience that took place three days after he was born when I woke in the middle of the night to an incredible sense of love and peace that filled the room. I knew instantly that it was Daniel's higher self present with us and I'll never forget the feeling of total love and acceptance that I was held in for those few moments. This experience was one of many that let me know that I was not alone.

The next few years of Daniel's life were the most difficult and transforming I have experienced. I spent most of that time feeling exhausted and separated by a layer of fog from the world as I'd known it. Yet I was rarely without the sense that I was doing exactly what Daniel needed me to do and that there was a greater meaning to all that was happening.

I learnt many times that my perceived limits were exactly that, just perceptions. I pushed through them time and time again, always to find a new place on the other side. There were many times I was in tears, sobbing with exhaustion and uncertainty while I held this precious child in my arms, as he finally slept. And many times I was aware of the presence of the spirit gently and lovingly holding me, letting me know that I was doing a wonderful job and that I would find the strength and courage to surrender and to continue. I struggle to find words to express the sacredness, the immenseness and sheer mystery of motherhood — an experience that is so central to our humanness.

Sonja Glamorgan 1999

4.15   This evening before bedtime we shared one of those rare episodes of peace in the hurly-burly of family life. Just quiet talk, a little reading, a little playing of the piano and Peter Kearney's *Songs of Hope* album in the background.

At one point, our sons (aged six and eight) lay close to the stereo, listening together and occasionally patting each other on the back. As I watched I reflected again how much I value our choice, taken years ago, to live without television: TV would make such evenings more rare, if not impossible.

My second reflection was gratitude for the impact of these peace and spirit songs on our three children. Our family went to Peter Kearney's concert in Townsville: we enjoyed the singing and the atmosphere and came home with the record album. For days it was played incessantly while the children alternately lost themselves in the music, or questioned us deeply about the lyrics of songs like 'Into the Light', 'George Zabelka' and 'Start from Here'.

Somehow, all our years of peace witness, of rejecting war-toys and television, of trying to be non-violent parents, were confirmed and strengthened.

At a recent Quaker gathering, we discussed turning points: those events and experiences that have changed our perceptions and directions in life. For our children, these songs have been such a point, inflaming their hearts to something of the pain, the passion and the love of the world.

Trish Johnson 1990

4.16   Neither teach ye them to strike in the least, nor provoke them to have any delight to see striking; for thereby afterwards they come to strike one another, and hurt one another. Neither teach ye them to speak wicked words, nor many words. Neither teach ye them to call Names in the least, nor any such thing, and in wisdom watch over them, and then you will know when to rebuke, and when to cherish.

Humphrey Smith 1660

4.17   I joined the Society at 16, which was the earliest age I could, but I stopped going to Friends in my late teens — it's a common pattern. The thing that brought me back to Friends and made sense of my life, in a way which no other move could have done, was when I had Suzi because she came along when I didn't have support from anyone else. I turned to Friends to give her an extended family because she was going to need more of a social setting than I, as a single parent, could give her. Having been brought up in Friends I just knew we would be accepted. The values of the Friends community would be positive for her; she wouldn't encounter any of the racism that I was worried she would encounter; attitudes about the circumstances in which she was born. So I came back to Friends for her but it was only a matter of months before it was for me.

Helen Bayes 1996

4.18   In 1985 when Nancy and I separated, I didn't want to talk to anybody. I didn't want to get into conversations, because I wasn't confident enough about how I was feeling. The men's group pressed me to talk about it some more. When I began to do that, I realised that talking about it had power in itself: it did provide a lift just to be able to identify what the issues were, rather than about whether it was right or wrong, or which direction I was going. I didn't have to hang on to a particular position or worry about it all the time. In sharing it I could let a bit of the struggle go and feel freer.

Harold Wilkinson 1995

4.19 Marital conflict may come in a variety of ways and reconciliation is not always possible. My husband and I, however, had a positive experience helped by a supportive Quaker meeting.

In the seventeenth year of our marriage we found that we had some seemingly irreconcilable differences. I had spent 10 years compromising, yelling, crying, discussing, and rationalising. We had worked hard with each other, through marriage enrichment courses and counselling, with support from family and friends, especially Quakers. We finally had one too many crises and I decided to move out.

Our plan to separate was open-ended; I intended to live in a house in an adjacent suburb with the children alternating between houses. A Friend at the clearness meeting, which we requested, asked why they needed to move. This led to a creative solution which I believe provided an environment for the rebuilding of our marriage: the children stayed at home with one parent while my husband and I each took three week 'turns' at living alone in the other house.

Much support was given to each of us by Friends and growth occurred in each of us in the next 11 months, after which we decided to return to our marriage with different expectations. This marriage has stood the test of 12 subsequent, increasingly happy years, with thanks from our children.

Nancy Wilkinson 1996

4.20   For me the worst thing was my 20-year-old son's perception of me as co-oppressor. He hadn't known of my anguish, my futile attempts to make things better. I'd followed my mother's injunction to present a united front to the children and work out our differences in private. What a lie.

With that conversation my reality was shattered. It was true. We, the happy, united family who attended Quaker gatherings and peace rallies, were a family of violence. The truth, having been spoken, could no longer be denied. The children and I shared our experiences and began the painful process of confronting and healing. I tried to talk to my husband; asked him to seek counselling with me. But I was met with denial, defensiveness and abuse. He is hurt, bewildered that, suddenly and unreasonably, his family have cast him off. After all that he's done. Indeed.

But he's not some kind of monster. In a way, I think it might have been easier if he were. He's a complex human being who can be charming, witty, vulnerable. He lacked the skills to deal with parenthood and coped the only way he knew how: with violence and aggression. I, in my turn, did not know how to cope with that and reacted with passive acquiescence. It was not until one of our children had the courage and wisdom to say 'Stop!' that the situation changed.

I've tried to make sense of it all and understand how it all happened; and I have, more or less. But no explanation can remove the horror, the guilt, the pain.

What I do know is that violence doesn't only happen out there with the rough and uncouth. It happens in nice, respectable Quaker families; and it's only by acknowledging this that we can begin to do something about it.

anon. 1991

4.21   Domestic violence is not conflict. It is the exercise of power by one person over another. It challenges the Quaker notion that people are equal, that there is that of God in everyone and that if we hurt one we hurt all.

So, when I began to work on domestic violence as an issue, that was my starting point. Conflict resolution would not work. What would work? It seemed, after much contact, work and experience, that the best initial approach was to encourage the victim to step back from the situation, leave if necessary and begin to look at building her own self-confidence, her belief in herself as a worthwhile person, her belief in that of God in herself, even if we didn't call it that. The violence perpetrated upon such people takes away their confidence, their belief in themselves as worthwhile. It lessens them as every violence does.

Of course it takes away from the perpetrator too in the long run. But it is usually too difficult to work on that while the same power relationship exists. Some perpetrators realise, when the victim is gone, what they have done, with help, of course. They need to see themselves as worthwhile also, and as people who do not need to destroy others in order to feel good about themselves.

Sabine Erika 1997

4.22   The worst thing about private violence and abuse is the damage it does to the victim's and the perpetrator's ability to feel and listen to the Spirit within. This injury is far above and beyond any physical damage. Interpersonal violence is an attack on God's presence. Early Friends rejected violence because of their sacred duty to greet and nurture that of God in everyone. Today, with all our knowledge and our reasons for caution, we can and, I believe must, ask the Spirit for guidance, in both our worship and our social witness, on how to care for those who are suffering, or have suffered, violence and sexual exploitation.

Helen Bayes 2003

4.23   To my former husband

We have been separated for quite some time and, although the relationship is over with no chance of reconciliation, I find myself grieving still.

I made a promise to you which, for reasons beyond my control, I am unable to keep. I resent that I have been put in this position. I find it difficult to promise anything like this again.

A legal divorce does not cover all aspects of a relationship that is over. There are many things that are not finished. For me, the promises I made were between you, me and God. I cannot live with a lie between me and God.

- I release you from any promise you made to me.
- I release you from the guilt of those broken promises.
- I leave this relationship behind and move toward my new life with new lightness of step.
- I bear no blame or negative thoughts about the marriage or the results of that marriage.

- I bear you no ill-will.

- I thank you for the gifts you have given me and the skills I now have from you.

- I understand that the pain may never be gone but I will no longer allow it, or any other negative feelings, to permeate my future relationships.

I have back my self-love. I can now love with truth and joy. I know of better ways of resolving problems and issues. I am a happy and capable person. I look good and am comfortable within my own skin.

Beth Reid 1997

4.24   Quakers talk so much about the Light but all I could see at this stage was the darkness. As I sensed the collapse of my personal pillars of relationship, health and professional life, I faced a stripping process. This metaphorical crucifixion could, however, be liberating and an avenue to personal freedom. Although trapped by circumstance, I could still attempt the rewriting of life's script and the reordering of priorities. It may have been that my cup had been spilled but also that it was ready to be refilled.

Brian Connor 1995

4.25 I feel fortunate to be part of a group that actively values its older members and looks to them for even greater usefulness in their later years than before. Although what they say may be of great significance to me at particular times, what endures and has become part of my own life awareness is how their lives speak.

They seem to welcome life's many transitions and move through them with increasing tranquillity and acceptance. This is no letting go of the temporal and embracing the spiritual. Rather, it seems an even deeper engagement with the reality of living in the world.

Susannah Brindle 1999

4.26 Times come when faith is like brittle and brown dry leaves of autumn,
Blowing in whispy winds,
Leaving the soil powdery, infertile.
I go to Meeting seeking — and offering — friendly smiles, loving words to fill the lonely empty spaces.
One day tender green sprouts of renewed faith tentatively break through the waiting earth,
Vulnerable, needing nurture.
Joyously I welcome the precious new growth,
A gift of grace.

Carol McLean 1987

4.27   There is no man, nor child, nor woman born who has not influenced those around them. What you and I do will either help or hinder to some extent, sustain or depress another. Our words, our courage or lack of it are contagious. If we are depressed, some of it rubs off on others. If we smile through it, that does too, with all the greater power for coming through our difficulty. If we feel lonely, there are others who feel likewise and by our seeking them out, we break their isolation as well as our own. By knowing this, faith in our worth reasserts itself and so purpose comes in infinitely small ways.

Slowly we find ourselves able to speak where once we were silent, and in the accumulating knowledge of contact, grow to know that we are not so different as we think: that though we all know the sense of isolation we are all, nevertheless, in this world together. We will come to realise that this is how the world is made and to some extent begin to understand the wisdom which so created it.

Olive Pell 1970

4.28   Some things that slow me down are:
watching a sunrise,
stopping and listening to street musicians,
hugging a baby,
folding sun-dried clothes,
just listening to the world go round.
God knocks very softly most of the time.

Elaine Edwards 1997

Death

4.29   We have given thought to the circumstances in which our fellows die and have found much to disturb us. We have considered the attention that society pays to the rituals of marriage and birth and contrasted it with the obscurity and neglect in which some people die — neglect which is not redeemed by attention to the funeral, however devout. The care that society devotes to its disadvantaged members is a measure of its civilisation and this is also true of the care it offers to those with terminal disease.

Dying, like living, is a very individual matter. We do not all wish to die in the same way, but we would all like some say in the matter of our dying. In many cases no such choice is possible. Death comes in an acute form that allows no scope for choice or control. But in many others there is an interval between the recognition of the terminal stages and the final loss of life. It is during this period that the wishes and needs of the individual concerned should be discovered and respected as far as it is possible to do so. The main requirement is not money or equipment but human time, thought and concern. Society needs to do more than it does now to protect the quality of what is left to the dying, but at the same time to pay more attention to the dying person's right to have a say in the manner of his or her death.

South Australian Friends 1992

4.30   I have recently returned from New Zealand after 18 weeks caring for my mother who had been extremely ill for many months. As I walked at last through Sydney airport to join my family I thought I felt emotionally strong, and confident I had done all that was possible to help her. But at the sight of my husband and Sarah waiting for me, the full load I had been carrying for so long fell away and, instead of giving a warm and loving greeting, I burst into tears and howled across the space between us, 'It was soooo awful'.

We may think of our deaths, but we seldom think of the long periods towards the end of our lives when we need extra care and attention as our bodies grow frail. Those who love us will do everything possible to help us at this time, but we may not be able to influence their decisions.
It is possible that with some preparatory care and forethought we could lessen the heartbreak, both to ourselves and those we love.

Cathy Davies 1998

4.31 Dying holds no terrors for me. I just wish society in general wasn't in such a state of denial. Dying is as much a miracle as birth. It isn't the end of something, just the continuation of a recycling process. I have recycled bits of me over most of Europe, Britain, Australia. As I watch the clouds and mists and swirls of rain drift over Kings Park I know that bits of me are recycled in those too. But so are bits of everyone! We are each other! We are breathing in the recycled air Chaucer breathed out. So, that means there is that of everyone in everyone. As a Quaker I believe there is that of God in everyone. Maybe that's what the word God really means — 'Everything, Everywhere, Everytime'; or maybe that's what eternity is — being part of an everlasting cycle. When I die I will still be here in a variety of forms. As long as any one person remembers me and thinks about me my energies will still be around.

Mary Mathews 2000

4.32   In 1989, after an operation for cancer, which had not bothered me, I was told I had to have radiation treatment. This seemed to bother me more — I was feeling very low. It registered with me that maybe I was facing my death. Suddenly I was full of incredible joy! I felt happy and excited way beyond my normal feelings of anticipation. The feeling only lasted a brief moment and there was a visual impression of a bright light. (I understand the technical term for this light is 'photism'.)

This experience has convinced me that there is life after death and it will be something wonderful.

Elaine Polglase 1997

4.33   *His dying words:* I am glad I was here. Now I am clear, I am fully clear... all is well; the Seed of God reigns over all and over death itself. And though I am weak in body, yet the power of God is over all, and the Seed reigns over all disorderly spirits.

George Fox 1691

4.34   I believe that modern biology has made us realise much more than was previously possible on a personal and emotional basis that life and death closely belong together. Those who have not yet learned the lesson will have to learn it in the population crisis which already has begun to teach us the dynamic steady state depending on the balance between life and death.

This lesson will be of great religious significance. We shall have to live our life in a manner that includes our coming death. Great men have always known this and have not succumbed to the cheap temptation that therefore all life is in vain, and the seeking of pleasure thereby justified. On the contrary, they have been stimulated to use the creative powers lent to them by God to the utmost of their strength.

Rudolf Lemberg 1979

4.35 The truest end of life is to know the life that never ends. He that makes this his care will find it his crown at last. And he that lives to live ever, never fears dying: nor can the means be terrible to him that heartily believes the end.

For though death be a dark passage, it leads to immortality, and that's recompense enough for suffering of it. And yet faith lights us, even through the grave, being the evidence of things not seen.

And this is the comfort of the good, that the grave cannot hold them, and that they live as soon as they die. For death is no more than a turning of us over from time to eternity. Death, then, being the way and condition of life, we cannot love to live, if we cannot bear to die.

They that love beyond the world cannot be separated by it. Death cannot kill what never dies. Nor can spirits ever be divided that love and live in the same Divine Principle, the root and record of their friendship. If absence be not death, neither is theirs.

Death is but crossing the world, as friends do the seas; they live in one another still. For they must needs be present, that love and live in that which is omnipresent. In this divine glass, they see face to face; and their converse is free, as well as pure.

This is the comfort of friends, that though they may be said to die, yet their friendship and society are, in the best sense, ever present because immortal.

William Penn 1693

Life Challenges

4.36 There is a spirit which I feel that delights to do no evil, nor to revenge any wrong, but delights to endure all things, in hope to enjoy its own in the end.

James Nayler 1660

4.37 Sometimes religion appears to be presented as offering easy cures for pain: have faith and God will mend your hurts; reach out to God and your woundedness will be healed. The beatitude, 'Blessed are they who mourn, for they shall be comforted', can be interpreted this way too, but the Latin root of the word 'comfort' means 'with strength' rather than 'at ease'. The beatitude is not promising to take away our pain; indeed, the inference is that the pain will remain with us. It does promise that God will cherish us and our wound, and help us draw a blessing from our distressed state.

S Jocelyn Burnell 1989

Disability

4.38   When the poet Milton became blind, he wrote a poem about his blindness. In it he stated, 'God took away my sight so that my soul might see.' I do not believe that. My God would not inflict blindness on anyone. But my God has given me the courage to step out into the coming darkness, the uncertainty, and to learn new skills, a greater appreciation of the colour and beauty that I can still see, and the hidden beauty in people and the world around me.

There are times of frustration when I cannot read the word I have typed or cannot see the strings of my harp. There are the days when the darkness seems to press in on me, the darkness of the day seems to increase the loss of sight.

I do not know what the future holds for me. Sometimes I feel that I am amongst the privileged ones as I am still mobile. I hope that there is still something of value I can do for the world. I shall march forward with faith and hope to the music of my own drummer.

Jean Carmen 1999

4.39   *Rufus Jones, describing the experience his friend John Wilhelm Rowntree had in 1894:*

Just as he was entering young manhood and was beginning to feel the dawning sense of a great mission before him, he discovered that he was slowly losing his sight. He was told that before middle life he would become totally blind. Dazed and overwhelmed he staggered from the doctor's office to the street and stood there in silence. Suddenly he felt the love of God wrap him about as though a visible presence enfolded him, and a joy filled him, such as he had never known before. From that time he was a gloriously joyous and happy man. His physical limitations have all along been turned into inward profit. His long, hard battle with a stubborn

> disease which was attacking the very citadel of his powers — his sight, his hearing and his memory — has only made him more heroic and gentle.
>
> Rufus Jones 1905

4.40 Life is become a canyon

Life is become a canyon.
The harsh rocky walls of my disablement press ever closer on me.
There is less sky; and the opening so far so very far ahead.
Sometimes I think it would be easier to be one of the mindless ones
and drift through the days unaware, seemingly uncaring.
Whereas I extrapolate the discouraging downward-sloping graph of
my performance
and find no comfort.
But into their half-light there creep sometimes bad and ugly dreams
of long-dead grievances and quarrelling
and no one can cheer them,
While I, with alert and wakeful mind,
cannot communicate.

But I must summon courage, patience.
I can enjoy a joke; I can direct my mind
to tackle problems, wrestle with fears, and face my challenges,
or browse at will among memories and pleasant thoughts,
to work the present transient moment into perspective.
I can get outside my canyon, and think of others
though I can give them little more than passed-on love.
I can delight in music;
I am not as isolated as the very deaf.
Count your blessings, fool!

Val Nichols 1989

4.41   Over the last eight years since I became aware that Red was starting to display indicators of dementia, I have learnt a lot. Gradually I have learnt to let go of things I might have thought important. Things like where are the scissors, or even going to the pictures with one sandal and one shoe, drinking coffee through a straw or even so-called anti-social behaviour. What people may think no longer matters to me, they are friends and so will understand or forgive, or they are strangers and will probably remain so.

Lost articles stay lost until they reappear and we can celebrate the find — if you can't do a job without the glasses, scissors etc, can't it be left to another day?

We cleared the house of bits and pieces so it was not cluttered, and I learnt not to be angry and tried not to be frustrated by jobs incomplete or even unable to be started.

We learnt to concentrate on what we could enjoy — a flower here (no botanical names now), following a trail of ants, walking on more level paths, shorter and shorter distances, sometimes over an hour to walk a kilometre. Red learnt that it is OK to forget a name, a person, an event or even a place.

Elizabeth Mitchell 1999

Illness

4.42 Many times in my life faith almost fails. There are times in all our lives when we 'look in a glass darkly', not because of our lives, but because of the unmerited suffering of others. We ask ourselves, 'Why?' We try to relate a loving God to the world's appalling tragedies, and yet we must never fail him by denying him. It is not for us to understand his ways, but to remember always that it is through us and his people everywhere that his love is expressed.

Rachel Kelly 1987

4.43 My favourite piece was, and is, the following account by John Woolman of his experience:

> In a time of Sickness with the pleurisy , a little upward of two years and a half ago, I was brought so near the gates of death I forgot my name. Being then desirous to know who I was, I saw a mass of matter of a dull gloomy colour between the south and the east, and was informed that this mass was human beings in as great misery as they could be, and live, and I was mixed in with them. And henceforth might not consider myself as a distinct or separate being. In this state I remained several hours. I then heard a soft melodious voice, more pure and harmonious than any voice I had heard with my ears before; and I believed it was the voice of an angel who spake to other angels. The words were 'John Woolman is dead'. I soon remembered that I was once John Woolman and being assured that I was alive in the body, I greatly wondered what that heavenly voice could mean. I believed beyond doubting that it was the voice of an holy angel, but as yet it was a mystery to me.

His words movingly describe his awareness of being mingled with the suffering of the world. This was very much my own experience at this time of my life, which was painful on all levels without my having any reliable source of comfort, except by clinging to my newfound spiritual beliefs. I was intensely sensitive to the great mass of suffering in the world and aware on a feeling level of the interweaving of it all in our global social structure.

Joan Mobey 2000

4.44   When I'm depressed it is as if a black wedge has been driven into my brain. There is no past, no future and no light. Please, don't ask me to phone and talk. I can't. Please don't phone me. I can't answer. Please don't ask me to cheer up or buck up. There is no up. Everything is down. It is all pain and the only thing I can do is withdraw and live through it. No, you don't die from sheer misery, but you wish you could! This one thing I know: it will pass. So I wait and it does.

I begin to feel better and more able to do and be, once more, a part of living. Once more to feel alive. To feel grateful for the past and to even plan a future. The contrast between light and dark is known and felt. Thanks be to God, that great giver of light. I stand in it, and bathe in it and am healed by it. Here, thanks to the grace of God, I am. Standing in the light. Although I could neither know nor feel it, you were holding me there all the time.

Joyce Hudson 1994

4.45   I was recovering in hospital from an operation. Somewhere about day three I was still in pain and closed my eyes in a deliberate attempt to separate myself from it. I had a little epiphany — feeling myself drawn into a room where Quakers of the seventeenth century were seated around a table on which was a lighted candle. They sat quietly with their hands folded and I knew they were holding me in the Light. I was flooded with a sensation of peace and joy and then gratitude.

When I finally opened my eyes, though I was still in pain, I knew that all would be well and was able to relax — which did much to help me manage my pain. Perhaps we may be part of some mystical chain of being which we cannot call up at will but which can reach us in our need when we are, for whatever reason, open to its manifestations.

Patricia Kerr 1999

4.46   In the last week of September 1994, things really started to change for my family. My sister and I were down in the park. My mum and dad were up in the hospital as my brother was there with a swollen leg. At least that's what we thought. Emily (my sister), Mum, Dad, Dylan (my brother) and I all knew that the tests were coming back that day. You see the doctors didn't know what was wrong with Dylan so what they did was they took some of the swollen tissue out to see what it was.

Mum and Dad called us up. When we got up there, we went into a small room. Dad shut the door gently. They were both in tears. 'What is it?' we said. 'Dylan's got cancer,' they said quietly. After that we were all in tears.

After a while, the doctors talked to us in another small room. Then the time came to tell Dylan. Mum and Dad went in to tell him. After they had told him, I went in to say hello. Then we left him to sleep. I can't imagine what it would be like to be told you had cancer. Soon we had to call all our relatives and a lot of visitors came and Dylan got a lot of presents.

In later weeks, I went to the hospital school while Dylan underwent his treatment. When we got back to school, there was a big crowd around Dylan in the wheelchair. Dylan's illness brought people together. For almost a year the people in the school have tolerated Dylan's illness and I have not heard one complaint about him. Even when he lost all his hair, people still accepted him without a word.

Dylan's treatment has been very powerful but it has been helped along by people coming together to help him when he needs it most.

Hannah Chapman–Searle (aged 9) 1995

4.47   Being diagnosed with a life-threatening illness when I thought I was doing everything I could to be in right relationship with Godde, once and for all has convinced me we do not control anything in our lives and all we can do is live in faith and trust, handing over our will and lives into Godde's hands.

In Quaker meeting for worship, most often I sit, waiting to hear what Godde has to say. Words come into my head as I sit, words in answer to questions spoken and unspoken in my life and they seem wise in my judgement so I trust them. 'What is the leading, the call I am being asked to live at this point?' is all I can ask on a daily basis, in my recovery from surgery. The answer comes, 'Be who you are — this is not a time for you to be doing.' This to me seems a wise answer and I can follow this.

At times I doubt and wonder if I'm fooling myself imagining I'm hearing messages from Godde. Sometimes when an action comes to me in words from Godde, I assume what the outcome will be when I do it. I have discovered time and time again that Godde's lessons are much much greater and deeper, and outcomes are rarely as I predict.

Sometime I see visions; sometimes I am suffused with a presence; sometimes there is nothing at all. At times Godde talks to me as a child, 'My child, you are much loved and you are lovable. You are safe, rest in me, know you are loved.' Other times he accompanies me as now. At times, he speaks urgently, loudly in my life, gives me challenges, laughs gently at my antics, or sends me in directions I do not want to go. And it is all mysterious and adventurous, rich and full. I am so so grateful to be alive.

Annabelle Cameron 2000

4.48 I feel that God had not caused my cancer but neither could God make it go away. In fact all I could do was to leave God to look after God's business while I got on with mine. My business was to cooperate with the treatment offered me by my doctors and the nurses who administered it. It was also to get on with living. Reason told me that to demand a cure, to be miserable and to hang out for one was actually to be dying. Accepting the fact that I could die — and we all have to die sometime — freed me to get on with living. The treatment made me feel dreadful. I slept a lot. When I was awake I lived — enjoying the good ordinary things of life, the company of my family and friends. I grew in love. I'm fortunate to live on a farm in the country and I am able to spend time looking at the scenery and watching the birds. From this I discovered happiness, and this happiness has never left me.

Heather Kelly 1997

4.49 Our journey with Dylan's cancer was a search for peace that needed to be carried out with a sense of faith in the healer and hope the outcome would be OK. I was immersed in AVP when Dylan was diagnosed and messages about expecting the best, and respecting oneself and others were so important.

We lived in the present and built community wherever we were — hospital wards, waiting rooms, everywhere.

Did we get the best? Absolutely no, because the best would have been a cancer-free teenager still here to hassle me. However in one sense we did get the best outcome because we learnt to deal with the pain and joy of life as it came to us. What has happened to my passion to change the world? I saw Dylan make his world a better place as he lived his short life with dignity. I have learnt that I do change the world when I live creatively with pain and seek just solutions to difficult problems.

Ronis Chapman 1997

4.50　I have recently given up family practice to work fulltime with people with AIDS, particularly those in the advanced stage of the disease. I could not keep going were it not for the strength God gives. This comes first and foremost in the love that I share with John; but also in prayer and worship, and in the support of Friends.

A whole generation of young gay men is being wiped out; we know devastation and grief on a scale normally experienced only from war. Yet it is the central Christian experience that as we express God's love to one another we can sometimes pass through such crucifying experiences to life, light, and new growth. In the gay community's response to the AIDS crisis I have experienced such courage and love that I can only describe it as God's grace.

Gordon Macphail 1989

4.51　Gratitude has been the key healing gift and my day now ends always with a prayer to God about the gifts of each day.

Annabelle Cameron 2000

Stress

4.52   One of the most potent, and sometimes most difficult ways of dealing with stress has been to sit with it, to allow it, and not to attempt to change it, analyse it, remove it or 'deal with it'. Sometimes in this process, I have discovered that my perception of the stress has changed. It may even be recognised as a potent teacher, containing within it healing energy. In just allowing the pain to be the pain (rather than telling myself it shouldn't be there), that pain may yield up its wisdom. Perhaps this is one aspect of that old favourite: 'Be still and know that I am God'.

Christine Pronger 1999

4.53   I believe that a vision is essential for those of us dedicated to work for justice and peace. It should be backed by the conviction that not only is God working through history, but there are many others working for change and against oppression around the world, as many others have done before us.

Peter Jones 1984

4.54   Science cannot make the claim of being the only way into truth. Its contributions to our knowledge of the good and beautiful, important though they are, are only those of a hand-maiden. Modern musical instruments, paints and materials as well as theories on harmony, perspective and stress, are essential for symphonies, pictures and houses, but they do not constitute them. An increasing amount of scientific advice may be necessary for finding the best way to the solution of ethical problems in our modern world, but purely scientific ethics remain utilitarian and relativistic. This is often hidden by ethical values, naively accepted as self-evident and incontestable (have we forgotten Hitler who did contest them?). The ethical character is inseparable from the act itself, and different from a scientific experiment; one's ethical decision cannot be suspended on account of insufficient evidence. The meeting of the I and the Thou (Buber) in its immediacy is different from the I and the It, the world.

Rudolf Lemberg 1966

4.55   I ask no favours for my sex. All I ask of our brethren is, that they will take their feet from off our necks and permit us to stand upright on the ground which God designed us to occupy.

Sarah Grimke 1837

4.56   I became so stressed out, my health began to deteriorate and I had grave doubts as to whether I might live to the ripe old age I'd always hoped for. Sometimes when I had difficulty in concealing my scratchiness, I would be gently reminded by other busier than busy people, 'it is the Lord's work you are doing!' When at an inter-church council meeting which seemed to be going nowhere, my obvious irritation and impatience caused someone else to begin singing, very quietly, 'Make me an instrument of your peace,' I knew I had to quit. I might have been doing the Lord's work, but somehow in the process, I was losing contact with Him.

So I resigned from the committees on which I had served, and yes, there were others to take my place. I was not indispensable. Personally, I never thought I was, but somehow I had felt guilty about bailing out. Today I do the things which bring me the greatest joy and inner peace. I read, I reflect, I write, I meditate, I pray and once a month I lead a small group for meditation and reflection on 'Living the Word'. Again I am close to God and 'my cup runneth over'.

Shirley Dunn 1996

4.57   I especially thought of you because our election fever [in the Philippines] is rising and there is much pressure all round. It is, again, a time for power shift and in developing democracies, power shifts are rarely peaceful.

I am so hesitant to go into the vortex of the action, yet also so eager to participate actively in our political process. We have attracted the progressive groups among the youth, people's organisations, non-government organisations. I feel so hesitant, even unwilling to take on the pressures of field operations. Inside me, I am quite unsure of self, vulnerable, perhaps even selfish, narcissistic. Inside me, I am also strong, steady, clear-minded and quite idealistic.

What makes political involvement so difficult for me is that I am quite an introvert. I enjoy thinking, being with myself, silence, daydreaming, imagining. I have much difficulty relating to crowds, strangers, loud people, 'back-slappers'. Yet, it is because of my nurturance during silence that I am pushed to political involvement

Cristina Montiel 1995

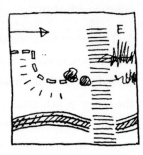

Deborah Faeyglenn

4.58   I am recovering from a long-term drug addiction. If my spirituality can't help me through a tough day, it's no use to me. The alternatives for me are drugs and alcohol and I don't want to go back to that. So I need something that's more attractive to help me cope with life. For me, trying to take a loving approach to life does it for me — to let go of anger and frustrations and put love and peace into my actions — changes me sufficiently to overcome the negative and feel okay about life. I use the breath awareness meditation that I learnt in the 70s.

It's taken a lot to rebuild my life from drug addiction, being a prisoner's wife for two and a half years, then suffering violence from him when he came out, and rejection by the church. I don't believe my ideas on love are starry-eyed romanticism; I'm too hard-headed now for that. It is more that love and peace are the only things that make sense, and trying to apply them via Christianity without being too idealistic or perfectionist, just as I can, a little bit, a day at a time.

I like the 'myth' of Christianity — that no matter what, there is always forgiveness, and renewal is possible, even if it takes a long time.

Lyn Traill 1995

4.59   In 1938 I lost my job with Lloyd's, London, for wearing a white poppy in my buttonhole on Armistice Day. 'We don't want any pacifists here!' declared my employer. Ironically, my next job as clerk to the principal probation officer of London came about because I was a conscientious objector, and worked in that position all through the war, being granted complete exemption from war service by the Conscientious Objectors Tribunal.

I hoped I was seen as witnessing against war as a result of my Christian belief about not taking life and a commitment to non-violence. Judging another's witness as right or wrong would not have been the way for me to go.

Now as a Friend I see the need always to test individual concerns with the gathered meeting and therein find support.

Ron Darvell 1989

4.60   Australia's first maternity hospital motel for newly confined mothers was built in our town.

An ageing elm tree extended its arms by way of welcome to the 500 new humans who passed under its branches each year to their new home on planet Earth. Situated between the hospital ward and the outside unit, its emerging buds have represented the new life of spring; its leaves have protected us from the fierce summer sun and coloured our autumn days while permitting the warmth of a fading winter light.

It was a shock to arrive one day and see our tree being brutally removed. No one took responsibility for the vandalism. There was talk of roots in pipes and leaves in drains but the managers were silent.

In our distress we had two choices: to vent our anger or deal with our own healing. We chose the latter option. We needed a ritual to help our mourning and it was devised with the help of Matthew Fox's Australian friends.

And so it came to pass that early one morning, as the sun was brightening the sky and the nurses were changing shifts, a small group gathered at the site where our tree had been torn from the ground. There was music from a violin and words:

I want you to think of the time when you saw a beautiful Elm.....

As we gather to mourn the loss of this Elm, we remember the words of wisdom of people from other lands and traditions much longer than ours.....

Brian Connor 1996

4.61   Only the passing of time,
the hours, the days and weeks
will show how healing can take place.

Love, patience and steadfastness
will be needed.

Remain yourself — constant.
Do not be undone by your distress.
Be strong.
I am with you always.

Penny Challis 1997

4.62   The sun went down
Bright orange flame, bold splash
Clump of trees silhouetted black against the sky
Glow illuminating landscapes in soft delicate pastels
Full of comforting shadows
As if tender hands were massaging day into night
A velvet cloak to sleep by.

Knowing those same hands
Will gently wake me in the morning

I am safe

Annabelle Cameron 2000

5

challenges

5 FACING THE CHALLENGES OF TIME AND PLACE

5.1   Would that we could love the whole world! But a special fragment is placed before us in the temporal now which puts a special responsibility for our present upon us.

Thomas Kelly 1941

Children and young people

5.2   Some of us, especially the younger, would like to know more about the unspoken rules and the history of Quakers. We feel like our ignorance in this prevents us from feeling comfortable speaking. We would like older Quakers to know that we often feel what we say in meeting is treated with disrespect. This disrespect either looks like what we have said is inappropriate and is ignored, or that we are gushed over and we feel patronised. We speak because the Spirit moves us. It seems strange that we should be gushed over for being moved by the Spirit. We don't want to stop you from thanking us for our contributions, but we'd like you to address the content rather than the age of the speaker. We would also like to affirm that though we may not articulate ourselves as readily when we are around adults, we do think as well as you do. We feel like because of Quakers' belief in that of God in everyone, you are much better at treating young people with respect than many adults. We would like to thank you very much for this.

Statement by Junior Young Friends and Young Friends
to Australia Yearly Meeting 1998

5.3   The most important thing we can do for children is to trust their inward light and encourage them as they follow it. This means steadfastly maintaining an egalitarian and respectful attitude to children and young people, and giving time to open-hearted listening. It means seeking corporate unity with them about the things they care about. It means giving the time to keep in dialogue with them so there will always be many and varied openings for them to influence what Friends do as a body and how we do it. It means giving resources and other forms of support so they may witness their seeking and insights in the wider world as 'Friends of the younger sort'.

Helen Bayes 2003

5.4   When thy children ask thee any questions of this nature — What is God, where he dwells; or whether he sees them in the dark — do not reject it; but wait to feel somewhat of God raised in thee, whether the question be put forth in sensibility or in vanity; and which can give thee an advantage of stirring the good.

Thou expectest, perhaps, from me, an outward rule; but I have no rule but the inward life, nor can I direct thee to any other, but to wait, that life may be revealed to thee.

As for praying, they will not need to be taught that outwardly; but if a true sense be kindled in them, though ever so young, from that sense will arise breathings to him that begat it, suitable to their state; which will cause growth and that sense of life in them.

Isaac Penington 1665

5.5   We need a closer participation with children today because we need fresh perspectives on our activities. We need their insights, and not only in the area of social action. We need their spiritual insights too.

Elise Boulding 1996

5.6   I recently came to Meeting for Worship bewildered. Someone was quoting one of Clive Sansom's most beautiful poems 'The Rabbi in the Temple'. The rabbi hears

> some firebrand causing trouble,
> Denouncing sellers and exchangers.
> Upsetting tables? Incredible!
> Young men today, they have no —
> No respect, no decency.
> 'Soiling my Father's House with trade'.

The ministry continued: 'The rabbi remembers the sincere voice of a beautiful lad 20 years ago saying to his mother 'Where should I be but in my father's house?' Jesus brought changes. Some like the rabbi, were horrified by them. His new patches began to tear the old fabric. Genuine Christianity has always involved readiness to examine what has become fixed, moribund…'

I came away somewhat restored. The future is not always born without pain. New wine was bursting the staid thought patterns of my mind.

Charles Stevenson 1989

5.7   It seems to me that some programmed and semi-programmed worship, in which our children participate as equals, would open us to new experiences of wonder, simple truths and joy. Let us give time to joyful, light-hearted ways to worship, for in these we will find healing and renewed humility. Let us also give as much respect to children's spiritual insights and discoveries as we give to those of older Friends.

Helen Bayes 2003

5.8   Participation and partnership involves working in such a way that the traditional power balance between generations shifts in favour of young people taking up more responsibility, and in consequence developing personally, socially and spiritually. It is not an abdication of responsibility, rather it is a change from a relationship of dependence to one of partnership. It is a way of relating that demands our full acceptance of their autonomy, independence and individuality.

Sandy Parker 2000

We journey on different paths, in many ways, from different directions. Yet when we join together in reverence and respect, we begin to see our connections to one another and to spirit.

We are all one. by L. Mooney

— Leanne Mooney

Indigenous people

5.9 **Lament**

two hundred years ago
an aborigine was killed
by a white

the conquerors did not note
who they killed
who they raped and tortured
the names of the first brave fallen
are lost to history

in every country town
stands a marble monument
bearing the mortal names
of the men who fought
(with borrowed honour)
and died
(for a borrowed cause)
we shall remember them

and yet
where is the monument of those
who did not travel across the world to fight
but sacrificed their lives
to protect their homes
their sacred lands
these people fought surely
and not men only but women
and terrified confused children
their names have been discarded

their lands confiscated
their lives debased

so two hundred years on
their sacrifice is finally noted
commemorated
if all was right
this should be the time for recognition
but it is the killing
not the dying that is made honourable
and still the people cry
and die

Philip Bywater (aged 16) 1987

5.10   In those parts of the Colony, in which the White Population have taken possession of the lands, the Kangaroos and Emus, which were among the chief animals on which the Blacks subsisted, have been generally destroyed, and the ground on which those animals fed, is now depastured by the flocks and herds of the usurpers of the country; who have also introduced profligate habits among the Blacks, that are rapidly wasting their race, some tribes of which have already become extinct, and others are on the verge of extinction.

It is scarcely to be supposed, that in the present day, any persons of reflection will be found, who will attempt to justify the measures adopted by the British, in taking possession of the territory of this people, who had committed no offence against our Nation; but who, being without strength to repel the invaders, had their lands usurped, without any attempt to purchase by treaty, or any offer of reasonable compensation, and a class of people introduced into their country, amongst which were many, both free and bond, who, regardless of law, and in great measure exempt from its operation, by the remoteness of their situation, practised appalling cruelties upon this almost helpless race. And when any of the latter have retaliated, they have brought upon themselves the vengeance of British strength.

Upon every hand, it is evident that a heavy responsibility has thus been brought upon the British Nation; in which also, the Colonial Government is deeply involved; and that it is their bounden duty, to make all the restitution in their power, by adopting efficient measures for the benefit of Aborigines of Australia, in affording them protection and support, and in endeavouring to civilise and settle them.

James Backhouse 1836

5.11   Therefore I trust that I shall not be accounted as improperly interfering in a political question in this plainly, yet respectfully urging it; seeing it is in the cause of humanity and on behalf of the oppressed — of a people who require to have justice done to them speedily, or the opportunity will be gone forever, and the unmitigated guilt before God of their extermination be fixed irremediably upon the British nation and its Australian descendants.

James Backhouse to Governor Bourke of NSW 1837

5.12   Twelfth Month 24th 1835: We sent some biscuit to the native family on the north side of the bay, by the mate and my son Charles; who saw two other families of these people in the course of their excursion.
Their debased condition is greater than can well be conceived, and such as to render every attempt to assist them fruitless: if money be handed to them, it is immediately exchanged for rum; or if clothes they are forthwith sold or exchanged for whatever will procure strong drink: such is the curse entailed upon them since their acquaintance with the British; who are doubtless chargeable, not only on this score, but for much of the demoralisation and degradation of these harmless people.

Daniel Wheeler 1842

5.13   *Joseph James Neave and Walter Robson had been travelling under concern in Brisbane in 1868.*

Thence we walked into town and called on a Mr Alfred Davidson. He wished to converse with us about the Aborigines of this colony, who he considers are most unjustly used. He told us of many instances of cruel injustice to them on the part of our fellow countrymen, who seem to think them in their way, and on the slightest provocation will shoot them down like dogs. Indeed before we had landed a week in Australia we heard the sad fact that an Englishman?, a farmer, finding the poor natives were stealing his flour, mixed arsenic with it and poisoned over 100 of the poor untaught savages, whom the Christian English have never cared to teach that God has said: 'Thou shalt not steal.' In this colony nothing is being done, except it be privately, to evangelise them and there is a large camp only 4 miles from Brisbane.

We have seen many of both sexes, the gaunt looking savages and their wives (or 'gins' as they are called here, or 'lubras' in South Australia and Victoria). Today before breakfast I had a long talk with a poor fellow who could speak a little English and seemed very glad to be spoken kindly to. The government of this colony have set up over them, native police, men picked from their number to keep order among the rest, but the result is they kill any who do not please them, and I fully believe, taking Australia through, the general feeling is that the colonists would be glad to get rid of them at any price.

Were I in England I would certainly lay some dark facts before the Aboriginal Protection Society and if I can collect facts will (D.V.) send them home for the information of those who are interested in this neglected race, the real rightful owners of Australia, which was originally planned out by them into huge hunting grounds. They are dying out very fast. Their babies (piccaninnies) often do not live to grow up. Our hearts are often sad to think of how badly the Christian settlers have treated the rightful owners of the soil.

Walter Robson 1868

5.14   Gilbert Foxcroft has told us something of the conditions under which some 6000 halfcastes are living in the south-west of Western Australia and the urgent need for something to be done. For a large proportion of them there are no homes, no school, no clothing except what they can beg, no work, no soap, and only a government ration of uncooked food.

Friends are concerned to go into many other countries to work amongst the people there. Have we anyone with concern for these people of our own land? We decide that the first step is to make the facts known and to this end suggest that there should be a series of articles in *The Friend of Australia and New Zealand*.

Australia General Meeting 1940

5.15 Assimilation is a policy which is not acceptable to the minority group. It is more a cause of group conflict than a means of avoiding it. Distinctive elements which Aborigines might preserve in a plural society are the attitudes and ideals which sustained the Aboriginal people in the past, which are still to be found among them and from which modern technological man may well learn.

Our task then is not to oppose group differences or nor to oppose legitimate group power (i.e. power which does not place one group in a position of dominance or privilege with respect to another), but to welcome such diversity and reciprocity as the basis of creative dialogue in a spirit of love. Our task is to gain the free, nonviolent, and voluntary acceptance by the white power structure of the legitimacy and value of sharing power with black people.

We need to act in love, truth and responsibility, but also with frankness and radical strength of purpose. We need to speak truth to power on race relations in a way which we have failed to do since the days of James Backhouse.

A Barrie Pittock 1969

5.16 *Australian Friends asked Charlotte Meacham, from the American Friends Service Committee, to visit among Aboriginal people in 1972 'to see what Quakers could or should do to support Aboriginal aspirations at a critical time'.*

This was an exciting time to be visiting Australia. After 200 years of white colonialism the first Australians were finding their voices and mounting demands for land rights and civil rights that startled the nation.

'Who has influenced them?' white Australians asked me over and over. Were these European-Australians really so unaware of the winds of change blowing through the world

as they sometimes appeared to be? I wondered who would need
to influence sick or hungry people to seek a better life?

Charlotte Meacham 1973

5.17 On Charlotte Meacham's *Listen to the Aborigines* and its outcomes.

The overriding 'leading of love and truth' which Charlotte left us, to enable us to confront the problem of white institutional racism was, 'Listen to the Aborigines, white Australia. Theirs is a message not of doom but of hope. They are demanding justice, autonomy and a future for their children — and yours.'

Friends made the following responses to Charlotte's calls:

- A consultation which included 30 Aborigines from four states and the Northern Territory as well as Quakers from all Regional Meetings was held 9–10 September 1972 at Devonshire Street Meeting House (before Charlotte left Australia).

- In 1973 the FWCC Triennial was held in Sydney and Len Watson, who had talked with Charlotte in Brisbane, spoke with great passion about how it felt to be subjected to discrimination and to watch his children suffering. His speech, which was confronting to the world family of Friends, was published by Australia Yearly Meeting as *From the Very Depths*. Later Len's sister, Lilla Watson and two young Aboriginal men, John Bayles and Ricky Clay, travelled around the USA for six months under the care of American Friends Service Committee. Lilla's report *Minority Groups in America: Their Struggle and Ours* was published by the Race Relations Committee of AYM.

- The Race Relations Committee helped to organise two land rights conferences, one in Darwin and one at Devonshire Street, Sydney.

Ruth Haig 2001

5.18   In her impressions on a session on inter-relationship of Cultures in the Regional Asian Pacific Conference, part of the Friends World Committee for Consultation Twelfth Triennial held at Sydney in 1973, Lau Wai Har of Singapore Friends Meeting reported how 'An Aborigine cried out with pain and, in vehement and forthright language, described the degrading and hurtful experience of his being an Aborigine. At the end of his speech, the whole audience remained absolutely silent for a few moments. It seemed that everyone was burdened with a deep sense of guilt and perhaps shock.'

Friends World News 1973

5.19   The Crusades, the Inquisition, and participation in World Wars I and II were all justified in their time by Christian thinkers. Aboriginal people were 'placed' in reserves, had their children taken from them, and were treated in ways which horrify us today, by sincere, devout Christian men and women.

We are prisoners of the thought forms of our own time, reflecting as they do the life experience of our time, as indeed were the men who established the canon of the Bible.

Margaret Bearlin 1984

5.20   On the occasion of the bicentennial of European settlement in Australia, we have considered deeply our role in any observances. We believe that, rather than being a time for celebration, this is a time for reflection and prayer: reflection on a history of cruelty and injustice to the original owners of this land and of broken promises by present and past governments over land rights legislation; prayers for forgiveness and for action to create an Australia where many races may live in harmony and where injustices towards Aborigines may be redressed.

The Yearly Meeting of the Religious Society of Friends lays down no rules as to the action of individual Friends concerning the observance of the Bicentennial celebrations but reminds Friends of our historical and spiritual witness in the field of social justice and racial inequality.

Australia Yearly Meeting asks its members to seek ways of expressing a commitment to an Australian society where harmonious relationships between our diverse cultures are valued and where special regard is given to the rights and aspirations of the Aborigines.

Statement from Yearly Meeting Officers 1987

5.21 A powerful statement [by heads of churches] reminded us that, though we have been living together for 200 years, ignorance, prejudice and discrimination divide us. In these 200 years many Aborigines have lost life, language, culture and dignity. 'While the past which many Aborigines have endured cannot be undone', continues the statement, 'we might shape a new future and become a nation to which all belong.'

Specific suggestions promulgated were (in brief):

- a secure land base for dispossessed Aboriginal communities
- a just process for the resolution of conflicting claims to land and its use, especially between Aborigines, pastoralists and miners
- an assured place for powerless Aborigines in our political processes with provision of Aboriginal Councils at local, state and federal levels
- a guaranteed future for Aboriginal culture and tradition with legal protection of Aboriginal heritage and public education of all Australians about Aboriginal history and the vitality of contemporary Aboriginal culture.

Bronwen Meredith 1988

5.22 A testimony to social justice and racial equality has been part of the Quaker witness to the world since the inception of our Religious Society of Friends in Britain in the seventeenth century. This witness has been expressed throughout our history by the actions of men and women guided by the Light as they saw it.

In 1691 William Penn signed a treaty of friendship with the Delaware tribes of American Indians, arranging for fair payment for lands taken and setting a pattern for good relationships between the European settlers and the indigenous people. John Woolman, an American Quaker of the eighteenth century, went alone and unarmed among warring American Indians in order to 'feel and understand their life and the spirit they live in'. In 1756 he persuaded Quakers in Philadelphia to pay for land stolen from the Indians by others. In the nineteenth century two British Friends, James Backhouse and George Washington Walker travelled through the Australian colonies and were forthright in their statements to influential figures in Australia and Britain concerning the cruelty and injustice meted to the Australian Aborigines, especially urging payment for land taken from them.

The Queensland Regional Meeting of the Religious Society of Friends had a small block of bushland near Greenbank and initially we discussed making this land available for the use of the Aboriginal and Islander Community. Over a period of two years, during which two Meetings seeking clearness were held and a discussion paper was circulated, it became clear that we should return this piece of land to the Aboriginal and Islander Community. For us, the decision to return this land was a deeply spiritual and joyous occasion.

Queensland Regional Meeting 1988

5.23 Footprints

Footprints alone remained
to tell of your presence,
a slight disturbance of dust
spoke of each sojourn.

In boots heavy with iron
the white man trampled
your mother the earth
as a locust plague stripped
the land with axe and saw.

Your people shed silent tears
watching the rape of their land.
Dreamtime spirits sighed as
the cloven-hoofed cattle
pounded the sacred soil.

Now in the season of giving
we return this land to you
though a fragment of the whole,
a symbol of hope for the long years ahead.

May the age old tales
echo anew through the trees
the laughter of little ones
float on the breeze
and the earth mother smile
as the dancing feet
of her children
heal her wounded spirit.

Sue Parritt 1988

Susanrah Brindle

5.24   *Brisbane's Aboriginal and Islander Independent School began about 1985.*

'How is the Murri school getting along?' a lot of you are asking.
The answer is, 'Above all that I had dared to ask or think.'

Friends helped this school to get started with a generous gift of money and, although it teetered on the edge of collapse during the first years, it kept going. There are serious problems that other schools do not have, but our numbers are growing, and so are our dreams: a really adequate building of our own with good grounds, a kindergarten; a high school too.

Muriel Langford 1989

5.25   We live in an exciting decade of change which presents enormous challenges — individually and collectively. One of the changes I see happening is the shift from material values being held supreme, to an inclusion of spiritual values. This involves an understanding of humans as part of the ecological web of life, not as dominators of it. This means having equal respect for all forms of life and for all peoples, including utmost respect for remaining indigenous people who have held on to their spiritual values in harmony with the environment.

Jo Vallentine 1991

5.26   Aborigines on a reserve outside our country town in the 1960s lived in bad conditions, some in humpies of old corrugated iron.
Also, the mothers held back their much-loved children from school until they were seven years old and able to stick up for themselves.
This handicapped their education from the start. However,
Save the Children Fund started a pre-school there and I was appointed as teacher. The children loved it. Just before they were five years old, we took them to the 'big school' kindergarten, to play with toys, some familiar and some excitingly new. So the children asked their mothers if they could go there. The mothers agreed and the children's education began well.

Thirty years later I revisited the reserve and met a man who had been a cheerful little pre-schooler. He recognised me, and we embraced. It was an emotional moment. He told me of the white friends he had made in kindergarten and kept since then, of his successful school career and training as a builder. He had helped to construct some of the new homes on the reserve, replacing inadequate houses and humpies.

Helen Linacre 1997

5.27   1997 Australia Yearly Meeting's strong concern to stand with Aboriginal people is still fresh in my heart. I feel privileged that Australian friends, therefore, were very much with me in the Spirit during that week of intense learning. In these times, when consciousness about the nature and extent of our racism is growing, I feel we are to be challenged to the foundations of our faith and integrity, in much the same way that Friends of the eighteenth and nineteenth century were in the face of their increased awareness of the iniquity of slavery. It has been coming, this no-turning-back time. We Friends, with our historic connections with the poor and oppressed, have always expressed concern for the plight of the Aboriginal peoples. To some extent this concern has tended to focus on what we might be able to do for them, an attitude which has its roots in the late nineteenth century belief that they were a doomed race and that we Europeans, from the superiority of our culture and wisdom, might be able to be kind to them and help them. Now we must face the fact that even we Friends have been and are an integral part of their distress.

The message, spoken so clearly — time and again, and from all quarters — was that all will be lost to the tidal wave of individualism, materialism and economic rationalism unless we stand with Aboriginal peoples, really listening to them and truly hearing the voice of this land.

Susannah Brindle 1997

5.28   At a meeting on cultural diversity I was shocked to hear myself accused of racism. Me? The most tolerant of souls, I had fondly thought. The issue was my preoccupation with getting on with the job. It took me some time to accept that some cultures find this task-orientation oppressive, ignoring as it does the value of process, of giving things due time.

Further, that people of other (more process-oriented) cultures could feel consistently devalued because of the domination of this value system in Australian society.

Laurel Thomas 1997

5.29   *Silent Vigil Melbourne 1997*

- Quakers acknowledge the Indigenous Australians on whose land we live.

- We wish to make a strong, visible statement of support to Indigenous Australians in their struggle for justice.

- We acknowledge the murder, the horror, the destruction of culture and communities that accompanied white invasion.

- We hear stories of the stolen children and of deaths in custody, and feel the pain, grief and anger.

- We believe that reconciliation cannot begin without justice and acknowledgment of past wrongs. Only after this can healing begin, and the building of a strong nation.

- We urge all Australians to look into their hearts: to recognise our common humanity, not a separateness, in our search for a way forward, embracing differences that strengthen and enrich the whole.

- Quakers want to be part of a process of reconciliation that will allow all Australians a share in the building and enjoyment of the good life this nation could offer.

    Quakers for a Reconciled Australia (QFARA) 1997

5.30 Pay the rent

Like most non-Aboriginal Australians, I had grown up quite ignorant of the ways my forebears had wrested this land from Indigenous people. It was not until 1969, while living in the Mount Isa area of north-west Queensland, that I became aware, in a moment of horrified awakening, of the magnitude of injustice done to these people, not only by my ancestors, but also by the present day governments which were supposed to represent me. For the next 20 years I felt helpless to do anything, however small, to redress the wrongs.

I first heard about the 'pay the rent' concept in January 1988. As I understood it then, it was a way forward offered by Aboriginal people to the non-Aboriginal Australians of good will who felt uncomfortable about living off stolen land and who wished that non-Aboriginal Australians could pay 2 per cent of their annual rates (or equivalent if they rented conventionally), in person, to a grass-roots Aboriginal body. At last I could acknowledge Aboriginal prior right to this land in a practical way. An annual payment of $12 seemed a ridiculously small amount.

Immediately I began to search for my local Aboriginal community and I soon found it was not so easy a matter as I had imagined. I can understand it when people say, 'I have never met an Aboriginal person and I wouldn't know how to go about it.' After six months, I tracked down the Biddi-Biddi community. Suddenly very nervous, I telephoned the manager. He listed patiently and attentively, and then suggested I come and see him at the community.

This meeting was the real beginning of an ongoing relationship with Aboriginal people and, in spite of many years of conscious nature conservation, I felt that for the first time in my life I was beginning to be 'in right relation' with the land.

Initially I simply felt glad that I had done the right thing. But with each year of paying the rent my feeling of being privileged to live on Aboriginaland has grown. For me paying the rent has been a *process* of becoming more aware of things my culture could not teach me. It is neither conscience money, nor a way in which I can *buy* the right to live on Aboriginaland. Things changed for me when I realised paying the rent means (in white terms) that I am a tenant. Although I may do so under white law I do not own the land morally; it will *always* be Aboriginaland and under their spiritual custodianship. For me this means they should, at least, know they can always walk upon it.

Paying the rent is a privilege. I now recognise I do not pay to keep the Indigenous people out, but rather I pay this pittance to begin to feel what has been taken from them, to be opened to the possibility of a valid relationship with them and this land, to begin to learn the rudiments of humility, and to become a true citizen of Australia.

Susannah Brindle 1997

5.31 Speaking out in support of the needs of the vulnerable people, whose voice is so often ignored, trivialised or ridiculed, is one way Quakers bear witness and let the world know what concerns lie in the depths of our hearts. We are not fractured parts isolated from the whole. Speaking out is one way to bear witness that all life is interconnected.

As long as I do not listen to the essence of what the Indigenous people of this land are saying, then I am not listening to myself. As long as I remain silent, not voicing my concern for their cultural-spiritual needs, then I silence the need for my own voice to be heard.

David–Rhys Owen 1997

5.32 Reconciliation

There's a song in my heart that is crying, crying crying
Stop the lying, lying lying

Echoes deep resound
we have to tell the truth
it's time, it's time
we did as a people
slaughter our own native born
we did take their land
we did take their children
we did take their bones
As if they weren't human
Non persons, didn't matter, didn't count
As if they were lesser

Denial, saying no
Opening the cracks, what then
Feeling underneath
Feeling the enormity of pain
Connecting with humanity
Taking responsibility with reference
Being accountable

I am sorry for white blindness
white disconnection
white arrogance
I am sorry for what has been done and
what is still being done
I am sorry
There's a song in my heart and it's crying, crying crying
Stop the lying, lying lying

Annabelle Cameron 1997

5.33 *The Quaker Sorry Statement to the Indigenous People of Australia 1998*

Quakers believe in reconciliation between Indigenous Australians, the original custodians of the land, and non-indigenous Australians, to be the cornerstone of a nonviolent inclusive Australian society.

Australia Yearly Meeting of the Religious Society of Friends (Quakers) acknowledges the injustices suffered by the indigenous people of Australia since 1788. We are ashamed that we have failed to recognise the extent of dispossession, deprivation and trauma over the past 200 years. We have been and are part of a culture that has dominated, dehumanised and devalued Aboriginal religious, cultural and family life.

For this we are sorry and express our heartfelt apology to Aboriginal and Torres Strait Islander Australians. We commit ourselves to working towards a reconciled Australia.

Australia Yearly Meeting 1998

5.34 For reconciliation to be effective, it must become more than a cosy word that makes us feel good. Real reconciliation reflects *actual relationship*. It demands the honesty and courage of self-knowledge, and the letting go of many previously held attitudes. To work for real reconciliation, we shall need to summon fresh Light to help us face what we must about ourselves and our culture. We shall need a spiritual awareness that challenges our comfortable parameters, and a faith strong enough for us willingly to go where we may never have ventured before.

> Oh that we who declare against wars, and acknowledge our trust to be in God only, may walk in the light and therein examine our foundation and motives in holding great estates! May we... try whether the seeds of war have nourishment in these our possessions. (John Woolman)

In our desire to redress the wrongs done to Aboriginal peoples, we have focused on alleviating their material suffering with measures we consider appropriate — better housing, education, health-care, greater representation in our whitefella political structures, more jobs, more money. We want to be fair; we want to be generous; we want to include them in our life here. It is often hard to accept that, as long as our ecocidal practices continue, our well-meant offerings are frequently experienced as a continuation of the genocidal policy of assimilation. How can we discover what Aboriginal peoples need if we consider ourselves to be the hosts in this land? How shall we ever listen to the Earth's needs if our own desires clamour above our ability to hear?

Susannah Brindle 2000

5.35 Finding connections

During 2001, our Brisbane Meeting explored points of connection between Quaker spirituality and that of the Indigenous peoples with whom we share this country. We used extracts from *Quaker Faith and Practice* as well as the Australian Quaker Faith and Practice working papers alongside readings on Aboriginal spirituality. We also considered the queries put forward in Documents in Advance for AYM 2001.

To prepare a framework for the discussions, Susan Addison and Lynne Laver, as co-convenors, met with Mary Graham, a Kombumerri person who is also affiliated with the Waka Waka group. Together, we identified much common ground including:

- appreciation of silence
- sense of awe in nature
- caring for the land (e.g. our meeting house rainforest) can be a spiritual act

- respect for the whole person, including those who are different
- deep sharing gathered in circles
- simplicity through non-hierarchical, non-competitive, non-materialistic society
- decision-making by general agreement and concord
- no priests as intermediaries — the individual contributes his or her abilities or gifts for the benefit of the whole society
- spirituality permeates the whole of life — no holy days, everyday life is sacred.

Susan Addison 2001

5.36   Anyone, anywhere can 'Come Right Way'. If reconciliation is about our coming into right relationship with Aboriginal peoples, coming right way is an important precondition of this process.

It will be challenging work to relinquish the superiority, rectitude and control we have never doubted was ours in every aspect of life in this country. I am reminded of the rich young man who asked Jesus how he could be saved. You will recall that, when Jesus suggested that he give up the wealth that was so important to him and follow the path of justice, mercy and humility, the young man sadly turned away. Jesus likened the difficulty he and materialistic others faced in achieving life abundant to the impossibility of an overloaded pack-camel passing through the narrow Jerusalem-wall gateway called the Needle's Eye.

Coming right way is like that too. Coming right way is about honesty to face the truth about the fundamental theft on which our lives are based; it is about commitment to change; it is about courage to enter realms unknown and perhaps undreamt of; and ultimately it is about action.

Aboriginal people continue to look to people of the Spirit to help them turn the tide for real justice. They mostly find us, however, locked into the racism inherent in being a Whitefella in this country — unconsciously addicted to the retention of materialistic power and possession, and to faith in the superiority of our new theories about how things are and should be. We need urgently to realise that connectedness to all Creation is physically, emotionally, mentally *and spiritually* fundamental to our own lives as well.

Coming right way begins with a single act of humility and contrition, the first step in a journey towards justice, community — and reconciliation. Coming right way can become non-indigenous Australia's uniquely significant contribution to a world hungering for just and peaceful alternatives. Individually becoming aware — of who we really are on this continent — and beginning to act from this awareness *can* help create the critical mass for real justice, a position from which it will ultimately become unthinkable for the rest of whitefella Australia to retreat. Coming right way, then, is about becoming fully human at last, and learning how to act as a humble, though integral member of the Earth's community.

I hope we will not find ourselves to be camels too fully laden to pass through this Needle's Eye, for I suspect that coming right way is potential salvation not only for us Australian whitefellas but, by extension, for the rest of humanity and for the Earth itself.

Susannah Brindle 2002

This land

5.37   The produce of the earth is a gift from our gracious creator to the inhabitants, and to impoverish the earth now to support outward greatness appears to be an injury to the succeeding age.

John Woolman 1772

5.38   There is a danger in the isolation and want of companionship of the dweller in the bush and there is a danger in the hurry, the activity, the excitement of the crowded city..... a roar of many voices on religion, on politics, on commerce, on pleasure daily distract.....

Epistle from Adelaide to Melbourne Annual Meeting 1871

5.39   The great Australian outback is awesome even to one familiar with the vastness of North America's western deserts. It stretches dark red and implacable as the tiny plane skims along, up through the centre of the continent's 3 million square miles. The low grey spinifex bush and a few scattered small trees seem to be the only vegetation. One is filled with wonder that the early peoples who roamed this harsh land for at least 20–30,000 years could have survived but so skilled were they and so sensitive their balance with the ecology that until the coming of the white settlers the land supported them. Outback survival was not comparatively easy, as in the south-east coastal areas and the lusher northern and eastern seaboard. But the Aborigines' discipline, ingenuity and respect for the land formed a very special bond with the areas that nourished them.

'The white man says the land belongs to me. We say, the Aborigine belongs to the land.' This I was to hear all over Australia from the Aboriginal people.

Charlotte Meacham 1973

5.40   Early Australian painters still saw gum trees as oaks and elms, just as our first poets ignored the wattle and remembered the primrose, and musicians echoed European rhythms. The struggle of the Australian arts for their own vision, fed by the landscape and seasons and the long silent vistas of the past, has to be paralleled in religious terms.

John Ormerod Greenwood 1982

5.41   It seems there are many Friends isolated by distance — those of us scattered in twos and threes across the vastness of Australia — Mackay, Herberton, Alice Springs, Leeton..... There are also Friends who are isolated not by these enormous distances, but by shorter distances where they are just out of easy access to a Meeting, or by family complexities or by shyness.

We can also take note of the many positive benefits we derive from isolation. Maybe what we miss is more than balanced by the advantages of isolation! Removed from the influence of other thoughts, we have the opportunity to hear God more clearly. In prayers we do require solitude as have many before us.

Let all of us remember in our isolation that we may be gathered very close to God when we are together in solitude.

David Johnson 1988

5.42   At the present time of ecological crisis, it's especially valuable to be able to draw on creation-centred traditions close at hand and evolved to fit the lands where we live. Metropolitan Europe is inclined to see Australia and New Zealand as frontier societies in a somewhat condescending sense; perhaps we are frontier societies in the other sense of being the settings where major discoveries can arise from the long-deferred true partnership between indigenous and settler cultures.

David James and Jillian Wychel 1991

5.43 No Stranger

A magic, mystic place,
feeling ancient Koori presence,
huge stones animated by
sheer eternity.
lichens to moss to ferns to
trees stretching up umbrellas of leaves
to catch the highest sun —
I am not a stranger here.
I am part of this golden eternity.

Scott Bywater 1991

5.44 Halfway through my holiday in England I experienced a profound change of direction as I sat in the familiar silence of meeting for worship. I understood that soft sunlight and gentle rain are not part of my present experience, they belong in my past. I do belong with the deep blue sky, the fierce heat and storms of my adopted land.

In this land drought always remains a possibility. Perhaps this explains why I use this metaphor to describe my spiritual and creative journey. There seems to be no middle path for me, no drizzle or gentle sunlight. All is heat and heartbreak, torrential rain and torment. I must learn to recognise the warning signs before the dry wind blows away the soil and exposes my roots to the burning sun. When my thoughts are blown hither and thither as I strive to centre down in meeting let me take the proffered stake and anchor my fragile faith in the gathered silence.

> When green begets brown
> swirling dust scatters my faith
> no anchor for words

Let me store water during the good seasons to nurture the crops during
drought. Teach me to care for this land, allowing it time to heal,
lest erosion and salinity create a desert where nothing can grow.

Sue Parritt 1992

5.45 Contemplating the wattle

A great shining bushel concealing a dark candle
That illuminates and shelters Godhead in its shade,
That offers unconditional balm, solace, aid,
To souls that pause, and flinch from too much light,
That crave the inner, blessed, holy sight.

.....this silver, green, gray bower,
Drooping, drawing us in, has more power
Than all the household shrines and Marian scents,
Where we 'do pause and give some reverence'.

The advertisement for Immanence is starkly plain,
But still we pass each time, and time again,
With no more than a perfunctory inward nod,
Then walk inside to look for God.

John Coe 1993

Susannah Brindle

5.46   For Nature (as for Aboriginal peoples) drought is not a malevolent disaster, but a seasonal phenomenon; one of the great lessons nature has for non-Aboriginal Australians is how to live with its rhythms.

It is possible our non-Aboriginal urge towards planting this country with exotic species is not just a desire to create the familiar scene (for there are now perhaps fewer of us who remember the motherlands of our forebears), but a primeval search for the 'ancient wisdom', the spiritual in nature. The old world abounds in folklore — so much of our present day gardening practices have grown out of an eons-old close relationship with the rhythms of the Earth, and an intimate and often non-verbal knowledge of the cycles and the essence of particular plants. We look for the same seasons in Australia and we plant the plants of the old world to reassure ourselves that the rhythms are the same. But we cannot cope with the Australian reality of droughts and floods, harsh, fire-bringing winds and ageing soils because they don't fit with our preconceived picture. We are only just beginning to realise that the Aboriginal peoples' knowledge of plants may be quite as refined as the Linnaean nomenclature system and that their specialised knowledge of Nature, born of careful observation and listening, may be what we need to be versed in to survive here.

Susannah Brindle 1995

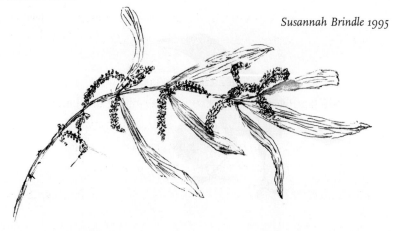

5.47

Four years ago — coming to Australia,
struck by strangeness..... and a beauty I did not understand.....
trees, birds, flowers I could not name
a night sky I did not recognise
a day-time sun travelling widdershins
a quality of light, a sky arc of unusual space.....
The brown grasslands of Avalon,
the salt flats of Avalon Beach,
the shore of Corio Bay and Hovell's Creek
became home.
Rare Cape Barren geese beside the road
Pacific gulls on the shore
penguins in the bay.....

I returned for a month to the USA and Europe
and found a familiar-unfamiliar night sky, upside-down Orion!
a confusing clockwise sun
gaunt bare skeletons of winter trees
in England
houses crowded together, claustrophobic density of people
yet beauty still on fell and in dale

Back in Victoria, the beauty of the gums
variety of leaves, bark, blossom and nut
black swan and blue wren
tiger snake and koala:
a familiar-unfamiliar country welcoming me 'home'
the spirit of the earth, no longer strange
a place of belonging, but not of ownership
a place of sojourn, but not of stasis.....

Sandy Parker 1996

5.48   Until recently I have felt guilty about my predecessors being party to the dispossession of Aboriginal people. Knowing that guilt is not productive, I have tried to engage with Aboriginal people in various ways, and to support their calls for land rights, which are fundamental to their spiritual lives. Aboriginal people belong to the land, not the other way round, as most non-Aboriginal people believe.

Cogitating on this matter as I sat at the top end of Australia — the northernmost tip of Cape York — I felt an overwhelming sense that finally, it was right for me to be here. With the whole of this magnificent and awesome island spread before me (or so it seemed) I felt passionately connected to all its aspects, including all its people.

Gratefully I acknowledged that I too belong to this land, and to it I shall always return.

Jo Vallentine 1996

5.49   I have grave concern for this earth that we are part of. I have fears that we, as a species, may not see that we are part of the whole and that we cannot go on destroying the earth and our own lives as we are currently doing. *But*, I am part of the crowd, I am human. If I cannot show compassion to others of my own species then I cannot show it beyond, to other species, to the Earth. It is the larger dimension of knowing that if we cannot love ourselves then we cannot love others.

It seems to me it is time to live in the larger dimension, the real world.

Gerard Fahey 1996

5.50   The Earth continues to speak to me in many voices and I am coming to sense its yearning for conscious communion with a humanity that has for so long almost severed its Life-connection. Since coming to live with Ray at 'Eldamar' (five hilly acres of granite boulders and honey-scented yellow box trees in Central Victoria) I have felt more at home in this Great South Land than ever before. The deeper I enter into this Earth-communion the more keenly I feel the dispossession of the Djadjawurung people. Recently I faced my territorial paranoia and asked their permission for us to live on this land, making it clear that if 'Eldamar' was a good 'sit-down place' they should feel free to have access to it. As they tell me the Dreaming stories associated with this sacred place, I begin to experience what it is like to live in a land which has been sung (a little) into life. I feel I no longer cling so tentatively to its surface. Some of its wisdom has entered into me and this connectedness gives me a greater sense of identity and integrity as a human being.

Susannah Brindle 1996

5.51   The real danger is that with the destruction of so much of the natural world, the spiritual basis of humanity will be threatened. We cannot afford to lose the reflective opportunity of the living desert, the sacred rainforest, the calm of still water. These are places where we can regain our sanity.

Brian Connor 1997

5.52   Early Quakers in Australia showed the range of inspiration and inadvertance that touches us still. We are human, with a glimpse of the divine to guide us. Backhouse spoke to the Australian colonists' condition when he challenged the 'plague in their own hearts' that scourged them even when worldly success had been wrought from the wilderness. He seemed to know that in searching for the unknown land, Europeans found nothing, but it was a *terra nullius* of the heart, not the landscape, which was feeding their imagination.

Australian Quakers, living in the vastness of a continent, have an opportunity through their collective stillness to envisage what this great emptiness inside offers the contemporary world, and the healing, the enormous healing, that might be done.

Dwelling in the deep silence the spirit may speak in its immediate way, or bide its time. Conceivably it may happen in special places writ in the landscape, or through Aboriginal voices, expressing aspects of this divine spirit which Friends uphold and are now beginning to hear in an Australian setting. How we discern such a meeting of cosmologies, and test the labour to justly share, may be one of the deepest mysteries our generation is led to celebrate.

Adrian Glamorgan 1997

Roberta Turner

Our region

5.53   We have found John Woolman's life of courageous seeking to be an inspiration and his message of pure wisdom, acquired by dying to oneself, by abandoning encumbrances and simplifying life, even more necessary today than when he lived. How often do our possessions and our instinctive defence of them weaken, or even endanger, our peace testimony.

Living as we do in the Asia-Pacific area, we realise how much this true caring is needed if we are to overcome, both in Aborigines and our Asian neighbours, the resistance aroused in them by past indignities. We realise we are bound with them in a common task of reconstruction. Our peace testimony must include the marshalling of constructive thought and action, which will overcome world hunger and the crying inequality of the distribution of the world's products.

General Meeting for Australia 1959

5.54   It is not part of our purpose to come here and condemn any act of government; we are in sympathy with those who bear the heavy responsibilities of government, and it is our concern to try to understand the problems which confront them. The belief by which we try to live is that no peace based on violence is ever really secure, and that we must always try, in ourselves and others, to discourage suspicion and fear, and develop trust, understanding and courage in working together.

We have come here to learn more about the fears and hopes, the joys and sorrows in which we are all involved so that, as neighbours in Australia and New Zealand, we may know better how we can help.

We would repeat the call made by our Friends World Conference in 1952:

> We call upon peoples everywhere to behave as nations with the same decency as men and brothers, and to substitute the institutions of peace for the institutions of war. Let us join together throughout the world to grow more food, to heal and prevent disease, to preserve and develop the resources of the good earth to the glory of God and the comfort of man's distress.
>
> These are among the tasks to which, in humility for our share in the world's shame, and in faith in the power of love, we call our own society and men and nations everywhere.

Quaker delegation to Indonesia 1965

5.55   We cannot salve our consciences by contributing to the appeal for bibles for the soldiers in Vietnam. Send the soldiers bibles by all means — they need all the spiritual succour they can get — but don't let us imagine that by so doing, or by supporting visits of prominent clergymen to the area, that we can turn this war into a holy crusade. You can't use bibles to bolster bullets. You can't spread the spirit of the nativity with napalm; you can't practise the love of God with a 'lazy-dog' slaughter weapon.

Can we, as Christians directly responsible to God, acquiesce in conscription whereby, at the behest of a few men, countless others are called to military service where they are taught to kill the enemy that we are required to love? Or should we use all our personal energy and ability and resources to bring this dispute to the conference table?

I do not wish anyone in Australia a 'happy' Christmas this year. I hope it will be the most mentally disturbing Christmas we have ever had.

This is an emergency rally. But the emergency is not only in Vietnam. It is right here in Australia and it is in the lives and the hearts of each one of us. Christmas is no time for mawkish sentimentality, nor is it merely a festival for children. It is a challenge to men and women to bring forth the Christlike spirit in their lives.

Jean Richards 1965

5.56   For the present and for the foreseeable future, there is little intrinsic basis for conflict between Australia and her Asian neighbours. However, if our policies continue to be motivated by fear and great power identification, rather than by constructive and purposeful national ideals, we will be inviting trouble. The years ahead in the Asian region will be tumultuous, for the modernising revolution in Asia is far from complete. Australians will be in a position similar to those Quakers of the American colonies who lived surrounded by racial wars. Shall we enclose ourselves in a fortress behind an immigration barrier, discriminating and taking sides against our neighbours? Or shall we, like the Quakers of early Pennsylvania, respect our neighbours as fellow humans and try to assist them to peaceful solutions to their problems, perhaps in so doing setting an example to the rest of the world?

Keith Crook 1970

5.57   On coming home from Kampuchea
I could cry for these people,
But tears will not come. So many things destroyed, so many people,
so many pillars of dead houses standing like naked, begging, agonised fingers
clutching at empty air.
Cry for the travesties of homes that now squat meagre on wide concrete bases,
flimsied in palm-leaf. They will not last, but they will have to do
in the thin hungry scrabble to survive.
I could cry for these people,
For the long haunted years of dwelling in caves and tunnels,
The brutalizing rain of bombs that made young girls and boys
grow into merciless savages,
whirled by the whipping winds of ideologies,
turning against their own.

I could cry for these people now, walking numb,
pretending, hoping to be real again —
Mind-wounds and aching memories of suffering unexplained,
The shadow of a demon and demonical cadres' raging whips.

Unscathed by the terror and the pain
which ravaged this once-lovely land, these gentle people,
I am a dazed onlooker, dismayed and sick, marvelling
that creatures so bruised can lift themselves to their feet again.
              — Old women with their eyes mercifully blank,
Young women lined and old, mainly their eyes alive,
watching over the precious children.
Theirs is the burden, mine the onlooker's emotionality.
Tears will not come to comfort my tight aching throat

as I look at shattered femurs disintegrating on the ground
(too far gone, to collect and display)
beside a chequerboard of gaping holes, unearthed mass graves.
    — So many empty pitted skulls,
so many children's garments in the filthy piled heaps,
so many bloodstains showing on the floors of the horror prison, Tuol Sleng,
so many ordinary faces in the weird display —
photos of torturers as well as victims —
How can I understand the *why* of it? but the sight
prickles the nape-hairs in broad daylight
with smell of whistling sorcery in the moonless dark of the spirit's night.

After the horror, after Tuol Sleng,
and the mind-paining, heart-jabbing booted-in-the-guts misery of one hour there,
It was a so blessed relief,
a merciful return to sanity
to find a group of children at the gate,
just a knot of giggling, peeping, curious kids
ready to burst out laughing at a foreigner, given the slightest chance —
God's good gift of young green grass
springing in a desert place.

Val Nichols 1984

5.58   We know that we live in a conservative country where security is traditionally seen as fighting someone else's war on the far side of the globe, in order to ensure that they will help us if we are invaded — while conveniently forgetting the effect of the last invasion in 1788 on the indigenous inhabitants of Australia. Raising our prophetic concerns about alternative concepts of security and defence, the need for an independent and non-aligned foreign policy, and an Asia-Pacific identity based on partnership rather than a preoccupation with the tyranny of distance from Europe and North America is no easy task.

Peter Jones 1987

5.59   In May I attended a consultation, 'Integrity of Creation: Our Land is our Life', which was held in Darwin. The initiators, the World Council of Churches Programme to Combat Racism, described it as a 'global meeting', and said: 'We feel it is a crucial time for the issue of land rights to be presented by indigenous people and a time for the churches to demonstrate their support'.

Listening was a harrowing experience. I think the thing that shocked me most was that everywhere the experience and the suffering was the same. Whether the speakers were from Hawaii or Australia, Guam or Japan, Aotearoa or Latin America; whether they were Indians from Canada or America, indigenous people from Timor, Fiji or the Philippines, and whether or not there had been a treaty or agreement with those who had invaded their land, the story was much the same. Some shouted and raved, some wept, some spoke quietly and shyly, and some spoke with calm determination. Most spoke bitterly of those who had taken away their land and their rights, and continue to deny them; most spoke of the churches as having played a large part in having caused the problem, and were bitter that they appeared to be doing so little to put matters right.

Joan Courtney 1989

5.60   [At a conference of social workers in a luxurious Seoul hotel] Ham Sok Hon, a Korean Quaker, said something and immediately there was silence and everyone closed their fans. Ham said, 'Is your comfort of more importance than my words... Jesus came to teach you love... I have come to teach you hate... to hate luxuries... to hate comforts... to hate your importance'. Ham spoke for a long time, and all was quiet — everyone listened.

Arthur 'Red' Mitchell 1989

5.61   Cambodia is a deeply disturbing experience. Words such as 'heart-rending', 'pitiable' and the like don't match it; they come from a sentimental view of the world. It isn't an intellectual experience either, though both the heart and the mind are involved.

Still trying to come to terms with the experience during Meeting for Worship last Sunday, I suddenly saw God comfortably at home in a nice clean house where the plumbing worked. It would have made me laugh except that it was a shock to realise that my notions were so shaped by my experience, and had caught me out by welling up from some unconscious depth. I obviously had to understand, and not just to think I knew, that the spirit of God is just as much at home where people have none of the things I take for granted, where flies walk on the food and mines blow off the legs of the hapless. The ministry with which Meeting began and ended, based on Matthew 25:31–46 ('Lord, when did we see thee hungry and feed thee?') could not have been more appropriate. The first requirement is that we see. I hope I have begun to see. Cambodia was a spiritual experience.

Frances Parsons 1992

Our world

5.62   O brother man, fold to thy heart thy brother:
where pity dwells, the peace of God is there;
to worship rightly is to love each other,
each smile a hymn, each kindly deed a prayer.

For he whom Jesus loved has truly spoken:
the holier worship which he deigns to bless
restores the lost, and binds the spirit broken,
and feeds the widow and the fatherless.

Follow with reverent steps the great example
of him whose holy work was doing good:
so shall the wide earth seem our Father's temple,
each loving life a psalm of gratitude.

Then shall all shackles fall: the stormy clangour
of wild war music o'er the earth shall cease;
love shall tread out the baleful fire of anger,
and in its ashes plant the tree of peace.

John Greenleaf Whittier 1848

THE TREE OF PEACE
("O Brother Man")

Words by J.G. Whittier

Music by A.E. Floyd

A Descant for optional use with the unison version in one or more of the later verses (e.g. the second and fourth).

5.63   We think it right at this our first Annual General Meeting to renew our protest against all war as opposed to the spirit and teaching of Christ. He came to give to the world a new commandment; a new rule of life to men, supplanting the old practices of hate and revenge. He came to reveal God as a Father, and to call upon men to live as brethren before Him.

Is it not dangerously akin to mockery for Christians to pray to God as our Father, and then to go forth and kill one another?

The sufferings of war fall most heavily upon the innocent. Its great cost adds to the hardness of the struggle of life in many homes. Preparations for war, instead of contributing to peace, produce suspicion, jealousy, and mistrust between the nations. It is far better to sow steadily and consistently the seeds of goodwill and concord. We appeal to all our members, and beyond them to our fellow Christians generally, to work earnestly in the cause of peace, and for the settlement of international differences by judicial tribunals instead of by resorting to fire and sword.

Australia General Meeting 1902

5.64   Believing war to be contrary to the Christian ideal and a crime against humanity, this General Meeting of the Society of Friends deplores the suggestion made in certain quarters of another war and preparations for war. We rejoice, however, in knowing that there is growing in the popular mind a keener opposition to war preparations and a desire for goodwill and peace among men. We desire to encourage all organisations working towards this end, and as a practical step in its direction we call upon our Commonwealth Government to carry into effect the proposal of the Council of Churches of New South Wales, the Women's Christian Temperance Union, Labour and other organisations who have asked for the abolition of the Compulsory Clauses of the Commonwealth Defence Act and thus prove to the world our sincere desire for peace.

Australia General Meeting 1927

5.65   At this General Meeting of the Society of Friends in Australia we reaffirm our historic testimony that all war and preparations for war are contrary to the spirit and teaching of our Lord Jesus Christ.

Changing conditions and new conceptions must not dim our knowledge of God, nor weaken our faith that through Jesus Christ the peoples of all nations will be brought into one great fellowship.

War is not inevitable. It can be done away with by the establishment of just relations between nations as between individuals. It is to the establishment of such relations that we would direct the minds of Christian men, urging them to work earnestly by all means open to them that the war now raging shall not be closed, as have so many wars in the past, by a peace that will become the seedbed of future wars but by a peace that will open up a lasting era of confidence, goodwill and mutual cooperation. 'The work of righteousness alone is enduring peace.'

Australia General Meeting 1940

5.66   One matter on which we are agreed and which reflects too the views of our Young Friends, is the need to emphasise not only a conscientious objection to war and killing, but our conscientious objective; our determination to take positive action to build a society where war will be unthinkable. We can cooperate with others in this objective but we should be distinguished by the depth of our spiritual inspiration, the breadth of our vision, and the energy of our devotion to this cause.

In bearing in mind the difficult decisions faced by Young Friends we should seek to join them in facing these decisions, hoping to find that corporate guidance from God we expect in our Meetings for Worship and Business. The fundamental basis of our testimony is in our understanding of the life and teaching of Jesus Christ.

Australia Yearly Meeting 1965

5.67   In the world there are wars and rumours of wars, confusion and darkness, danger and doubt. Troubles crowd in upon our daily lives.

Light shouts of morning, but the heavy clouds weigh down.
Where is the mountain?

We gain strength from the gathered Meeting. Far from perfect we are caught up by the Spirit which works through each one.

The path leads upwards into the mist. We can reach for what we can't see.

We are moved to speak out our message to the world; to draw closer to others of like mind. Our way seems clearer.

Sometimes the light strikes on the trees up there, so sharp. It brings them close.

Now we are moved to go out, to tell and to live the vital word. 'Love with My love, and you can save the world.'

Australia Yearly Meeting Epistle 1980

5.68   Friends may have difficulty in recognising the implications of the remark of one member that Quakers are almost an ethnic group. But it might be well for us to consider to what extent we, along with many other well-meaning Christians, are still imprisoned in our Quakerly ghettos (programmed or unprogrammed, pastoral or non-pastoral, evangelical or universalist); in our Christian sectarian national, or hemispherical ghettos; in our ignorance, arrogance, pride or complacency; in the constraints of prejudice arising from race, class or sex.

Few, if any of us, can claim to have escaped the bonds of all these forms of personal imprisonment or intolerance. But we can seek to recognise the limitations to our growth and begin to work on at least one area. We can ensure that in one measure or another we are escaping the confines of one of our personal ghettos, and that we are making some visible contribution towards the development of the global society — of Friends, and of humankind.

Richard Meredith 1982

5.69   Cutting the fence down was a powerful experience. Weeks of discussion in small groups all over the country eventually led to this decision to remove the fence which divides us and replace it with a thread of hope. There are so many divisions and great efforts are made to maintain them: between countries, peoples, classes, women and between the American and British soldiers and between them and us. Removing the fence was a powerful, symbolic act carried out with great calmness. As long as we could we took it down, not to enter the base but to remove the division. The women were wonderful; we started at 4pm with about 2000 women and by midnight had taken down eight of the 15 kilometres perimeter fence. As each section came down a flare was lit to celebrate and to let other women know. Arrests were made continuously.

In the court women told their stories and it was very moving. This afternoon we had a meeting to explore our feelings about some of the violence of the past days. Paratroopers fresh from Ireland and trained to respond violently had abused a number of the women. One woman was rolled in barbed wire and kicked along. It was very hard talking with these men, although we tried as we do with all of them. I found myself thinking, we mustn't encourage these men to be violent and then remembered that that was old thinking, blaming the victim. We talked of the need to find more creative ways of dealing with violence. But women are very creative. Our meetings are creative with singing and silences and a great regard for the uniqueness of each woman's contribution, not always easy for a great planner like myself, but I'm learning.

Sabine Erika 1983

5.70   As Quakers we reject war and other violent responses to conflict. At the same time we recognise that conflict does and will continue to exist in the world. The crisis in the Gulf is of overriding concern at the present time. We recognise the appalling potential for bloodshed and environmental destruction.

There has been a Quaker presence in the Middle East for more than 100 years. Both at the educational level and, since 1948, working with refugees and supporting various projects. Through this continuing presence we are very conscious of the way in which Western intervention in the region is perceived by many people in the Arab world.

Once more, Western forces in the region are serving to inflame the ill feeling of many people in the Middle East. This in turn is undermining what stability there is left in this part of the world. We feel that further such intervention will, in the long run, only serve to exacerbate their anger and strengthen extremist forces.

We are conscious of the double standards practised by the West in the Middle East for many years. This ranges from the drawing of arbitrary boundaries of nation-states in the region after 1918, to the refusal to implement UN resolutions on Palestine/Israel and Lebanon over the last 25 years. The people of the region deserve a constructive response to the crisis — a response which encourages listening and understanding rather than reinforcing religious and cultural differences.

We urge the Australian Government to withdraw our forces from the Gulf, and to work, instead, for a non-military solution, based on sanctions and negotiations through the United Nations.

Australia Yearly Meeting 1991

5.71   If we are to break the feedback loops of market-driven growth, population growth, and high technology serving consumerism, inequity and the arms race, we must work together and pool our strength, integrity and resources. This will involve political lobbying and developing new ideas and alternative institutions.

In the end we must decide what kind of a society we want to live in. Do we want to live in a society that maintains its high consumption lifestyle by condemning others to live in poverty? If not, what steps are we prepared to take to make the kind of society we want into a reality?

Robin Arnold and Dale Hess 1994

5.72   You cannot imagine what it is like here now. Stepping onto the bus, the Chinese women do not look you in the face any more. I used to pick up some of them who lived in our street, but now I don't see them. What can we do? And yet this is the country where people integrate faster than I have ever seen. When I came here in 1950, Greeks, Syrians and Lebanese had a hard time for only a few years. And now you notice hardly any difference at all, and it will be so again, I hope.

I want to walk, if perhaps not always cheerfully over the earth, then at least in the little patches of light there is still left to me in life. And then this [injustice and racism] came along. But I guess God will, as ever, know the best what he wants.

Aase Pryor 1996

5.73   In 1980 I came to Quakers and, marvelling, rejoined my heritage.

My cosy relationship with the Almighty became enormously extended. Jehovah, Allah, Baiami, God — I found to be aspects of the Great Brooding Spirit, dimly revealing itself as we become willing to learn and comprehend. I found that the Indigenous people had always known that everything in the cosmos was family and sacred, inextricably joined together. Science is only discovering that today! But Quaker beliefs also reached out through the cosmos. And that was beautiful.

But I am also afraid, and often angry, because those links which join animate and inanimate together are being broken with savage wars, extinction of species and forests, rending the fabric of that great relationship well understood by Indigenous people, but insolently desecrated and trampled by others.

It's not that I am looking for '... and they lived happily ever after' — end of story — for the Great Spirit must still be weeping over Jerusalem, and Bosnia, and Zaire, and Somalia, and..... and..... That cannot be brushed aside.

An Indian village sadhu, devoted to white magic, urged one in imminent danger to repeat constantly: 'Goodness shall overcome evil, righteousness shall prevail'. George Fox saw that the ocean of Light was greater than the ocean of darkness. Those teachings are sweet.

Muriel Langford 1997

5.74   How to 'speak truth to power' when surrounded by madness, grief, and hopelessness? Here in Budapest I do not hear the NATO bombers lumbering their way to Yugoslavia. I do not hear the whine of the fighter jets, nor am I awakened every hour by the dogs in the neighbourhood who do hear them, and who begin to howl long minutes before their engines are audible to human ears. In Szeged, to the south these sounds are the constant reminders of a war occurring just a few kilometres away.

Most frightening to me is the deafening silence here. No one speaks, or speaks only in whispers, of peace and pacifism. Of the sanctity and value of all fragile human lives. Of the utter futility and cruelty of all organised, coordinated violence and death. There is such grief and hopelessness here, drifting listless through these corridors of learning. Yes, arguments are provoked, and debates concerning human rights, sovereign states, and US economic interests in the region are carried on. But there is not the anguished cry I keep expecting to hear howled into the night air.

Only the dogs in Szeged, confronted every hour with yet another NATO sortie, give vocal protest to this violence. Dear power, listen then to the dogs of Szeged. Stop this madness now, and in place of 200,000 ground troops send in 400,000 civilians armed with food and blankets and medicines and books and clothes and toys and hammers and nails and shovels and saws and music and care. Flood the country, all of Yugoslavia, with aid workers. Do it now, before another life, another home, another town, another train, another bridge, another bird's nest is destroyed. Do it now before another half-world war is triggered. Listen. Come with me beneath the media hype, beneath the political rhetoric. Come lie down in the dirt and grass and let us howl together the only truth I know. Lives are sacred. All lives. Bodies are holy. All bodies. Lives are sacred. All. All. All.

Lucy Tatman 1999

5.75   Friends place much importance on living our lives in such a way that we will 'come to walk cheerfully over the world answering that of God in everyone.' Our strength lies in the inclusive nature of this phrase: it encompasses children, women and men, people of other faiths and denominations, the secular community, refugees, asylum seekers and the 'more than human' world. We remind ourselves that it includes those on all sides of all conflicts and national leaders who shame us.

In a session on facing our own racism we read, 'This work of the heart is essential to living out our Quaker testimony of equality — the deep moral recognition that we are all equal in the Spirit. It is work we must do.' When we find space for the heart, our work for peace and reconciliation has begun. We believe that every human being is entitled to a space in the world which enhances their dignity.

Australia Yearly Meeting Epistle 2003

5.76   And dear Friends, do all that you do in peace and love, and in the fear of God, condescending one unto another, in the simplicity and innocency of life, and truth, and in the wisdom of God... that nothing may be done in strife, to occasion words; for you are called to peace and holiness... and to serve one another in love.

George Fox 1669

5.77   The Light in all your consciences... will let you see Creation, and the Goodness thereof, and will teach you how to use it, and order it in its place... and how to do good with it, so that there will be no Want in creation, nor Cry of oppression; but the Hungry will be fed and the Naked clothed, and the Oppressed set free; and here is the blessing restored to the Creation.

James Parnell (aged 17) 1665

advices & queries

6

6 ADVICES AND QUERIES
(BRITAIN YEARLY MEETING 1994)

We include the Advices and Queries from Britain Yearly Meeting 1994, which are widely used in Australian meetings. (The Australian *Handbook of Practice and Procedure* still contains the 1964 British edition of Advices and Queries, awaiting the development of our own Australian version.)

Introduction

As Friends we commit ourselves to a way of worship which allows God to teach and transform us. We have found corporately that the Spirit, if rightly followed, will lead us into truth, unity and love: all our testimonies grow from this leading.

Although the corporate use of advices and queries is governed by more flexible regulations than in the past, they should continue to be a challenge and inspiration to Friends in their personal lives and in their life as a religious community which knows the guidance of the universal spirit of Christ, witnessed to in the life and teachings of Jesus of Nazareth.

Advices and queries are not a call to increased activity by each individual Friend but a reminder of the insights of the Society. Within the community there is a diversity of gifts. We are all therefore asked to consider how far the advices and queries affect us personally and where our own service lies. There will also be diversity of experience, of belief and of language. Friends maintain that expressions of faith must be related to personal experience. Some find traditional Christian language full of meaning; some do not. Our understanding of our own religious tradition may sometimes be enhanced by insights of other faiths. The deeper realities of our faith are beyond precise verbal formulation and our way of worship based on silent waiting testifies to this.

Our diversity invites us both to speak what we know to be true in our lives and to learn from others. Friends are encouraged to listen to each other in humility and understanding, trusting in the Spirit that goes beyond our human effort and comprehension. So it is for the comfort and discomfort of Friends that these advices and queries are offered, with the hope that we may all be more faithful and find deeper joy in God's service.

Dearly beloved Friends, these things we do not lay upon you as a rule or form to walk by, but that all, with the measure of light which is pure and holy, may be guided; and so in the light walking and abiding, these may be fulfilled in the Spirit, not from the letter, for the letter killeth, but the Spirit giveth life.

Postscript to an epistle to 'the brethren in the north'
issued by a meeting of elders at Balby, 1656

ADVICES AND QUERIES

6.1 Take heed, dear Friends, to the promptings of love and truth in your hearts. Trust them as the leadings of God whose Light shows us our darkness and brings us to new life.

6.2 Bring the whole of your life under the ordering of the spirit of Christ. Are you open to the healing power of God's love? Cherish that of God within you, so that this love may grow in you and guide you. Let your worship and your daily life enrich each other. Treasure your experience of God, however it comes to you. Remember that Christianity is not a notion but a way.

6.3 Do you try to set aside times of quiet for openness to the Holy Spirit? All of us need to find a way into silence which allows us to deepen our awareness of the divine and to find the inward source of our strength. Seek to know an inward stillness, even amid the activities of daily life. Do you encourage in yourself and in others a habit of dependence on God's guidance for each day? Hold yourself and others in the Light, knowing that all are cherished by God.

6.4 The Religious Society of Friends is rooted in Christianity and has always found inspiration in the life and teachings of Jesus. How do you interpret your faith in the light of this heritage? How does Jesus speak to you today? Are you following Jesus' example of love in action? Are you learning from his life the reality and cost of obedience to God? How does his relationship with God challenge and inspire you?

6.5 Take time to learn about other people's experiences of the Light. Remember the importance of the Bible, the writings of Friends and all writings which reveal the ways of God. As you learn from others, can you in turn give freely from what you have gained? While respecting the experiences and opinions of others, do not be afraid to say what you have found and what you value. Appreciate that doubt and questioning can also lead to spiritual growth and to a greater awareness of the Light that is in us all.

6.6 Do you work gladly with other religious groups in the pursuit of common goals? While remaining faithful to Quaker insights, try to enter imaginatively into the life and witness of other communities of faith, creating together the bonds of friendship.

6.7 Be aware of the spirit of God at work in the ordinary activities and experience of your daily life. Spiritual learning continues throughout life, and often in unexpected ways. There is inspiration to be found all around us, in the natural world, in the sciences and arts, in our work and friendships, in our sorrows as well as in our joys. Are you open to new light, from whatever source it may come? Do you approach new ideas with discernment?

6.8 Worship is our response to an awareness of God. We can worship alone, but when we join with others in expectant waiting we may discover a deeper sense of God's presence. We seek a gathered stillness in our meetings for worship so that all may feel the power of God's love drawing us together and leading us.

6.9 In worship we enter with reverence into communion with God and respond to the promptings of the Holy Spirit. Come to meeting for worship with heart and mind prepared. Yield yourself and all your outward concerns to God's guidance so that you may find 'the evil weakening in you and the good raised up'.

6.10 Come regularly to meeting for worship even when you are angry, depressed, tired or spiritually cold. In the silence ask for and accept the prayerful support of others joined with you in worship. Try to find a spiritual wholeness which encompasses suffering as well as thankfulness and joy. Prayer, springing from a deep place in the heart, may bring healing and unity as nothing else can. Let meeting for worship nourish your whole life.

6.11 Be honest with yourself. What unpalatable truths might you be evading? When you recognise your shortcomings, do not let that discourage you. In worship together we can find the assurance of God's love and the strength to go on with renewed courage.

6.12 When you are preoccupied and distracted in meeting let wayward and disturbing thoughts give way quietly to your awareness of God's presence among us and in the world. Receive the vocal ministry of others in a tender and creative spirit. Reach for the meaning deep within it, recognising that even if it is not God's word for you, it may be so for others. Remember that we all share responsibility for the meeting for worship whether our ministry is in silence or through the spoken word.

6.13 Do not assume that vocal ministry is never to be your part. Faithfulness and sincerity in speaking, even very briefly, may open the way to fuller ministry from others. When prompted to speak, wait patiently to know that the leading and the time are right, but do not let a sense of your own unworthiness hold you back. Pray that your ministry may arise from deep experience, and trust that words will be given to you.

Try to speak audibly and distinctly, and with sensitivity to the needs of others. Beware of speaking predictably or too often, and of making additions towards the end of a meeting when it was well left before.

6.14 Are your meetings for church affairs held in a spirit of worship and in dependence on the guidance of God? Remember that we do not seek a majority decision nor even consensus. As we wait patiently for divine guidance our experience is that the right way will open and we shall be led into unity.

6.15 Do you take part as often as you can in meetings for church affairs? Are you familiar enough with our church government to contribute to its disciplined processes? Do you consider difficult questions with an informed mind as well as a generous and loving spirit? Are you prepared to let your insights and personal wishes take their place alongside those of others or be set aside as the meeting seeks the right way forward? If you cannot attend, uphold the meeting prayerfully.

6.16 Do you welcome the diversity of culture, language and expressions of faith in our yearly meeting and in the world community of Friends? Seek to increase your understanding and to gain from this rich heritage and wide range of spiritual insights. Uphold your own and other yearly meetings in your prayers.

6.17 Do you respect that of God in everyone though it may be expressed in unfamiliar ways or be difficult to discern? Each of us has a particular experience of God and each must find the way to be true to it. When words are strange or disturbing to you, try to sense where they come from and what has nourished the lives of others. Listen patiently and seek the truth which other people's opinions may contain for you. Avoid hurtful criticism and provocative language. Do not allow the strength of your convictions to betray you into making statements or allegations that are unfair or untrue. Think it possible that you may be mistaken.

6.18 How can we make the meeting a community in which each person is accepted and nurtured, and strangers are welcome? Seek to know one another in the things which are eternal, bear the burden of each other's failings and pray for one another. As we enter with tender sympathy into the joys and sorrows of each other's lives, ready to give help and to receive it, our meeting can be a channel for God's love and forgiveness.

6.19 Rejoice in the presence of children and young people in your meeting and recognise the gifts they bring. Remember that the meeting as a whole shares a responsibility for every child in its care. Seek for them as for yourself a full development of God's gifts and the abundant life Jesus tells us can be ours. How do you share you deepest beliefs with them, while leaving them free to develop as the spirit of God may lead them? Do you invite them to share their insights with you? Are you ready both to learn from them and to accept your responsibilities towards them?

6.20 Do you give sufficient time to sharing with others in the meeting, both newcomers and longtime members, your understanding of worship, of service, and of commitment to the Society's witness? Do you give a right proportion of your money to support Quaker work?

6.21 Do you cherish your friendships, so that they grow in depth and understanding and mutual respect? In close relationships we may risk pain as well as finding joy. When experiencing great happiness or great hurt we may be more open to the working of the Spirit.

6.22 Respect the wide diversity among us in our lives and relationships. Refrain from making prejudiced judgments about the life journeys of others. Do you foster the spirit of mutual understanding and forgiveness which our discipleship asks of us? Remember that each one of us is unique, precious, a child of God.

6.23   Marriage has always been regarded by Friends as a religious commitment rather than a merely civil contract. Both partners should offer with God's help an intention to cherish one another for life. Remember that happiness depends on an understanding and steadfast love on both sides. In times of difficulty remind yourself of the value of prayer, of perseverance and of a sense of humour.

6.24   Children and young people need love and stability. Are we doing all we can to uphold and sustain parents and others who carry the responsibility for providing this care?

6.25   A long-term relationship brings tensions as well as fulfilment. If your relationship with your partner is under strain, seek help in understanding the other's point of view and in exploring your own feelings, which may be powerful and destructive. Consider the wishes and feelings of any children involved, and remember their enduring need for love and security. Seek God's guidance. If you undergo the distress of separation or divorce, try to maintain some compassionate communication so that arrangements can be made with the minimum of bitterness.

6.26   Do you recognise the needs and gifts of each member of your family and household, not forgetting your own? Try to make your home a place of loving friendship and enjoyment, where all who live or visit may find the peace and refreshment of God's presence.

6.27   Live adventurously. When choices arise, do you take the way that offers the fullest opportunity for the use of your gifts in the service of God and the community? Let your life speak. When decisions have to be made, are you ready to join with others in seeking clearness, asking for God's guidance and offering counsel to one another?

6.28 Every stage of our lives offers fresh opportunities. Responding to divine guidance, try to discern the right time to undertake or relinquish responsibilities without undue pride or guilt. Attend to what love requires of you, which may not be great busyness.

6.29 Approach old age with courage and hope. As far as possible make arrangements for your care in good time, so that an undue burden does not fall on others. Although old age may bring increasing disability and loneliness, it can also bring serenity, detachment and wisdom. Pray that in your final years you may be enabled to find new ways of receiving and reflecting God's love.

6.30 Are you able to contemplate your death and the death of those closest to you? Accepting the fact of death, we are freed to live more fully. In bereavement, give yourself time to grieve. When others mourn, let your love embrace them.

6.31 We are called to live 'in the virtue of that life and power that takes away the occasion of all wars'. Do you faithfully maintain our testimony that war and the preparation for war are inconsistent with the spirit of Christ? Search out whatever in your own way of life may contain the seeds of war. Stand firm in our testimony, even when others commit or prepare to commit acts of violence, yet always remember that they too are children of God.

6.32 Bring into God's light those emotions, attitudes and prejudices in yourself which lie at the root of destructive conflict, acknowledging your need for forgiveness and grace. In what ways are you involved in the work of reconciliation between individuals, groups and nations?

6.33 Are you alert to practices here and throughout the world which discriminate against people on the basis of who or what they are or because of their beliefs? Bear witness to the humanity of all people, including those who break society's conventions or its laws. Try to discern new growing points in social and economic life. Seek to understand the causes of injustice, social unrest and fear. Are you working to bring about a just and compassionate society which allows everyone to develop their capacities and fosters the desire to serve?

6.34 Remember your responsibilities as a citizen for the conduct of local, national, and international affairs. Do not shrink from the time and effort your involvement may demand.

6.35 Respect the laws of the state but let your first loyalty be to God's purposes. If you feel impelled by strong conviction to break the law, search your conscience deeply. Ask your meeting for the prayerful support which will give you strength as a right way becomes clear.

6.36 Do you uphold those who are acting under concern, even if their way is not yours? Can you lay aside your own wishes and prejudices while seeking with others to find God's will for them?

6.37 Are you honest and truthful in all you say and do? Do you maintain strict integrity in business transactions and in your dealings with individuals and organisations? Do you use money and information entrusted to you with discretion and responsibility? Taking oaths implies a double standard of truth; in choosing to affirm instead, be aware of the claim to integrity that you are making.

6.38 If pressure is brought upon you to lower your standard of integrity, are you prepared to resist it? Our responsibilities to God and our neighbour may involve us in taking unpopular stands. Do not let the desire to be sociable, or the fear of seeming peculiar, determine your decisions.

6.39   Consider which of the ways to happiness offered by society are truly fulfilling and which are potentially corrupting and destructive. Be discriminating when choosing means of entertainment and information. Resist the desire to acquire possessions or income through unethical investment, speculation or games of chance.

6.40   In view of the harm done by the use of alcohol, tobacco and other habit-forming drugs, consider whether you should limit your use of them or refrain from using them altogether. Remember that any use of alcohol or drugs may impair judgment and put both the user and others in danger.

6.41   Try to live simply. A simple lifestyle freely chosen is a source of strength. Do not be persuaded into buying what you do not need or cannot afford. Do you keep yourself informed about the effects your style of living is having on the global economy and environment?

6.42   We do not own the world, and its riches are not ours to dispose of at will. Show a loving consideration for all creatures, and seek to maintain the beauty and variety of the world. Work to ensure that our increasing power over nature is used responsibly, with reverence for life. Rejoice in the splendour of God's continuing creation.

6.43   Be patterns, be examples in all countries, places, islands, nations, wherever you come, that your carriage and life may preach among all sorts of people, and to them; then you will come to walk cheerfully over the world, answering that of God in every one.

George Fox, 1656

7

historical

Fairfield, Mt Barker, Joseph May's residence, 1854.
Pencil drawing by Frederick Mackie, 1812–1893. Sketches taken
in the Australian Colonies, Rex Nan Kivell collection NK2092/54,
National Library of Australia PIC T837 nla. pic–an4769570.

7 HISTORICAL PERSPECTIVE

7.1 Beginnings

The movement to which the name 'Quakers' was attributed arose largely from the insights and leadership of George Fox (1624–1690). Individuals who were 'convinced' met in meetings for worship without paid ministers. As organisation developed, the unit became the Monthly Meeting. Monthly Meetings were grouped into Quarterly Meetings and these in turn into a London Yearly Meeting. A continuing part of London Yearly Meeting was Meeting for Sufferings, so named because of the persecution that Friends were subjected to, especially in the 1660s. Other Yearly Meetings developed, among settlers in the North American continent.

On Captain Cook's expedition to Australia in 1770 was Sydney Parkinson, a Quaker, a natural history painter assisting Sir Joseph Banks. He made a remarkable beginning to documenting Australian flora and fauna. The ship's company had been kept in good health as far as Batavia, where the *Endeavour* had to spend two months for repairs. Sickness broke out and the young Sydney Parkinson was one of 23 who died.

The European colonisation of Australia began with the establishment of Sydney as a British penal colony in 1788. Convict centres after Sydney were in Norfolk Island, Van Diemen's Land (the present Tasmania), Moreton Bay and Port Macquarie. For the first decades the new population mostly arrived as convicts, including many Irish political prisoners, with comparatively few free settlers. Many convicts remained as 'emancipists' at the expiration of their sentences.

Quaker concern about the transportation was expressed in England. Elizabeth Fry is remembered for visiting women prisoners and for her efforts to ensure tolerable conditions on the ships carrying them to Australia.

James Backhouse, a nurseryman from the north of England, had sensed a call to service in far-off countries. In time the focus of vision sharpened to identify the far-off country as Australia. Years later he tested his concern before his Monthly Meeting, then the Quarterly Meeting and ultimately before the Yearly Meeting of Ministers and Elders in London in 1830 where it was supported.

He chose as a companion George Washington Walker, a Friend from Newcastle on Tyne. They set out from London in September 1831, arrived in Hobart in February 1832, and left Australia in February 1838. They had spent most of that time in the colony of Van Diemen's Land and less in the then colony of New South Wales, including visits to Port Macquarie and Moreton Bay. There was also a visit to Norfolk Island entailing a three-and-a-half months absence from Sydney, and brief calls in very early Melbourne, Adelaide, Albany and Fremantle.

After two years in Mauritius and South Africa, Backhouse returned to England, and published *A Narrative of a Visit to the Australian Colonies* in 1843. Walker returned to Hobart to settle and to marry Sarah Mather. He became a draper, and established a savings bank.

They came to the Australian colonies primarily 'to discharge a duty of Christian love'. This covered four specific objectives: to preach the gospel to scattered settlers whether bond or free; to investigate the penal system; to find out how the Aboriginals were being treated by the white settlers; and to promote the cause of temperance. Backhouse found time to study natural history and his name has been given to various Australian small trees and shrubs.

7.2   Van Diemen's Land

There were few free settlers' homes in Van Diemen's Land where Backhouse and Walker were not known and welcome. They visited also all the penal establishments — the road-gang camps, the hulks, the town lock-ups, the penitentiaries, the 'female factory', the isolated Macquarie Harbour and the early years of the Port Arthur experiment. Their reports on 'the habits, appearance, disposition and treatment' of Aboriginals are detailed and thorough. The Van Diemen's Land Aboriginals were still being gathered together and drafted to Flinders Island.

Revulsion against white brutality and laudable curiosity based on a respect for the Aborigines as fellow human beings were characteristic of Backhouse and Walker. Their consciences were deeply troubled and they did their best to stir those of their fellow Christians in the colonies and at home in England. They wrote frank reports on Aboriginal settlements, not only on Flinders Island but also on the mainland. They also spoke the truth as they saw it to Governor Bourke in New South Wales, to Lieutenant-Governor Arthur in Van Diemen's Land and to the
British Government.

Though the primary purpose of their journey was a religious and not simply a Quaker duty, they made every effort to seek out Quaker settlers and to establish Quaker meetings. In Hobart, some met for worship with them in their lodgings when they were in town. By March 1833 these meetings were held publicly and regularly in a schoolroom hired for the purpose. They had been in Van Diemen's Land for almost two years before they felt it right, in September 1833, to form a monthly Meeting for Discipline, and the first minutes were made. It was not a promising beginning but they established a small group of Friends which was to be the mainstay of the movement in Australia at least until the 1860s. Quite early in its history the meeting was strengthened by the addition of the Mather family from Lauderdale, formerly Methodists, the Cotton family and Henry Propsting. Monthly meetings alternated between Hobart and Kelvedon, the Cotton home on the east coast at Swanport.

A Van Diemen's Land Yearly Meeting was established in October 1834. Backhouse and Walker were present at its sessions in 1834, 1835 and 1837. Backhouse in 1837 had advanced the money to buy a cottage in Murray Street which became the Hobart Meeting House and was in use until replaced, on the same site, in 1880.

7.3   New South Wales

In December 1834 Backhouse and Walker had come to Sydney from Hobart in company with Daniel and Charles Wheeler in the sloop *Henry Freeling*. English Friends had provided this vessel for the use of the Wheelers in a visit to 'the Pacific Islands and other parts of the Southern World'. Meetings were held on the *Henry Freeling*, and they held the first Friends meeting in Sydney, on land, at a private house when 22 persons were present. A week later a meeting for public worship was held in the Old Court House, four to five hundred people being present. Three weeks later another such meeting was held. The four English Friends then departed on the *Henry Freeling* for Norfolk Island.

After their departure the few persons professing with Friends kept up the meeting for worship and one of them, John Tawell, in 1835 built a meeting house in Macquarie Street. Backhouse and Walker returned to Sydney after three months and continued their mission in New South Wales. After a long tour in the country districts, largely on foot, they returned briefly to Sydney. Backhouse obtained a piece of land in Sydney, facing Devonshire Street, as a burial ground for Friends.

In 1842 Sydney Monthly Meeting was recognised by the Yearly Meeting of Van Diemen's Land as a constituent. However, as years went on numbers fell and the monthly meeting was discontinued. The meeting house was lost to members and sold in 1845. The Friends continued to meet and in 1854 adapted a cottage on the burial ground that Backhouse had obtained, as their second meeting house. In 1860 A Meeting for Discipline was re-established.

7.4   South Australia

South Australia was established as a province without convicts in 1834 and public idealism was evident in the venture. Several Quaker families were among the earliest settlers, one being the large family of Joseph May, arriving in 1839. Motives for emigration were principally economic. A piece of land in North Adelaide was bought for a burial ground. Friends in England had a meeting house constructed and shipped to Adelaide. Its erection on the burial ground was completed in June 1840. It did not come into use as the principal meeting house because Friend settlers who had made their homes in the Mount Barker district were meeting there. A business meeting for South Australia was established in 1843, meeting every two months alternatively in Adelaide and at Fairfield, the May's farmhouse at Mount Barker. A meeting house in Mount Barker was built in 1855.

Backhouse and Walker's westward journey on the *Edora* at the end of 1837 took them first to Melbourne. They were critical of the way arrangements for settlement worked out by John Batman with the Aboriginals of Port Phillip were not being honoured. During their short visit to Adelaide, Friends' meetings for worship were begun. They had no encouraging words to say for the settlements of Albany, Fremantle or Perth.

7.5   Western Australia

An early attempt at European settlement in Western Australia was made at Swan River in 1829, but with little success. In 1841 Marshall Waller Clifton, his wife Elinor and a large family came to Australind, 160 kilometres south of Fremantle. Some of Elinor's friends in England furnished a small meeting house which was erected in Australind. No other Friends were in Western Australia, but she kept in touch by correspondence with Friends in Hobart.

It was not until 1930 that a regular meeting for worship was established in Perth following an extensive visit to Friends in Western Australia by two South Australian Friends, Edwin Ashby and F Watson Coleman. Regular business meetings were held from October 1933.

7.6 Victoria

In the 1850s transportation ceased and the gold rush brought a great increase in population, particularly to New South Wales and Victoria, affecting Friends in common with all others. Melbourne Monthly Meeting was founded. London Yearly Meeting addressed an epistle to 'the Meetings now established as Meetings for Discipline' at Hobart Town, Adelaide, Melbourne and Sydney.

In 1852 Robert Lindsey and Frederick Mackie arrived from England on a mission of religious service. They spent over two years in the colonies — in Van Diemen's Land, New South Wales, South Australia, Victoria, where they were in Ballarat days after the Eureka Stockade. They then sailed to Fremantle where they visited Australind and members of the Clifton family settled in neighbouring places before going north to Perth. At the conclusion of their visiting Mackie remained in the colonies and married Rachel May. Frederick and Rachel became a source of strength to meetings, first in Hobart where they conducted a successful Friends school for some years, and then in Mount Barker where they made a home with Rachel's father, Joseph May.

7.7 Queensland

Queensland became a separate colony in 1859. Two of the first Friend families to arrive were the Smiths and the Hopkins. They had known each other in England and came to Brisbane in l861 and 1862. Friends meetings were held at the home of Rachel Hopkins. By 1866, with the help of English Friends, a meeting house had been built in Makerston Street. Francis Hopkins had married Felicia Smith and was established in Rockhampton, to be joined later by his brother William. Their Quakerly activities led eventually to the building of a meeting house in Rockhampton in 1880. Rosamond Smith established a home for female servants arriving in the colony.

In 1912 the Brisbane, Rockhampton and Toowoomba meetings, which were formerly part of Sydney monthly meeting, were permitted to form themselves into a Queensland Six Months Meeting, which met for the first time in Rockhampton at Easter 1913.

7.8 Deputations

In 1867 Joseph J Neave, accompanied by a cousin Walter Robson, arrived from England, and engaged in earnest labours among the meetings and scattered families of Friends. They witnessed dissension in Sydney meeting, visited Ballarat, Brisbane and Rockhampton and Neave went alone to Capella. In 1869 Robson returned to England. Neave also went back but returned in 1876 with wife and child to settle in Sydney.

In 1874 the London Yearly Meeting, being strongly impressed with a sense of the difficulties under which some of the Australian Friends were labouring, approved of the sending out of a deputation 'to visit them in the love of Christ, trusting that their representatives would have the sympathy and cooperation of those amongst whom they might labour'. The Friends forming this deputation were Joseph J Dymond, Alfred Wright and William Beck.

Although the deputation visited individual Friends wherever possible, they concentrated on the settled meetings, believing that Neave and Robson had carried out pastoral visiting of outlying Friends much more effectively than they could do in the limited time available to them. The deputation saw that the main difficulty was the distance separating Friends from each other, in the cities as well as in the outback, and therefore the lack of social contact so necessary for mutual encouragement and inspiration.

They soon realised that their main objective must be to arrest the disintegration of the Society of Friends in the Australian colonies. Strong support was expressed for the moves to set up an Australian Yearly Meeting, to promote inter-meeting contacts. The need for personal visitation from Friends in England and America was stressed as a means of developing a more confident ministry in Australian meetings.

7.9 Friends School

The deputation recommended in 1876 that the highest priority be given to establishing a Friends School, for the children of Friends in Melbourne. It was realised that financial as well as moral support would be needed if a Friends School was to be established successfully. For almost a decade there was no positive follow up to this move, due to lack of initiative in Australia.

In 1885 Hobart Friends suddenly took the initiative and appointed a committee to investigate the possibility of setting up a school in Hobart. Joseph Mather, Clerk of Hobart Monthly Meeting, became the central figure in the move. It was taken up, without delay, to the Continental Committee of London Yearly Meeting. The clerk of that committee, Edward R Ransome, might be regarded as one of the founders of the school even though he never crossed the equator to visit it. By means of massive personal correspondence with Friends in Hobart he provided invaluable help and encouragement, particularly during crises which the school had to face in its early years.

The first principal, Samuel Clemes, came from teaching in a Friends school in Wigton in Cumberland. He favoured a school that was coeducational and unsectarian, though firmly based on a non-dogmatic approach to the scriptures. He was anxious to include adequate teaching of science. The school had been first proposed as an elementary school catering for about twenty children of Friends, but Joseph Mather anticipated the possibility of some parents of other denominations sending their children to 'a well-conducted Friends' school'. In fact, the school in its first year attracted an unexpected number of non-Friends in its senior classes.

The school opened in leased premises in Warwick Street, Hobart, on 31 January 1887 with an attendance of 33. By the close of that year the numbers had increased to 75. Only a handful of boarders could be accepted because they had to lodge with the headmaster's family. In August 1888 the committee bought a five acre site, Hobartville, on the eastern side of Commercial Road, North Hobart. The school changed its site to Hobartville at the beginning of 1889 and its name to Friends High School.

By 1900 the current number enrolled had risen to 185. Total enrolments up to that time were 678. Of that total Friends' children represented a little more than ten per cent or nineteen per cent if the category 'connected with Friends' is included. But in the boarder group, which represented twenty per cent of total enrolments, the proportion of 'Friends and connected with Friends' was relatively high at sixty per cent. In that same year Samuel Clemes left the school and formed a smaller school on a nearby site which came to be known as Clemes College. This continued for over forty years, but in 1945 there was a reunion under the headmastership of William Oats, who was headmaster until 1973.

The school had begun under a committee chosen by Hobart Friends Meeting and continued so until 1903 when London Yearly Meeting agreed on a future constitution under which LYM appointed the committee of management including therein representatives of other Australian meetings. In 1923 LYM's responsibility was handed over to the Australia General Meeting.

The original name 'The Friends' School' was restored about 1930. Over the years it has grown to be a large school with an enrolment of over 1100. Boarder numbers did not increase but declined to the point where in 1985 boarding facilities at the school were closed down. However, more recently there has been an increase in demand for student accommodation and student residences are provided, enabling the school to establish a more diverse student body and to cater for exchange students and others from overseas.

7.10 Late 1800s initiatives

The year 1887 saw not only the beginning of the Friends School but also the appearance of *The Australian Friend*, a quarterly publication. William Benson, the first editor, who had come to Australia in 1866, married Elizabeth Mather, and settled in Hobart in 1885. In 1890 he transferred to Melbourne and then in 1903 to Sydney. He filled the position of clerk to the meetings in both those towns. In 1887 London Yearly Meeting recognised Sydney as a Meeting for Discipline in unity with LYM and on the same footing as meetings in Tasmania, Victoria and
South Australia.

The first meeting to make a serious move to bring Australian Friends together in conference was Melbourne. Their suggestion for a conference in 1879 was not accepted by the colony meetings, but a repeated offer in 1887 resulted in a Melbourne conference in 1888. Friends came from London, New Zealand, Rockhampton, Sydney, Hobart and Adelaide. William Benson was appointed clerk. The major agenda item concerned the establishment of a General Meeting with the disciplinary powers of a Quarterly Meeting of London Yearly Meeting. However, this move was still considered premature.

The last quarter of the nineteenth century gave promise of an outward looking Society. Members of Melbourne meeting established the Elizabeth Fry Retreat for women in South Yarra and also started a Sunday School for poor children. In Sydney an Adult School, begun in 1879 but discontinued, was revived in 1884 and continued for many years.

By the turn of the century Australian Quakers had begun to establish an identity of their own. The success of their school and their journal gave confidence. A General Australasian Friends Conference was held in Melbourne in May 1901 at the time of the opening of Australia's first Federal Parliament. There was striking unanimity in support of the proposal to establish a General Australasian Meeting or a Standing Federal Committee. This was referred back to monthly meetings. Only New Zealand remained outside. The first General Meeting was held in Melbourne in 1902. A Standing Committee was appointed. Thereafter general meetings were held each September in strict rotation — Melbourne, Sydney, Hobart, Adelaide — until in 1933 a change was made to January. Brisbane (1950), Canberra (1961) and Perth (1966) were later brought into the sequence.

7.11   Young Friends

In 1909 a deputation of two young Friends from Meeting for Sufferings, Wilfred Littleboy and J Eliott Thorp, came to Australia. During their visit four weekend camps for young Friends were held in four different States. Younger Friends have continued to be valued by Quakers, and today Young Friends and Junior Young Friends have their own meetings associated with Australia Yearly Meeting.

Several years later Eliott Thorp came to live in Australia where he became an active member of Adelaide meeting. Another visit of 1909 was that of Thomas Hodgkin accompanied by his wife, his daughter Violet and his son George. They visited all states and attended the General Meeting in Adelaide. Thomas Hodgkin was favourably impressed with the Friends School and made an initial gift towards the building of a new dining hall which is named after him.

7.12   The peace movement

The late 1800s and the Boer War saw a growing attention to the need for public witness against the growth of militarism. The peace movement in Australia received great stimulus in 1888–89 from the visit of the English Friend William Jones who awakened Australian Friends to the importance of the Quaker Peace Testimony. The need for Australians to formulate a corporate judgement on national issues of defence and racial policy was becoming more insistent as Australian colonies moved towards Federation.

In 1909 a Bill to amend the Commonwealth Defence Act proposed to introduce compulsory military training for boys, beginning at age 14. It passed through Parliament in 1910 and the first call to register was made in January 1911. The 1910 General Meeting minuted as follows:

> As those who desire to remain law-abiding citizens of the Commonwealth, we are reluctantly compelled to declare that if these proposals are passed into law we shall be bound by our Christian consciences to refuse to yield them obedience.

The Peace Committee of London Yearly Meeting was particularly interested in developments in Australia and in 1912 sent a deputation of concerned Friends to help in the struggle against the compulsory clauses of the Defence Act. Friends in South Australia took an initiative in founding an Anti-Military Service League, later changed to Australian Freedom League. Percy Fletcher, Commonwealth organiser of the League and editor of its journal *Freedom*, helped organise branches in Melbourne, Hobart and Sydney. The League remained strongest in South Australia. A number of boys suffered military detention for refusing to obey military orders and a number of parents were prosecuted for not permitting their boys to be registered.

These early efforts against boy conscription helped lay the groundwork for the successful 'No' voting in the wartime conscription referenda of 1916 and 1917. The compulsory training law continued until 1929, though latterly it was not strictly enforced. Two Queensland Quaker families moved their residence from town into the country because the compulsion did not apply to children living more than five miles from the nearest training centre.

In 1912 there came to the Friends School, as acting principal while the head Edmund Gower was on leave, J Herbert Thorp, accompanied by his wife and daughter Margaret. Margaret Thorp, later Watts, was an active peace worker in Queensland during the war and later travelled overseas on War Victims Relief work. She returned to Sydney, where as a member of Sydney meeting she gave her time to crippled children, newly arrived immigrants and students from overseas.

During the 1914–1918 war years British Friends established the Friends' Ambulance Unit, and the War Victims Relief Committee, which continued into the 1920s, and a committee for the relief of enemy aliens. Some Australian young members went overseas to join the Ambulance Unit or to help with relief work. Friends had oversight of the distressed aliens — chiefly wives and families of internees. A campaign for collecting clothing resulted in sending many cases of excellent garments overseas which were distributed by Friend workers on the spot.

In the late 1930s Friends helped refugees from persecution in Europe to settle in Australia. In 1940 a boatload of enemy aliens was hurriedly shipped from England on the *Dunera*. On arrival in Australia they were taken to camps in Hay (NSW) and Tatura (Victoria). Meetings for worship after the manner of Friends were held even on the voyage and subsequently in the camps. Later some became Jewish Friends and married within meetings.

The concern for refugees has continued in several waves, through refugee support groups, relationships with individuals, protests and political action.

At the time of the Vietnam war there were vigils in front of Parliament House in Canberra, and in public places in other states. Meetings were held with young men liable to be conscripted under the 'ballot of birthdays' scheme, and some of them became conscientious objectors. The Australian Campaign Against the Arms Trade (ACAAT) began in the 1980s in Townsville among Friends and others, and provides information and a newsletter. At the AIDEX arms exhibition in Canberra in 1989–90 Friends had a stall opposing the promotion of such weapons.

In the 1980s Yearly Meeting Peace Committee supported Peter Jones and David Purnell as peace workers, and two young friends as part-time peace interns. In the 1990s peace work was continued by regional meeting peace and justice committees. Simon Weber of Hobart was accepted as a peace worker for 1992–3 by agreement of these committees.

Friends have been organisers and participants in innumerable imaginative and sustained peace actions — vigils, pilgrimages, camps, seminars, books and articles, radio programs, deputations, letter-writing, nonviolence training including the Alternatives to Violence Program (AVP). Friends have participated in community and ecumenical groups working for peace and social justice. Resources were exchanged with international Quaker bodies such as Quaker UN offices and American Friends Service Committee.

7.13 Indigenous concerns

British Friends were concerned for Australia's indigenous people from earliest settlement. Backhouse and Walker shared their observations forthrightly, both here and in England. For more than two centuries, with other well-meaning people, we have tried (albeit with waves of energy) to 'listen to the Aborigines', and address the trauma of our impact on their world.

Some of our efforts have been: the 'pay-the-rent' response, initiated by settler Robert Cock in 1838 and adopted by AYM in 1988; Barrie Pittock's 1969 Backhouse Lecture, *Towards a Multiracial Society* and Charlotte Meacham's 1972 visit and its aftermath (items 5.16, 5.17); racism workshops; and support for many Aboriginal and Islander projects, particular to the regional meetings involved.

Queensland Regional Meeting in 1988 returned a small block of bushland to the Aboriginal and Islander community, and in 2001 explored points of connection between Quaker and Aboriginal and Islander spirituality. They and QSA are giving support to a current Aboriginal native plant project at Purga.

In the late 90s Quakers for a Reconciled Australia formed, based in Victoria, to circulate concerns and empower action, and in 2001 AYM Indigenous Concerns Committee was established, based in Canberra. In 2002 the Condobolin project, to study racism, and spend time with Aboriginal elders and community at Condobolin, and visit various sacred and important sites, was an invaluable experience for those involved.

Susannah Brindle's 2000 Backhouse Lecture, *To Learn a New Song*, and 2002 *Coming Right Way* (YMICC publication) have informed and challenged us. The Werona committee is currently discerning the right relationship for the Werona property with its Aboriginal custodians.

Friends have been slowly recognising and acknowledging our white cultural arrogance, and grieving how much ancient knowledge and wisdom has been lost to the world.

7.14 Quaker Service Australia

In 1961 Friends Service Council Australia (FSCA) was meeting monthly, under Olive Hirschfeld in Melbourne, and contributing, among other recipients, to South African relief and Aboriginal and Islander welfare. It continued under AYM which made a change of name to Quaker Service Council Australia (QSCA), later shortened to Quaker Service Australia (QSA), and established a Management Committee, centred first in South Australia where the meetings were held. A representative of each Regional Meeting was appointed to keep in touch with the committee.

In 1969 over $8,000 was distributed. In 1971 a contribution was received from the newly-formed Austcare. In 1976 the centre was moved to Tasmania and Valerie Nichols became the convener, later secretary. Disbursements in that year amounted to $28,000, the largest recipient amounts being to Rasulia (India), Vietnam, Guatemala for flood relief, African famine and Hlekweni Rural Development Centre in Southern Rhodesia (now Zimbabwe). In later years there was a link with Australian Development Assistance Bureau (ADAB), now AUSAID, which became the largest source of funds for a time. A paid administrator was employed in the Hobart Office.

QSA funds have come from direct donations, and from fund-raising efforts in each regional meeting. A major contributor has been the Adelaide Quaker shop. It began in 1967 with jumble sales from donated boxes of goods dropped in a basket at Adelaide Railway Station labelled 'For the relief of civilian victims of war in Vietnam' with 'Quaker Service' added. The premises were in Kensington Rd, moved later to a larger site in Norwood South. Voluntary helpers include Friends and attenders and other well-wishers.

By 1998, consideration was being given to passing the substantial responsibility of managing QSA to another regional meeting. This became urgent when Richard Meredith, clerk of the management committee, suddenly died and Sieneke Martin, administrator, left to work overseas. After a review of QSA programs and processes the office was moved into the care of Sydney Regional Meeting. Recent programs have included post-war work in Vietnam, Cambodia and East Timor, as well as projects in Africa and India, and Australian Aboriginal projects.

7.15 Current organisation

The changeover from General Meeting, equivalent to a Quarterly Meeting of London Yearly Meeting, to a new status as an independent Yearly Meeting, was accomplished in 1964 when the first yearly meeting of the new body was held in Melbourne under the clerkship of David Hodgkin.

While they are responsible for clerking sessions of Australia Yearly Meeting and Standing Committee, Presiding Clerks also represent Friends as 'head of church' at national occasions in the community. This is a voluntary position nominated for three-year terms. We have been gifted with wisdom from a variety of experience and knowledge brought by men and women from around Australia: David Hodgkin, Canberra; Richard Meredith, Hobart; Eric Pollard, Sydney; Margaret Roberts, Perth; Bronwen Meredith, Hobart; Ruth Haig, Sydney; Bill Oats, Hobart; Joan Courtney, Hobart; David Purnell, Canberra; Patricia Firkin, Newcastle; Colin Wendell–Smith, Hobart; and Ruth Watson, Perth.

The Religious Society of Friends (Quakers) was incorporated under ACT law on 6 July 1967. In the same year a *Handbook of Practice and Procedure* was printed under the auspices of AYM.

In the first revision of the *Handbook*, in the early 1980s, there was a request for a recognition of committed relationships other then marriage, particularly same sex partnerships. A number of Friends were not able to accept such a statement of recognition and at several successive Yearly Meetings it was not possible to reach a group decision. Finally, at Yearly Meeting 1985 it was agreed to accept a subsection in the *Handbook* which recognised 'a need to offer loving support to those who are sharers in relationships other than marriage — which includes unmarried couples and homosexual pairs'. There was also a need to recognise that 'not all Friends feel able to support these relationships and there is a need for sensitivity to those who have a conscientious belief that heterosexual marriage is the appropriate commitment'. A number of Friends resigned from AYM membership following the Yearly Meeting decision.

A salary payment for a Secretary was introduced in 1961. This appointment would relieve the Clerk of General Meeting of routine work and enable him/her to concentrate more on broader questions of policy and influence of the Society. Eric Pollard, who had been editor of *The Australian Friend* filled the position on a part-time basis for a number of years, but in 1969 applications were invited for a fulltime position.

The successful applicant was Donald Groom, an English Friend, a peace activist who with his wife Erica (nee Hodgkin) had spent sixteen years in India at the Rasulia Friends' Centre. He had worked with Vinoba Bhave in the Land Gifts

Movement, walking long distances and addressing village meetings in the Hindi language. He came to Sydney in March 1970 and operated from an office in the Friends meeting house there, where he established a school for nonviolence. Later in 1970 they moved to Melbourne where he was able to establish an office, as well as to live, in Friends House of which Erica became the warden.

In 1972 he was given leave to attend a triennial of War Resisters International in Sheffield. On his way home he was killed in a plane crash in India. Donald Groom is remembered in Australia by the establishment of the Donald Groom Fellowship which encourages and finds funding for specific projects within a framework of fostering nonviolence, justice and peace. Over 20 awards have been made from the Fellowship.

The work of secretary, following Donald Groom's death, after an interim in which it was done by Enid Haarhoff and Erica Groom, was taken up by David Hodgkin operating from a Friend's house in Canberra. David remained secretary until his death in 1977. Next came David Purnell, until 1985. Topsy Evans of Hobart was then secretary until 1996. Then came Beverley Polzin in Melbourne, until 2004, when Judith Pembleton in Queensland will take over the task.

The Yearly Meeting Secretary is the executive officer of the Society of Friends in Australia and should 'follow the leadings of the Spirit in furthering the activities of the Society in a creative and flexible way'.

In preparation for each Yearly Meeting the secretary assembles Documents in Advance, containing reports of the activities of regional meetings, of Yearly Meeting officers and committees, and other matters for consideration.

Standing Committee meets twice yearly — once immediately before the January Yearly Meeting and again in mid-year. Minutes are circulated in the secretary's newsletters. Minutes of Yearly Meeting and of the associated Standing Committee meeting and also Epistles, attachments to the minutes, testimonies read in respect of Friends who have died, lists of registrants and membership of the current Yearly Meeting committees are all assembled into a document entitled Documents in Retrospect and issued as soon as possible after Yearly Meeting.

In the post-war period there have been a number of changes to places of meeting in the capital cities. Melbourne's meeting house changed from its central city site to a large house in Orrong Road, Toorak in 1953. In Adelaide extensive rooms were added to the old meeting house in 1958, while in 1959 the Eden Hills meeting house, built in 1912 adjoining Edwin Ashby's botanical garden Wittunga, was taken down. Hobart built a new meeting house close to Friends School in 1960. Canberra established its meeting house in 1961. The second Sydney meeting, in Wahroonga, built its meeting house in 1964. Perth moved to its house in Mount Lawley in 1967. Brisbane built on a new site at Kelvin Grove in 1973. Sydney celebrated one hundred years at its Devonshire Street site in 2003.

In 1999 the Avon Valley Meeting in WA disassociated itself from AYM and affiliated with Ohio (conservative) Meeting in the US.

In 1964 the number of members of AYM was just over 900. It grew to 1100 in the early 1980s, but then declined to below 1000 in the first years of the new century. The number of attenders rose from under 200 to 600 in the early 1980s, and to 900 in 2002. Those numbers are based on returns from regional meetings for Documents in Advance. The census of 2001 recorded 1815 people who gave their religion as Religious Society of Friends.

7.16 Spiritual nourishment

From their beginnings, Quakers have shared their spiritual experience and understandings. With Australian distances, letters, newsletters, and now email play a vital role. We have always had 'epistles', and pamphlets, discussions and workshops around Quaker basics, exploration of our Testimonies and Advices and Queries and how we apply them in current circumstances.

Since the later 1900s an Australian edition of the *Wider Quaker Fellowship/Network* newsletter shares articles from overseas; *Seekers Open Letter* carries an Australian conversation on spiritual issues; *Wholeness* (from the Fellowship of Healing), and articles offered with the Yearly Meeting Secretary's newsletter have supplemented *The Australian Friend*. The advent of electronic mail has opened access to Quaker websites worldwide and we continue to develop our own.

An initiative of Nancy Wilkinson, Penn Friends, has linked older Friends with younger friends in correspondence.

Also in the early 90s, in Victoria Frances Thorsen and others developed the Meeting for Learning — including a silent retreat program, a year-long program beginning and ending with retreat weeks, on the ministry of listening and care, for Quakers and like-minded seekers to deepen their own spiritual journey, including projects done at home with support groups from their own meetings. AYM has adopted the program, and Sheila Keane has developed distance learning materials on Quaker Basics which are being used by individuals and groups.

The annual James Backhouse Lectures, initiated at our first Australia Yearly Meeting, in 1964, are an ongoing source of inspiration.

Friends Book Supplies, initiated by Leo Menka of Sydney, was taken up by Yearly Meeting in 1989 to promote the awareness and sale of Quaker publications. It was managed by different regions, the longest stay being in Queensland as Margaret Fell Bookshop. It was wound up at AYM 2000. Internet ordering has taken over its role. Libraries are an important resource of regional meetings and many local meetings.

Several properties have been adapted as accommodation for spiritual refreshment, eg the Fellowship of Healing Friends Lodge in New Norfolk, Tasmania, and Werona bushland in Kangaroo Valley, for camping — particularly loved by Young Friends.

The sharing and support continue — in meetings and Meeting, in clearness meetings, in work groups, over cups of tea and dinner tables, wherever Quakers gather.

HISTORY SOURCES

WN Oats, – *A Question of Survival*, Queensland University Press, Brisbane 1985
    – *Backhouse and Walker*, Blubber Head Press, Tasmania 1981
    – *The Rose and the Waratah*, The Friends School, Hobart 1975
    – *I could Cry for These People*, Quaker Service Australia 1994
Victoria Rigney, *Peace Comes Walking*, Glasshouse Books, Queensland, 2002
Charles Stevenson, – *With Unhurried Pace*, The Religious Society of Friends 1973
    – *The Millionth Snowflake*, The Religious Society of Friends, Adelaide 1987
The Centenary of Australian Quakerism 1832–1932, Hobart Society of Friends 1933
The Australian Friend, Current Editorial State Capital, Bimonthly from 1964

Documents in Advance*	annual
Documents in Retrospect*	annual
Yearly Meeting Minutes*	annual
Standing Committee Minutes*	semi-annual

* Obtained from the central office of the Religious Society of Friends

references

Glossary

Sources

Contributors

Subject Index

Acknowledgments

James Backhouse Lectures

Glossary

Attender – one who, not being in membership, regularly attends a recognised meeting for worship. Attenders, listed with lower-case first names in the list of members, often contribute significantly to the life and support of the meeting.

Australia Yearly Meeting (AYM) – the national body and the annual gathering. As a body AYM consists of all members of regional meetings in Australia, incorporated in the ACT as Australia Yearly Meeting of The Religious Society of Friends (Quakers) Inc. The Yearly Meeting is usually held in January and hosted by regional meetings in rotation.

(James) Backhouse Lecture – an annual lecture, usually given at AYM by a Friend selected several years earlier. Published lectures form a body of perspectives on contemporary and Quaker issues in Australia. The equivalent in Britain is the **Swarthmore Lecture**.

Britain Yearly Meeting (BYM) – (until recently known as London Yearly Meeting LYM) with headquarters in Friends House, London — was the parent body of AYM until 1964 when AYM became autonomous.

Christian faith and practice in the experience of the Society of Friends (CFP) – An anthology of Quaker inspirational writing approved by LYM in 1959. Often referred to as 'the blue book' in Australia, it still lies on the central table during many meetings for worship, along with the larger, later volume *(QF&P)*, 'the red book'.

Clerk – each local meeting and regional meeting has a clerk or co-clerks, nominated usually for three years. The clerk's role is to handle correspondence, to prepare and facilitate business meetings, and to minute decisions and 'the feeling of the meeting' on agenda items. The members present amend or accept each minute during the meeting. Yearly meeting clerk has an assistant clerk and a secretary.

Convincement – belief which is related to convincing experience, apart from doctrine or logical argument.

Elders – also called ministry committee, nominated for three years to help care for the spiritual life and the quality of worship of the meeting.

Friends World Committee for Consultation (FWCC) – the international organisation linking Friends around the world. They have a triennial meeting in different countries.

'Gathered meeting' – a meeting for worship which reaches a depth of silence that touches each person taking part. Spoken prayer or other ministry may emerge from the silence.

Handbook of Practice and Procedure – a loose-leafed book of accumulated wisdom about the running of the Society of Friends, approved by AYM.

Leading – the sense of being directed by the Spirit to act in a particular way.

Light – the inner light, which enlightens each individual and guides our sense of truth or rightness, also referred to as 'the seed', or 'that of God within'. The universal spirit that creates, sustains and heals.

Local meeting – holds a meeting for worship after the manner of Friends at least twice a month, with members of the Society actively associated with the meeting. It is responsible for its own local affairs and is part of a regional meeting.

Meeting – used in several ways by Quakers: the event of corporate worship; a community focused around corporate worship; and a legal entity (AYM Incorporated).

Meeting for learning – an annual retreat program to deepen the capacity for listening and care, often generating year-long projects by the participants. Now includes a distance learning program on Quaker Basics.

Meeting for worship – corporate worship which is central to life as a Quaker. In Australia, meetings are usually held in silence, without any planned ministry or prayer. Every participant is responsible for the quality of the corporate worship. Spontaneous ministry may be given by anyone. Regular worship is a public, advertised event, and all are welcome.

Meeting for worship for business – regular meetings at which decisions are made together, guided by the light in each one present and in the gathered meeting. Minutes are composed by the clerk and accepted at the time.

Members – those who have become committed to a way of worship and life as lived within the Society of Friends and have been admitted into membership by a regional meeting. They share responsibility for the upholding of their meeting.

Ministry – general care and nurture of each other. Also some thoughts, a prayer, perhaps a song one may feel led to stand and share aloud during meeting for worship.

Pendle Hill – Quaker study centre in Wallingford, Pennsylvania USA, named after Pendle Hill in Lancashire, England. In 1652 Firbank Fell and Pendle Hill in England were the scenes of large gatherings inspired by George Fox, which energised the early Friends movement.

Quaker faith & practice – the book of Christian discipline of the Yearly Meeting of the Religious Society of Friends (Quakers) in Britain, 1995, second edition 1999 **(QF&P)**, 'the red book' — the current British anthology used widely in Australia.

Quaker ways – edited by Elizabeth Stevenson and published by AYM in 1996 especially for young people, it gives information about Friends' history, faith and practice.

Recognised meeting/worshipping group – holds a meeting for worship at least once a month and appoints a correspondent to maintain contact with a regional meeting.

Regional meeting (RM) – the primary religious and administrative unit within AYM. RMs have a high level of autonomy and hold a monthly or bi-monthly regional meeting for worship for business. A RM will usually include local meetings and worshipping groups.

Seekers open letter (SOL) – occasional informal publication for sharing thoughts on spiritual matters.

Summer school – a participatory day held in association with yearly meeting each year and arranged by the host meeting on a theme of interest to Australian Quakers.

Testimony – to the grace of God in the life of a deceased Friend, generated by their regional meeting, sometimes read at yearly meeting, and stored in regional meeting files as the Australian Dictionary of Quaker Biography.

The Australian Friend (AF) – is the official journal of AYM, founded in 1887. Published five times a year, it is mailed free to members and by subscription to others.

Wholeness – periodical publication of the Fellowship of Healing, a special interest network within AYM.

Woodbrooke – Quaker study centre in Birmingham UK.

Young Friends(YFs) – a recognised network for members and attenders aged 16 to 30 years. Important gathering times are before and at YM and Easter Camp. YFs nominate 1–2 representatives to all AYM committees.

References of Glossary

Harvey Gillman, *You and the Quaker Tradition*, BYM, 1994.

Handbook of Practice and Procedure, 4th edition, AYM, 1995.

Sources

1 INSPIRATION: OUR FAITH

p.iii   Quoted by M. Fell *QF&P* 19.07.

1.1   Australia Yearly Meeting 2001, Summer School summary 'For Affirming'.

1.2   Jenny Spinks, talk given at Canberra RM residential weekend, 1996.

1.3   George Fox (1624–1691), Journal, edited by J L Nickalls, 1952, p. 2f (entry for 1647). Also *QF&P* 1995, No. 19.02.

1.4   Elaine Polglase, *What Canst Thou Say?*, study held at Sydney RM, 1997.

1.5   Edward Linacre, talk given at Canberra RM residential weekend, 2000.

1.6   Isaac Penington (1616–79) *QF&P* No. 19.14.

1.7   Ruth Sansom (1906–1994), *The Australian Friend*, Oct., 1971.

1.8   Reginald Naulty, 1998 — Marmaduke Stevenson, *QF&P* 1917.

1.9   Michael Jones, 'Convincement', *Quaker Explorations*, Northern Suburbs Local Meeting, Melbourne, 2000.

1.10   Malcolm Whyte, 1991.

1.11   Drew Lawson, *The Australian Friend*, May 1995.

1.12   Sue Wilson, 1996.

1.13   Ursula Jane O'Shea, Living the Way: Quaker Spirituality and Community, (*Backhouse Lecture* 1993), p. 12.

1.14   Nancie Hewitt (1908–89), *The Australian Friend*, Nov. 1982.

1.15   Thomas Kelly (1893–1941), 1938, *QF&P* 26.72, *A Testament of Devotion*, 1941.

1.16   Ruth Sansom (1906–1994), *The Australian Friend*, May, 1987.

1.17   Rufus Jones, 1937, *QF&P* No. 2.16, from the 1937 World Conference, report of Commission 1, p. 13, 'The spiritual message of the Religious Society of Friends'.

1.18   Max Raupach, *The Australian Friend*, July 1990.

1.19   Clive Sansom (1910–81), *The Cathedral*, Methuen, London, 1958.

1.20   Clive Sansom (1910–81), *The Shaping Spirit* (Backhouse Lecture 1965).

1.21   Roberta Turner, 2003.

1.22   Horace Pointing (1891–1976), *QF&P* 21.32, *Art, Religion and the Common Life*, SCM Press, London, 1944, p. 29, 45.

1.23   Frances Parsons, *The Australian Friend*, May 1997.

p.14   Rufus Jones letter to Violet Holdsworth *QF&P* 24.56.

1.24   Bridget Hodgkin (1909–87), *The Canberra Times*, 7 May 1966, and in Vol. 1 of *Quaker Poets*, 1988.

1.25   Jo Farrow, 1994, *QF&P* 21.38.

1.26   Kerstin Reimers, *Seekers Open Letter*, Sept. 1996.

1.27   Dorothy Gibbons (1895–1990) *Wholeness*, 1988.

1.28   Ernest Unwin (1881–1944), 'School Echoes', Dec. 1935, p. 245.

1.29   Clive Sansom (1901–81), op. cit.

1.30   Kelsey Aves, *Hither and Thither. A Personal Anthology of a Tasmanian by Choice*, 1996, p. 32.

1.31   Leanne Mooney, *Seekers Open Letter*, July 1997.

1.32   Deborah Faeyrglenn, 2001.

1.33   William Charles Braithwaite (1862–1922), .CFP 461, from 'Has Quakerism a message to the world today?', *Report of Proceedings of the Manchester Conference 1895*, p. 44. CFP 461.

1.34 Joan Roberts, 1995.

1.35 Andrew Glikson, 2000.

1.36 Howard Brinton, 1931, *QF&P* 21.42, *Creative Worship,(Swarthmore Lecture)*, G. Allen and Unwin, London, 1931, p. 13.

1.37 Rudolf Lemberg (1895–1975), 'The Complementarity of Religion and Science: A Trialogue', *Zygon*, Dec. 1979.

1.38 Gabrielle Watt, 2000.

1.39 Leonce Richards, 1994.

1.40 Rudolf Lemberg (1895–1975), op. cit.

1.41 Kenneth Boulding (1910–93), 1993, *There is a Spirit – The Nayler Sonnets*.

1.42 Max Raupach, *The Australian Friend*, Nov. 1989.

1.43 David Carline, *The Australian Friend*, May 1995.

1.44 Ken Carroll, 1998.

1.45 John Ormerod Greenwood, *Celebration: A Missing Element in Quaker Worship*, *(Backhouse Lecture 1982)*

1.46 Lloyd Williams, *The Australian Friend*, Sept. 1995.

1.47 Susannah Brindle, *To Learn a New Song (Backhouse Lecture 2000)*, p. 60f.

1.48 Eleanor Morphet, *The Australian Friend*, July 1995.

1.49 Ruth Haig, *The Australian Friend*, July 1995.

1.50 Valwyn Beggs, 1995.

1.51 Helen Gould, 1989.

1.52 Mary Mathews (1936–2001), *The Australian Friend*, July 1995.

1.53 Annabelle Cameron (1949–2001), 1999.

1.54 Fiona Gardner, 1996.

1.55 Judith Aitchison, 1999.

1.56 Catherine Heywood, 1996.

1.57 David King, *Seekers Open Letter*, Sept. 1996.

1.58 Jean Talbot, 1996.

1.59 Val Gargett, *The Australian Friend*, May 1990.

1.60 Norman Talbot, *Australian Quaker Christmases*, 1993.

1.61 Charlotte Meacham, *Listen to the Aborigines*, Rel. Soc. of F., Toorak, 1973.

1.62 Lilla Watson, 1998. For Lilla's connection with Quakers see item 5.17.

1.63 John Kelsall, (c. 1700) *Journal of John Kelsall*, quoted in Arnold Lloyd's *Quaker Social History 1669–1738*, Longmans, Green, London/New York, 1950, p. 172f.

1.64 John Woolman (1720–72), CFP 47, *Journal and essays*, ed. A M Gummere, 1922, p. 156.

1.65 William Oats (1912–99), *The Nurture of the Human Spirit*, Friends School, Hobart, 1990.

1.66 Chris Castle, 1999.

1.67 Helen Gould, *The Australian Friend*, Nov. 1992.

1.68 Jewish-Quaker group at Australia Yearly Meeting, 1996.

1.69 David Thomas, *The Australian Friend*, July 1989.

1.70 Margaret Watts (1892–1978), *The Australian Friend*, April 1964.

1.71 Ursula Jane O'Shea, *Living the Way: Quaker Spirituality and Community*, *(Backhouse Lecture 1993)*, p. 23.

1.72 Frank Lindsey (1913–2001), *The Australian Friend*, May, 1997.

1.73 Helen Bayes, *Respecting the Rights of Children and Young People (Backhouse Lecture 2003)* p. 80.

1.74 Shay Jones (1926–67), *Personal Thoughts at Easter*, printed 1967.

1.75 Brigid Walsh, *The Australian Friend*, July, 1992.

1.76 William Oats (1912–1999), op. cit.

1.77 Hector Kinloch (1927–1993), *The Australian Friend*, Nov., 1992.

1.78 David Evans, *The Australian Friend*, May, 1998.

1.79 Warwick Everson (1932–2003) from study held at Canberra RM, 2000 — Isaac Penington, *QF&P* 27.27.

1.80 Jo Vallentine, *Inspirational Talks from the World of Worship*, ABC Books, 1990.

1.81 Otto van der Sprenkel (1906–78), *Friends and other Faiths*, (Backhouse Lecture 1973 – Jan.). Alec Vidler, *The Church in an age of revolution, 1789 to the present day*, Pelican History of the Church, Vol. 5, Harmondsworth, 1961, and Emile Léonard, *A History of Protestantism II*, London 1967.

1.82 Sydney Carter, 1964, whose song has been sung by generations of Australian Quakers. From *Songs of the Spirit*, Religious Education Committee, Friends General Conference, Philadelphia, 1978.

1.83 Monika Smith, *The Australian Friend*, May 1996.

1.84 Ursula Jane O'Shea, *Living the Way: Quaker Spirituality and Community*, (Backhouse Lecture No.28 1993) p. 13f.

1.85 Kenneth Wright (1923–1996), 1992.

1.86 Elizabeth Stevenson, *As the Seed Grows*, ed. C. Stevenson, AYM, North Hobart, 1997, p. 93.

1.87 *Quaker Ways*, ed. Elizabeth Stevenson, 1996 p. 58.

1.88 Sarah Hancock, *The Australian Friend*, May 1987.

1.89 Susannah Brindle, *The Australian Friend*, March 1991.

1.90 John Edwards 1998.

1.91 Peter Wilde, talk given at Hobart study 1998.

1.92 Brian Connor, 2000.

1.93 Sheila Given, 1999.

1.94 Judith Aitchison, ABC program made at Australia Yearly Meeting in Brisbane 2000, by David Busch.

1.95 Annie Wilton (1857–1932), extract from an article in *The Advertiser* Adelaide, 20 December 1924, to mark the tercentenary of the birth of George Fox.

1.96 David Hodgkin (1914–1977), *Quakerism–A Mature Religion for Today*, AYM 1971, republished and revised by Quaker Universalist Fellowship 1995.

1.97 Elizabeth Fry (1780–1845) *Memoir of the life of Elizabeth Fry*, 2nd ed. 1848, Vol. 1, p. 34f. Also CFP 65.

1.98 William Oats (1912–99), op. cit.

2 THE RELIGIOUS SOCIETY OF FRIENDS: OUR PRACTICE

2.1 William Oats (1912–99), *The Nurture of the Human Spirit*, Friends School, Hobart, 1990, p.108.

2.2 Eric Pollard (1905–78), *The Australian Friend*, Dec. 1964.

2.3 Christopher Nordin, 'Is there a Quaker religion' in LYM journal *The Friend*, 1999.

2.4 Chris Castle, 1999.

2.5 Elizabeth Stevenson, *As the Seed Grows*, ed. C. Stevenson, AYM, North Hobart, 1997, p. 44f.

2.6 Gerard Guiton, *Stillness*, 1994.

2.7 Carol McLean, *The Australian Friend*, May 1976.

2.8 Anna Bell, 1997, Jo Farrow, *World in my Heart*, Quaker Home Service, London, 1990.
2.9 Leonce Richards, *The Australian Friend*, May 1993.
2.10 Annabelle Cameron (1949–2001), 1998.
2.11 Brian Connor, *Towards a Theology of Silence*, 1997.
2.12 Ursula Jane O'Shea, leading Britain Yearly Meeting into worship, *The Friend*, May 1995.
2.13 Caroline Stephen (1835–1909), *QF&P* No. 2.39, *Light Arising*, 1908, p. 68.
2.14 Max Raupach, 1999.
2.15 Clive Sansom (1910–81), *The Witnesses*, Methuen, London, 1957.
2.16 Doreen Cope, *The Australian Friend*, July 2000.
2.17 Cathy Davies, 1997.
2.18 Adrian Glamorgan, *As the Seed Grows*, op. cit.
2.19 Australia General Meeting, 1927.
2.20 Anon. from *What do you do in Meeting for Worship?* ed. Margaret Woodward, 1996.
2.21 George Bewley (1684–1749), *A Narrative of the Christian Experiences of GB written by himself*, 1750, p 5f.
2.22 Barbara Wright, 1992.
2.23 Barbara Wright, 1996.
2.24 Jo Vallentine, from Caroline Jones, *The Search for Meaning*, Vol. 2, 1990.
2.25 *The Australian Friend*, Oct. 1903.
2.26 Kenneth Wright (1923–96), 1980.
2.27 L. V. Hodgkin (1869–?), *George Lloyd Hodgkin*, Edinburgh Press, Scotland, 1921.
2.28 Leonce Richards, *The Australian Friend*, Nov. 1992.
2.29 Britain Yearly Meeting *Advices and Queries*, 1994, Point 9.
2.30 Dorothy Gregory (1898–1969), *The Australian Friend*, June 1963.
2.31 Pierre Lacout, *QF&P* 2.12.
2.32 Australia Yearly Meeting Epistle, 1975.
2.33 Frances Parsons, 1990.
2.34 Anon., contribution to a meeting for worship, Tasmania, 1995.
2.35 Sue Parritt, *The Australian Friend*, Nov. 1993.
2.36 Jan de Voogd, 1996.
p.85 Pierre Lacout, God is Silence, Quaker Home Service 1993
2.37 Roger Walmsley, 2003.
2.38 Ernest Unwin (1881–1944), from an article published in *The Sydney Morning Herald*, 24 June 1933.
2.39 Roger Walmsley, from an Irish Famine commemoration address, Perth, 1996.
2.40 *The Australian Friend*, 1981.
2.41 *QF&P* 12.26.
2.42 Reg Naulty, *The Australian Friend*, Nov. 1986.
2.43 Roger Walmsley, 2003.
2.44 Drew Lawson, 1996.
2.45 Quaker Home Service, London, *Am I a Quaker?* pamphlet, 1993.
2.46 *The Australian Friend*, Oct. 1896.
2.47 Epistle to the Meetings now established as Meetings for Discipline of Friends at Hobart Town, Adelaide, Melbourne and Sydney from a Committee of a Meeting for Sufferings, London, July 1855.

2.48 Edgar G. Dunstan, 1956, *QF&P* 11.18, *Quakers and the Religious Quest* (Swarthmore Lecture 1956).

2.49 *QF&P* 12.23.

2.50 Jan Hoffman, *Clearness Committees and their use in personal discernment*, Philadelphia pamphlet, 1996.

2.51 Mark Deasey, *To Do Justly, and to Love Mercy: Learning from Quaker Service*, (Backhouse Lecture 2002), p. 50.

2.52 Helen Bayes, *Respecting the Rights of Children and Young People* (Backhouse Lecture 2003) p. 76.

2.53 William Oats (1912–99), 1981.

2.54 Helen Bayes, op. cit., p. 76f.

2.55 Nancie Hewitt (1908–89), *The Australian Friend*, April 1971.

2.56 Ron Frey, *The Australian Friend*, March 1990.

2.57 Helen Bayes, 2003.

2.58 Helen Bayes, *Respecting the Rights of Children and Young People* (Backhouse Lecture 2003), p. 85f.

2.59 Ursula Jane O'Shea, *Living the Way: Quaker Spirituality and Community* (Backhouse Lecture 1993), p. 12f.

2.60 Charles Stevenson, *With Unhurried Pace*, Rel. Soc. of F., Toorak, 1973.

2.61 Margaret May (1822–?), May family papers, State Library of South Australia, quoted in Elizabeth Kwan, *Living in South Australia: A Social History*, S. A. Govt. Printer, Vol. 1, 1987, p. 30f.

2.62 Devonshire House (London) Monthly Meeting, to members resident in the Southern Hemisphere, 1855.

2.63 Epistle of Iowa Women Friends to Australia, 1873.

2.64 Australia General Meeting, Epistle to New Zealand, 1902.

2.65 Testimony to the grace of God in the life of Margaret Roberts (1910–78), *The Australian Friend*, March 1979.

2.66 Annette Wallis, international visitor, *The Australian Friend*, Sept. 1985.

2.67 Charles Stevenson, op. cit.

2.68 Anna Wilkinson, *The Australian Friend*, 2000.

2.69 *Children and Quaker Meeting: Queries and Ideas*, Australia Yearly Meeting Children's Committee, 1996.

2.70 Thomas Hodgkin (1831–1913), from Louise Creighton, *Life and Letters of Thomas Hodgkin*, Longman, Green & Co., London, 1917.

2.71 Joan Humphreys, Review of Ursula Jane O'Shea's Backhouse Lecture in *The Australian Friend*, March 1993.

2.72 Reg Naulty, *The Australian Friend*, Nov. 1990.

2.73 Gerard Guiton, *The Australian Friend*, July 1991.

3 LIVING OUR FAITH

3.1 David James and Jillian Wychel, *Loving the Distances Between: Racism, Culture and Spirituality*, (Backhouse Lecture 1991) p. 43.

3.2 Margaret Bearlin, *Douglas Hobson Lecture*, Canberra, 1984.

3.3 William Oats (1912–99), *The Nurture of the Human Spirit*, Friends School, Hobart, 1990, p. 13.

3.4 Donald Pescod, *The Australian Friend*, Dec. 1960.

3.5 Jean Richards, 'Christ's Way to Peace', an address to a Weekend of Dedication to Peace, Sydney, 1962.

3.6 Adam Curle, quoted in Australia Yearly Meeting Epistle, 1990.

3.7 Margaret Olesen (1916–97), *Seekers Open Letter*, June 1981.

3.8 Susannah Brindle, 2001.

3.9 William Littleboy (1853–1936), *QF&P* 2.24.

3.10 Frank Lindsey (1913–2001), *Seekers Open Letter*, June 1981.

3.11 Rowe Morrow, 2001.

3.12 Doreen Cope, *The Australian Friend*, July 2000.

3.13 Eric Gargett, *The Australian Friend*, Sept. 1991.

3.14 Anon.

3.15 Jack Dobbs, *QF&P* 21.73.

3.16 Australia Yearly Meeting Epistle, 1975.

3.17 Peter Jones, *The Australian Friend*, Nov. 1979.

3.18 Stewart and Charlotte Meacham, *Imperialism without Invading Armies*, (Backhouse Lecture), 1976.

3.19 Eric Gargett, *As the Seed Grows*, ed. C. Stevenson, AYM, North Hobart, 1997.

3.20 Rowe Morrow, 1998.

3.21 Penny Duckworth, *The Australian Friend*, May 1991.

3.22 Mark Deasey, *To Do Justly, and to Love Mercy, Learning from Quaker Service*, (Backhouse Lecture 2002).

3.23 Annie Wilton (1857–1932), from an article in *The Advertiser*, Adelaide, 20 December, 1924, to mark the tercentenary of the birth of George Fox.

3.24 Sarah Briggs, *The Australian Friend*, May 1992.

3.25 Cyril Gare (1903–85), message to Perth Meeting, 1961.

3.26 Helen Bayes, *Respecting the Rights of Children and Young People*, (Backhouse Lecture 2003), p. 16.

3.27 Helen Gould, *The Australian Friend*, Nov. 1995.

3.28 Bronwen Meredith, *The Australian Friend*, Nov. 1993.

3.29 Brian Connor, *The Australian Friend*, Sept. 1994.

3.30 Australian General Meeting, 1956.

3.31 John Woolman (1720–72) *QF&P* 27.02.

3.32 Florence James (1902–93), *The Australian Friend*, 1982.

3.33 Maureen Powles, from a talk to Victoria Regional Meeting, c. 1985.

3.34 William Oats (1912–99), *A Question of Survival*, U. of Q. Press, St Lucia, 1985, p. 39.

3.35 Statement at the time of the death of Frank Fryer (1875–1942), Adelaide, 1942.

3.36 Mollie Skinner (1876–1955), *The Australian Friend*, 1947.

3.37 Charles Stevenson, *The Australian Friend*, July 1991.

3.38 Quoted on back cover of *Quaker Ways*, ed. Elizabeth Stevenson, 1996.

3.39 David Martin, *The Australian Friend*, July 1972.

3.40 Kevin Clements, *The Australian Friend*, May 1993. Kenneth Boulding gave the first Backhouse Lecture in 1964.

3.41 Sabine Erika, 1997.

3.42 Leslie Storey, 1997.

3.43 Jo Vallentine, 1999.

3.44 Pat Firkin, 2000.

3.45 John Woolman (1720–72), *QF&P* 26.61.

3.46 Helen Bayes, *Respecting the Rights of Children and Young People*, (Backhouse Lecture 2003), p. 10.

3.47 James Backhouse (1794–1869), *A Narrative of a Visit to the Australian Colonies*, 1843.

3.48 Charles Howie, 1910.

3.49 Sabine Willis (Erika), *An Adventure into Feminism with Friends, (Backhouse Lecture* 1983).

3.50 Annabelle Cameron (1949–2001), 2000.

3.51 David Purnell, *The Australian Friend*, Sept. 1988.

3.52 *Gay and Lesbian People in the Religious Society of Friends (Quakers)*, Australia Yearly Meeting leaflet, 1996.

3.53 Judith Aitchison, 1996.

3.54 Margaret Fell (1614–1702), 1664, *QF&P* 19.38.

3.55 Australia General Meeting, 1929.

3.56 Leonce Richards, *The Australian Friend*, 1989.

3.57 Sue Wilson, 1999.

3.58 Isaac Penington (1616–79), 1667, *QF&P* 10.01.

3.59 William Oats (1912–99), *The Nurture of the Human Spirit*, Friends School, Hobart, 1990.

3.60 Helen Bayes, op. cit, p. 88f.

3.61 Gerard Guiton, *The Australian Friend*, Nov. 1991.

3.62 David Purnell, *Changing Men—A Reflection*, 1994.

3.63 Irene Speight (1903–93), *Wholeness*, 1991.

3.64 Katherine McNamara, 1997.

3.65 Reg Naulty, 2000.

3.66 Raymond Wilton (1885–1944), *These Three: Love, Faith, Hope*, Advertiser Pr. Office, Adelaide, 1945.

3.67 Joyce Hudson, *Wholeness*, 1991.

3.68 Malcolm Whyte, 1999.

3.69 David Hodgkin (1914–77), *Quakerism—a mature religion for today*, 1971.

3.70 Katherine Purnell, *Canberra Quakers Newsletter*, Nov. 1996.

3.71 Jenny Spinks, 1996.

3.72 Annabelle Cameron (1949–2001), 1999.

3.73 David Purnell, *The Australian Friend*, May 1992.

3.74 Ruth Watson, 1997.

3.75 Joy Storey, *The Australian Friend*, July 1996.

3.76 Joseph James Neave, concerning an incident in Mansfield, Victoria, 1879, just after three policemen had been killed by Ned Kelly, *The Friend* (London), Sept. 1879.

3.77 Helen Gould, *Wholeness*, Sept. 1990.

3.78 Jean Harkins, 1997.

3.79 *QF&P* 20.28.

3.80 Royal Buscombe, 1987.

3.81 Howard Brinton (1884–1973), *Creative Worship, (Swarthmore Lecture)*, G. Allen and Unwin, London, 1931.

3.82 Jenny Spinks, 1999.

3.83 Roxanne Hendry, *The Australian Friend*, July 1989.

3.84 Jenny Spinks, *Towards an understanding of the Simplicity Testimony*, Canberra Regional Meeting Brochure, 2002.

3.85 Inazo Nitobe (1862–1933), *QF&P* 20.01.

3.86 Richard Griffith (1923–2002), *The Australian Friend*, July 1992.

3.87 David Purnell, *The Australian Friend*, July 1992.

3.88 Frederick Mackie, *Traveller Under Concern*, p. 253f.

3.89 Australia General Meeting, 1925.

3.90 Australia General Meeting, 1935.

3.91 William Oats (1912–99), *Choose your dilemma, an Australian pacifist in Hitler's Europe*, Montpelier Press, Hobart, 1999.

3.92 Australia General Meeting, 1947.

3.93 David Jones, letter to the Minister for Labour and National Service, 1970.

3.94 David Martin, statement made to Brisbane Magistrate's Court, quoted in *The Australian Friend*, June 1971.

3.95 Charles Stevenson, *With Unhurried Pace*, Rel. Soc. of F., Toorak, 1973, p. 39f.

3.96 Jo Vallentine, *The Search for Meaning*, Book Two, Caroline Jones, 1990, p. 106f.

3.97 Mark Deasey, *The Australian Friend*, Sept. 1982.

3.98 Editorial, *The Australian Friend*, March 1991.

3.99 Andrew Wells, *The Australian Friend*, July 1989.

3.100 Ronis Chapman, *The Australian Friend*, March 1990.

3.101 *The Australian Friend*, Nov. 1991.

3.102 Peter Low (New Zealand), visited Australia 1997.

3.103 Brian Connor, *The Australian Friend*, Sept. 1994.

3.104 Donald Groom (1913–72), Vietnam Moratorium Campaign: National Anti-War Conference, 1971.

3.105 William Oats (1912–99), *The Nurture of the Human Spirit*, Friends School, Hobart, 1990.

3.106 Tom Silcock (1910–83), *The Australian Friend*, Sept. 1987.

3.107 Topsy Evans, *The Australian Friend*, May 1990.

3.108 Ronis Chapman, 1997.

3.109 Nancy Shelley, from 'Peace: Who are the Peacemakers?', address to the Australian Association for Religious Education conference, Brisbane, 1986.

p.185 "A declaration from the harmless and innocent people of God called Quakers" given to Charles II on 21 Jan 1661, and printed and sold up and down the streets–*QF&P* 24.04

3.110 Terry Pinnell, *The Australian Friend*, Sept. 1992.

3.111 Laurel Thomas, 1997.

3.112 Wilhelmina Walker, 1999.

3.113 Jane Vaughan Donnelly, 2000 — describing part of Australia's contribution to the 24 hour televised millennial celebration.

3.114 Margaret Bearlin, *Douglas Hobson Lecture*, Canberra, 1984.

3.115 Rose Dryzek, speech written and spoken by Rose at the opening of the Children of the Gulf War photo exhibition, Canberra, 2003.

3.116 Nancy Shelley, address to Symposium on Australia and Nuclear War, Canberra, 1983.

3.117 Stephanie Dowrick, extract from peace meditation at Interfaith Prayers for Peace ceremony, Sydney, 2003.

4 FINDING OUR WAY THROUGH LIFE

4.1 Trish Roberts, talk on 'Community' at Overdale, 1996.

4.2 Helen Bayes, *Respecting the Rights of Children and Young People* (Backhouse Lecture 2003), p. 94.

4.3 Ronis Chapman, *The Australian Friend*, July 1991.

4.4 Helen Bayes, op. cit., p. 46f.

4.5 Norman Talbot, *The Australian Friend*, May 1995.

4.6   William Howitt (1792–1879), unpublished autobiography in A W Howitt Papers, La Trobe Library, State Library of Victoria, p. 68.

4.7   Helen Bayes, *The Australian Friend*, May 1994.

4.8   Elise Boulding, *Our Children, our Partners* (Backhouse Lecture 1996) p. 6.

4.9   Suzi Bayes–Morton, May 1998.

4.10 Christine Larkin, *Experiences of Young People*, a Meeting for Learning Quaker Project, 1999.

4.11 Adrian Glamorgan, *Life–Five Questions*, ed. K. Purnell, a Meeting for Learning Quaker Project, 1996.

4.12 Sue Wilson, 1999.

4.13 John Olive (1952–1992), *The Australian Friend*, July 1982.

4.14 Sonja Glamorgan, October 1999.

4.15 Trish Johnson, *The Australian Friend*, July 1990.

4.16 Humphrey Smith, *To all Parents of Children Upon the Face of the Earth*, 1660, in *Works*, 1683.

4.17 Helen Bayes, in *Life–Five Questions*, op. cit.

4.18 Harold Wilkinson, in *Life–Five Questions*, op. cit.

4.19 Nancy Wilkinson, 1996.

4.20 Anon., *The Australian Friend*, July 1991.

4.21 Sabine Erica, 1997.

4.22 Helen Bayes, *Respecting the Rights of Children and Young People* (Backhouse Lecture 2003), p. 32.

4.23 Beth Reid, 1997.

4.24 Brian Connor, *Australia Wide Quaker Fellowship*, 1995.

4.25 Susannah Brindle, *Seekers Open Letter*, Nov. 1999.

4.26 Carol McLean, *For My Friends*, 1987.

4.27 Olive Pell, Radio broadcast, *By the Way*, 1970.

4.28 Elaine Edwards, *Seekers Open Letter*, Jan.–Feb. 1997.

4.29 South Australian Friends' submission to the South Australian Parliamentary Committee on the Law and Practice relating to Death and Dying, *The Australian Friend*, March 1992.

4.30 Cathy Davies, *Sydney Regional Newsletter*, April, 1998.

4.31 Mary Mathews (1937–2002), 2000.

4.32 Elaine Polglase, 1997.

4.33 George Fox (1624–91), 1691, *QF&P* 21.49.

4.34 Rudolf Lemberg (1897–1975), *Zygon*, Dec. 1979.

4.35 William Penn (1644–1718), 1693, *QF&P* 22.95.

4.36 James Nayler (1617?–1660), 1660, *QF&P* 19.12.

4.37 S. Jocelyn Burnell, 1989, *QF&P* 21.66.

4.38 Jean Carmen, *Queensland Friends Newsletter*, May 1999.

4.39 Rufus Jones (1863–1948), *QF&P* 26.06.

4.40 Val Nichols (1920–1990), *A Sort of Therapy*, V. Nichols, Hobart, 1989.

4.41 Elizabeth Mitchell, *Seekers Open Letter*, March 1999.

4.42 Rachel Kelly (1905–1995) *Seekers Open Letter*, Series 3, No. 1, 1978.

4.43 Joan Mobey, 2000 — John Woolman, *QF&P* 21.64..

4.44 Joyce Hudson, *Wholeness*, 1994.

4.45 Patricia Kerr, *Seekers Open Letter*, March 1999.

4.46 Hannah Chapman–Searle, 1995.

4.47	Annabelle Cameron (1949–2001), *This I Know Experimentally (Experientialy)*, 2000.	**5**	**FACING THE CHALLENGES OF TIME AND PLACE**	
4.48	Heather Kelly (1939–2002), 1997.	5.1	Thomas Kelly (1893–1941), *A Testament of Devotion*, Harper and Bros., New York, 1941.	
4.49	Ronis Chapman, 1997.			
4.50	Gordon Macphail, (1956–1991) *The Australian Friend*, Nov. 1989.	5.2	Australia Yearly Meeting, 1998.	
4.51	Annabelle Cameron (1949–2001), 2000.	5.3	Helen Bayes, *Respecting the Rights of Children and Young People (Backhouse Lecture* 2003), p. 94.	
4.52	Christine Pronger, 1999.	5.4	Isaac Penington (1616–79), 1665, *Letter to a Parent*, 1665.	
4.53	Peter Jones, 1984.			
4.54	Rudolf Lemberg (1897–1975), *Seeking in an Age of Imbalance*, *(Backhouse Lecture* 1966) — Martin Buber, *I and Thou*, T&T Clark, Edinburgh, 1937.	5.5	Elise Boulding, *Our Children, our Partners (Backhouse Lecture* 1996).	
		5.6	Charles Stevenson, *The Australian Friend*, Sept. 1989.	
		5.7	Helen Bayes, op. cit. p. 28f.	
4.55	Sarah Grimke, 1837, quoted in Erica Fisher, *A new-born sense of dignity and freedom (Backhouse Lecture* 1989) p. 10, from Miriam Schneir, *Feminism, the Essential Historical Writings*, Vintage Books, 1972, p. 38.	5.8	Sandy Parker, *The Experience of Caring for One Another Amongst Friends (Quakers)*, unpublished Master of Theology thesis, Melbourne College of Divinity, 2000.	
		5.9	Philip Bywater, *The Australian Friend*, Sept. 1987.	
4.56	Shirley Dunn, *Seekers Open Letter*, May 1996.	5.10	James Backhouse (1794–1869), from a letter to the Governor of New South Wales, *A Narrative of the Visit to the Australian Colonies*, 1836, Appendix P.	
4.57	Cristina Montiel (attended Canberra Regional Meeting while at the Australian National University), 1995.			
4.58	Lyn Traill, in *Life–Five Questions*, op. cit.	5.11	James Backhouse (1794–1869), *James Backhouse Letterbook, No. 2*, 1837, p. 80.	
4.59	Ron Darvell, 1997.			
4.60	Brian Connor, *Seekers Open Letter*, Sept. 1996.	5.12	Daniel Wheeler, *The Memoirs of the Life and Gospel of the late Daniel Wheeler, a Minister of the Society of Friends*, 1842.	
4.61	Penny Challis, 1997.			
4.62	Annabelle Cameron (1949–2001), 2000.			
		5.13	Walter Robson, 1868.	
		5.14	Australia General Meeting, 1940.	
		5.15	A. Barrie Pittock, *Toward a Multi-racial Society (Backhouse Lecture* 1969).	
		5.16	Charlotte Meacham, *Listen to the Aborigines*, Rel. Soc. of F., Toorak, 1973.	

5.17 Ruth Haig, 2001.
5.18 *Friends World News* 101, 1973.
5.19 Margaret Bearlin, *Douglas Hobson Lecture*, 1984.
5.20 *The Australian Friend*, Sept. 1987.
5.21 Bronwen Meredith, *The Australian Friend*, Sept. 1988.
5.22 *The Australian Friend*, Sept. 1988.
5.23 Sue Parritt, *The Australian Friend*, March 1988.
5.24 Muriel Langford (1913–2003), *The Australian Friend*, May 1989.
5.25 Jo Vallentine, *The Australian Friend*, Nov. 1991, from an address given at the Fifth World Conference of Friends at Chevakali, Kenya, Aug. 1991.
5.26 Helen Linacre, 1997.
5.27 Susannah Brindle, *The Australian Friends Newsletter*, July 1997.
5.28 Quakers for a Reconciled Australia, Victoria, 1997.
5.29 Laurel Thomas, 1997.
5.30 Susannah Brindle, 1997.
5.31 David–Rhys Owen, 1997.
5.32 Annabelle Cameron (1949–2001), 1997.
5.33 Australia Yearly Meeting, 1998.
5.34 Susannah Brindle, *To Learn a New Song (Backhouse Lecture* 2000).
5.35 Susan Addison, 2001.
5.36 Susannah Brindle, *Coming Right Way*, YM Indigenous Concerns Committee, 2002, p. 21ff.
5.37 John Woolman (1720–72), *The journal of John Woolman and a plea for the poor: the spiritual autobiography of the great colonial Quaker*, The Citadel Press, N.J., 1961.
5.38 Epistle from Adelaide to Melbourne Annual Meeting 1871.

5.39 Charlotte Meacham, op cit.
5.40 John Ormerod Greenwood (1907–89), *Celebration: A Missing Element in Quaker Worship (Backhouse Lecture* 1982).
5.41 David Johnson, *The Australian Friend*, May 1988.
5.42 David James and Jillian Wychel, *Loving the Distances Between: Racism, Culture and Spirituality (Backhouse Lecture* 1991).
5.43 Scott Bywater, *Quaker Poets 2*, Rel. Soc. of F., Canberra, 1991.
5.44 Sue Parritt, adapted from 'After the Drought: Spiritual and Creative Rebirth', BYM *Quaker Monthly*, June/July 1992.
5.45 John Coe, 1993.
5.46 Susannah Brindle, *The Australian Friend*, 1995.
5.47 Sandy Parker, from a Meeting for Learning Retreat, 1996.
5.48 Jo Vallentine, 1996.
5.49 Susannah Brindle, *The Australian Friend*, Sept. 1996.
5.50 Gerard Fahey, *Seekers Open Letter*, March 1996.
5.51 Brian Connor, *Towards a Theology of Silence*, 1997.
5.52 Adrian Glamorgan, from *As the Seed Grows*, ed. C. Stevenson, AYM, Hobart, 1997.
5.53 General Meeting for Australia, 1959.
5.54 Report of Australian and New Zealand Quaker Delegation to Indonesia, Malaysia and Singapore, at the time of 'Confrontation' of Malaysia by Indonesia, 1965.
5.55 Jean Richards, from an address given as the convener of the Australian Quaker Peace Committee to Sydney Town Hall Christmas Rally, 1965.

5.56 Keith Crook, *Security for Australia* (*Backhouse Lecture* 1970)

5.57 Val Nichols (1920–90) *The Australian Friend*, Sept. 1984.

5.58 Peter Jones, *The Australian Friend*, July 1987.

5.59 Joan Courtney, *The Australian Friend*, Sept. 1989.

5.60 Arthur 'Red' Mitchell, *The Australian Friend*, July 1989.

5.61 Frances Parsons, *The Australian Friend*, July 1992.

5.62 John Greenleaf Whittier (1807–92), from his 'Worship', 1848.

p.284–5 A.E. Floyd, from "The Tree of Peace". H.A. Evans & Son, Melbourne 1950

5.63 Australia General Meeting, 1902. Australians fought in the Boer War in South Africa, 1899–1902.

5.64 Australia General Meeting, 1927.

5.65 Australia General Meeting, 1940.

5.66 Australia Yearly Meeting, 1965.

5.67 Australia Yearly Meeting Epistle, 1980.

5.68 Richard Meredith (1913–98) then General Secretary of Friends World Committee for Consultation, from *Quakerism a Way of Life*, 1982.

5.69 Sabine Erica, *A Day at Greenham Common*, 1983.

5.70 Call for the Non-military Solution to the Gulf Crisis, Australia Yearly Meeting, 1991.

5.71 Robin Arnold and Dale Hess, *The Paradox of Economic Growth and Inequity* (Victorian Association of Peace Studies), 1994.

5.72 Aase Pryor, *Seekers Open Letter*, Dec. 1996.

5.73 Muriel Langford (1913–2003), *The Australian Friend*, May 1997.

5.74 Lucy Tatman, 1999.

5.75 Australia Yearly Meeting Epistle, 2003.

5.76 George Fox (1624–91), Epistle No. E264 1669, 7,341.

5.77 James Parnell (1637–1656), *The Trumpet of the Lord Blown*, 1655, in *Works*, p. 38f. James Parnell met George Fox at 15, became a travelling minister at 16, wrote several influential tracts and died after 11 months of cruel and degrading treatment in Colchester Prison, aged 18.

Visuals from other publications

p. 1, 271 from *A Lake in the Forest*, Kay and Rupert Russell, Hisine Technique, Herberton, 1976

p. 193 from Tasmania Regional Meeting Newsletter, Sept. 1995

p. 214f *The Australian Friend*, May 1994

p. 307 from the Rex Nan Kivell Collection, National Library of Australia (an 4769570)

Contributors

Addison, Susan: 5.35
Aitchison (Pembleton), Judith: 1.55, 1.94, 3.53
anon.: 2.20, 2.34, 3.14, 3.35, 4.20
Arnold, Robin: 5.71
Aves, Kelsey: 1.30

Backhouse, James: 3.47, 5.10, 5.11
Balby elders: p. 300
Bayes, Helen: 1.73, 2.52, 2.54, 2.57, 2.58, 3.26, 3.46, 3.60, 4.2, 4.4, 4.7, 4.17, 4.22, 5.3, 5.7, p. 249
Bayes–Morton, Suzi: 4.9
Bearlin, Margaret: 3.2, 3.114, 5.19
Beggs, Valwyn: 1.50
Bell, Anna: 2.8
Bewley, George: 2.21
Boulding, Elise: 4.8, 5.5
Boulding, Kenneth: 1.41
Braithwaite, William Charles: 1.33
Briggs, Sarah: 3.24
Brindle, Susannah: 1.47, 1.89, 3.8, 4.25, 5.27, 5.30, 5.34, 5.36, 5.46, 5.50, p. 1, 73, 105, 257, 271
Brinton, Howard: 1.36, 3.81
Burnell, S Jocelyn: 4.37
Buscombe, Royal: 3.80
Bywater, Philip: 5.9
Bywater, Scott: 5.43

Cameron, Annabelle: 1.53, 2.10, 3.50, 3.72, 4.47, 4.51, 4.62, 5.32
Carline, David: 1.43
Carmen, Jean: 4.38
Carroll, Ken: 1.44
Carter, Sydney: 1.82, p. 53f
Castle, Chris: 1.66, 2.4
Chapman, Ronis: 3.100, 3.108, 4.3, 4.49
Chapman–Searle, Hannah: 4.46
Challis, Penny: 4.61
Clements, Kevin: 3.40
Coe, John: 5.45
Connor, Brian: 1.92, 2.11, 3.29, 3.103, 4.24, 4.60, 5.51
Cope, Doreen: 2.16, 3.12
Courtney, Joan: 5.59
Crook, Keith: 5.56
Curle, Adam: 3.6

Darvell, Ron: 4.59
Davies, Cathy: 2.17, 4.30
Deasey, Mark: 2.51, 3.22, 3.97
de Voogd, Jan: 2.36
Dobbs, Jack: 3.15
Donnelly, Jane Vaughan: 3.113
Dowrick, Stephanie: 3.117
Dryzek, Rose: 3.116
Duckworth, Penny: 3.21
Dunn, Shirley: 4.56
Dunstan, Edward G.: 2.48

Edwards, Elaine: 4.28
Edwards, John: 1.90
Erika, Sabine: 3.41, 3.49, 4.21, 5.69
Evans, David 1.78
Evans, Halcyon: p. 108, 143, 241
Evans, Topsy: 3.107
Everson, Warwick: 1.79

Faeyrglenn, Deborah: 1.32, p. 132, 197, 234
Fahey, Gerard: 5.49
Farrow, Jo: 1.25
Fell, Margaret: 3.54
Firkin, Pat: 3.44
Fisher, Erica: p. 113
Floyd, A E: p. 285f
Fox, George: p. iii, 1.3, 4.33, 5.75, 6.43
Frey, Ron: 2.56
Fry, Elizabeth: 1.97

Gardner, Fiona: 1.54
Gare, Cyril: 3.25
Gargett, Eric: 3.13, 3.19
Gargett, Val: 1.59
Gibbons, Dorothy: 1.27
Given, Sheila: 1.93
Glamorgan, Adrian: 2.18, 4.11, 5.52
Glamorgan, Sonja: 4.14
Glikson, Andrew: 1.35
Gould, Helen: 1.51, 1.67, 3.27, 3.77, p. 31
Greenwood, John Ormerod: 1.45, 5.40
Gregory, Dorothy: 2.30
Griffith, Richard: 3.86
Grimke, Sarah: 4.55
Groom, Donald: 3.104
Guiton, Gerard: 2.6, 2.73, 3.61

Haig, Ruth: 1.49, 5.17
Hancock, Sarah: 1.88
Harkins, Jean: 3.78

Hendry, Roxanne: 3.83
Hess, Dale: 5.71
Hewitt, Nancie: 1.14, 2.55
Heywood, Catherine: 1.56
Hodgkin, Bridget: 1.24, p. 222
Hodgkin, David: 1.96, 3.69
Hodgkin, L V: 2.27
Hodgkin, Thomas: 2.70
Hoffman, Jan: 2.50
Howie, Charles: 3.48
Howitt, William: 4.6
Hudson, Joyce: 3.67, 4.44
Humphreys, Joan: 2.71

Inazo Nitobe: 3.85

James, David: 3.1, 5.42
James, Florence: 3.32
Johnson, David: 5.41
Johnson, Trish: 4.15
Jones, David: 3.93
Jones, Michael: 1.9
Jones, Peter: 3.17, 4.53, 5.58
Jones, Rufus: 1.17, 4.39, p.14
Jones, Shay: 1.74

Kelly, Heather: 4.48
Kelly, Rachel: 4.42
Kelly, Thomas: 1.15, 5.1
Kelsall, John: 1.63
Kerr, Patricia: 4.45
King, David: 1.57
Kinloch, Hector: 1.77

Lacout, Pierre: 2.31
Langford, Muriel: 5.24, 5.73
Larkin, Christine: 4.10
Lawson, Drew: 1.11, 2.44
Lemberg, Rudolf: 1.37, 1.40, 4.34, 4.54
Linacre, Edward: 1.5
Linacre, Helen: 5.26
Lindsey, Frank: 1.72, 3.10
Littleboy, William: 3.9
Low, Peter: 3.102, p. 177ff

Mackie, Frederick: 3.88, p. 309
McLean, Carol: 2.7, 4.26
McNamara, Katherine: 3.64
Macphail, Gordon: 4.50
Martin, David: 3.39, 3.94
Mathews, Mary: 1.52, 4.31
May, Margaret: 2.61

Meacham, Charlotte: 1.61, 3.18, 5.16, 5.39
Meacham, Stewart: 3.18
Meredith, Bronwen: 3.28, 5.21
Meredith, Richard: 5.68
Mitchell, Arthur 'Red': 5.60
Mitchell, Elizabeth: 4.41
Mobey, Joan: 4.43
Mobey, Justine: p. 193
Montiel, Cristina: 4.57
Mooney, Leanne: 1.31, p. 40, 90, 118, 245
Morphet, Eleanor: 1.48
Morrow, Rowe: 3.11, 3.20

Naulty, Reg: 1.8, 2.42, 2.72, 3.65
Nayler, James: 4.36
Neave, Joseph James: 3.76
Nichols, Val: 4.40, 5.57
Nitobe, Inazo: 3.85
Nordin, Christopher: 2.3

Oats, William: 1.65, 1.76, 1.98, 2.1,
  2.53, 3.3, 3.34, 3.59, 3.91, 3.105
Olesen, Margaret: 3.7
Olive, John: 4.13
O'Shea, Ursula Jane: 1.13, 1.71,
  1.84, 2.12, 2.59
Owen, David–Rhys: 5.31

Parker, Sandy: 5.8, 5.47
Parnell, James: 5.77
Parritt, Sue: 2.35, 5.23, 5.44
Parsons, Frances: 1.23, 2.33, 5.61
Pell, Olive: 4.27
Penington, Isaac: 1.6, 3.58, 5.4
Penn, William: 4.35
Pescod, Don 3.4
Pinnell, Terry: 3.110
Pittock, A Barrie: 5.15
Pointing, Horace: 1.22
Polglase, Elaine: 1.4, 4.32
Pollard, Eric: 2.2
Powles, Maureen: 3.33
Pronger, Christine: 4.52
Pryor, Aase: 5.72
Purnell, Katherine: 3.70
Purnell, David: 3.51, 3.62, 3.73, 3.87

Quakers
  Adelaide Annual Meeting: 5.38
  Australia General Meeting: 2.19 2.64,
    3.30, 3.55, 3.89, 3.90, 3.92, 5.14,
    5.53, 5.63, 5.64, 5.65

Australia Yearly Meeting: 1.1, 2.32, 3.16, 3.52, 5.2, 5.20, 5.33, 5.66, 5.67, 5.70, 5.76
Britain Yearly Meeting: 2.29, 2.41, 2.49
Children's Committee, Australia Yearly Meeting: 2.69
Committee of the Meeting for Sufferings, London: 2.47
Delegation to Indonesia: 5.54
Devonshire House (London) Monthly Meeting: 2.62
Friends World News: 5.18
German internees: 3.38
Iowa Women Friends: 2.63
Jewish–Quaker group: 1.68
Junior Young Friends: 5.2
London Yearly Meeting: 3.79
Margaret Roberts, Testimony to: 2.65
Peace retreat: 3.101
Quakers for a Reconciled Australia: 5.29
Quaker Home Service, London: 2.45
Quaker Ways: 1.87
Queensland Regional Meeting: 5.22
South Australian Friends: 4.29
Summer School: 1.1
The Australian Friend: 2.25, 2.40, 2.46, 3.98
Young Friends: 5.2

Raupach, Max: 1.18, 1.42, 2.14, p. 23, 24, 25, 38, 127, 131, 189f
Reid, Beth: 4.23
Reimers, Kerstin: 1.26
Richards, Jean: 3.5, 5.55
Richards, Leonce: 1.39, 2.9, 2.28, 3.56
Roberts, Joan: 1.34
Roberts, Trish: 4.1
Robson, Walter: 5.13

Sansom, Clive: 1.19, 1.20, 1.29, 2.15
Sansom, Ruth 1.7, 1.16
Shelley, Nancy: 3.109, 3.115
Shelton, Justine: p. 65
Silcock, Tom: 3.106
Skinner, Mollie: 3.36
Smith, Monika: 1.83
Smith, Humphrey: 4.16
Speight, Irene: 3.63
Spinks, Jenny: 1.2, 3.71, 3.82, 3.84

Stephen, Caroline: 2.13
Stevenson, Charles: 2.60, 2.67, 3.37, 3.95, 5.6
Stevenson, Elizabeth: 1.86, 2.5
Storey, Joy: 3.75
Storey, Leslie: 3.42

Talbot, Jean: 1.58
Talbot, Norman: 1.60, 4.5
Tatman, Lucy: 5.74
Thomas, David: 1.69
Thomas, Laurel: 3.111, 5.28
Traill, Lyn: 4.58
Turner, Roberta: 1.21, p. 69, 272, 276

Unwin, Ernest: 1.28, 2.38

van der Sprenkel, Otto: 1.81
Vallentine, Jo: 1.80, 2.24, 3.43, 3.96, 5.25, 5.48

Walker, Wilhelmina: 3.112
Wallis, Annette: 2.66
Walmsley, Roger: 2.37, 2.39, 2.43
Walsh, Brigid: 1.75
Watson, Lilla: 1.62
Watson, Ruth: 3.74
Watt, Gabrielle: 1.38
Watts, Margaret: 1.70
Wells, Andrew: 3.99
Wheeler, Daniel: 5.12
Whittier, John Greenleaf: 5.62
Whyte, Malcolm: 1.10, 3.68
Wilde, Peter: 1.91
Wilkinson, Anna: 2.68
Wilkinson, Harold: 4.18
Wilkinson, Nancy: 4.19
Williams, Lloyd: 1.46
Wilson, Sue: 1.12, 3.57, 4.12
Wilton, Annie 1.95, 3.23
Wilton, Raymond: 3.66
Wood, Patricia: p. 14, 85, 185
Woolman, John: 1.64, 3.31, 3.45, 5.37
Wright, Barbara: 2.22, 2.23
Wright, Kenneth: 1.85, 2.26
Wychel, Jillian: 3.1, 5.42

Subject index

The Table of Contents, p. iv, may also provide useful clues

Aboriginal and Torres Strait Islander Australians,
  advocacy for, 5.11, 5.13, 5.31, 7.2, 7.4
  aspirations, 5.16, 5.17
  assistance, support for, 5.10, 5.14–17, 5.20, 5.27, 7.13, 7.14
  knowledge, talents, 1.44, 1.61, 3.47, 3.113, 5.46
  land, 1.52, 1.54, 1.61, 1.62, 5.23, 5.39, 5.43, 5.48, 7.13
  maltreated, 5.9, 5.10, 5.12, 5.13, 5.18–21, 5.50, 5.58, 7.2
  paying the rent, 3.34, 5.30, 7.13
  reconciliation, reparation, 5.21–23, 5.28, 5.32, 5.34–36, 5.53, 7.13
  schooling, 5.24, 5.26
  spirit, 3.8, 5.25, 5.35, 5.52, 7.13
  tradition, beliefs, culture, 1.43, 1.45, 1.47, 1.62, 7.13
  see also indigenous people
action, 3.6, 3.69, 4.57, 5.71
Adelaide, *see* South Australia
Advices and Queries, 2.45, 2.56, *and see* Chapter 6
ageing, 6.29, *see also* elderly
Albany, *see* Western Australia
American Friends Service Committee, 5.16, 5.17, 7.12
anti conscription, *see* conscription
anti war, *see* war, anti *and* conscription
Anti-Military Service League, 7.12
arms trade, 3.29, 3.100
art, artists, artistry, 1.21–23, 1.28, 1.31–33, 5.40, *see also* creativity
Ashby, Edwin, 7.5
Asia Pacific region,
  Cambodia, Kampuchea, 5.57, 5.61
  India, 3.21, 3.116
  Japan, 3.92
  Korea, 5.60
  neighbours, 3.30, 3.33, 5.18, 5.53, 5.56, 5.58, *see also* New Zealand
  Vietnam, 3.95, 5.55, 7.12, 7.14

atheism, 1.8, 1.89
Aurelius, Marcus, 1.39
Australian Campaign Against the Arms Trade (ACAAT), 7.12
Australian Freedom League, 7.12
Australian Friend, 7.10, 7.16
Australian Friends Fellowship Union, 2.67
Avon Valley Meeting, 7.15
AVP, *see* violence, non, AVP (Alternatives to Violence Project)
awe, 1.55, 1.57
Backhouse Lecture, 7.13, 7.16
Backhouse, James, 2.53, 3.32, 3.34, 5.22, 5.52, 7.1–7.4
Ballarat, *see* Victoria
beauty, 1.19, 1.23, 1.28, 1.46
Beck, William, 7.8
being heard, 3.64
Benson, William, 7.10
Bible, 1.72, 1.75, 1.78, 1.79, 2.16, 2.19, 5.55
bicentennial celebrations, 5.20
blessings, 1.80, 4.40
Boulding, Kenneth and Elise, 3.40
Brummana High School, 3.97
business, *see* meeting for worship for business
Canberra, 7.10, 7.12, 7.13, 7.15
Capella, 7.8 *and see* Queensland
caring, 4.12
centreing, 1.31, 2.8, 2.15, 2.22, 2.26
childhood, children,
  encouragement, respect, support 4.2, 4.4, 4.7, 5.3, 5.4, 6.24
  experiences, 1.55–58, 4.5, 4.6,
  learning, 2.46, 4.3
  participation, ministry, 2.69, 5.5, 5.7
  rearing, 4.15
  valued, 2.69, 3.113, 4.7, 5.57, 6.19
  vulnerability, illness, death, 4.4, 4.9, 4.46
Christ, *see* Jesus
Christianity, 1.65, 1.81, 1.98, 4.58, 5.6, 6.2, 6.4
church, 1.65, 1.66, 1.70, 1.90, 1.96, 5.59
Churches, Australian Council of, 1.70
citizenship, 6.34, 6.35
clearness, clearness meetings, 2.58, 4.19, 6.27
Clemes, Samuel, 7.9

Clifton, Marshall Waller, and Elinor, 7.5, 7.6,
Cock, Robert, 3.34, 7.13
Coleman, F Watson, 7.5
comfort, 4.37, 5.60, 5.61
communication, 2.11, 2.54
community,
    creating, 4.49, 6.18
    spiritual, 2.11, 2.59,
    vows, 2.44
companions, 1.93, *see also* isolation, gathered meeting
concerns, 2.57, 2.58, 4.59, 6.36
Condobolin project, 7.13
Conference, Australian, 7.10
conflict,
    dealing with, 3.72, 3.73
    marital, 4.19
    positive effects 3.74
    settlement of, 3.89
connectedness, 1.11, 1.34, 1.39, 2.54, 5.73, *see also* oneness
conscientious objection, 3.39, 4.59, 5.66, 6.35, 7.12
conscription, anti, 2.67, 3.39, 3.93, 3.94, 3.95, 5.55, 5.64, 7.12
consumerism, material values, possessions, 5.25, 5.53, 5.71, 6.39
convincement, 1.9
coping, 4.41, 4.46, 4.47, 4.49, 4.58
cosmos, 1.39, 1.41, 5.73
Cotton family, 7.2
countryside, 1.57, *see also* environment *and* outback
courage, 4.38, 4.40
Courtney, Joan, 7.15
creation, 1.14, 1.34, 1.38, 6.42
creativity, 1.23–25, 1.27, 1.29, 1.31, 1.32, *see also* art, artists, artistry
creeds, 1.65, 1.70, 1.87
crisis, 3.3, 4.24
Crosland, Herbert, 3.36
cultures, meeting of, 5.20, 5.35, 5.42, 5.52
death,
    dying, 2.49, 4.9, 4.29–35, 4.48, 4.49, 6.30
    life after, 4.32, *see also* immortality
deputations, 7.8, 7.9, 7.11, 7.12

despair, depression, 4.10, 4.24, 4.40, 4.42, 4.44
difference, diversity, 3.52, 3.78, 3.105, 5.15, 5.28, 5.69, 6.16, 6.22
disability, 4.38–40
discernment, 2.37, 2.54, 2.59, 6.7, 6.28, 6.39
disease, *see* illness
disobedience, civil, 3.43
distance learning, 7.16
divided beings, 1.29
divine centre, 1.15
division, removal of, 5.69
divorce, 4.23, 6.25
Donald Groom Fellowship, 7.15
dreaming, 1.44, 5.50
drugs, 4.58, 6.40
Dunera, 3,37, 7.12
Dymond, Joseph J, 7.8
earth , 5.34, 5.37, 5.47, 5.49, 5.50, *see also* land
ecology, 1.38, 5.39, 5.42
ecumenism, other faiths, 1.70, 2.68, 6.6
elderly, 4.25, *and see* ageing
Elizabeth Fry Retreat, 7.10
enlightenment, 1.5–8, 1.10, 1.11, 1.13, 1.63, 1.71, 1.89, 3.44, 4.39, 4.45, 6.7
environment, 3.27–29, *see also* earth, land *and* nature
epiphany, *see* enlightenment
equality, 3.48, 3.52, 5.75
ethics, 4.54
Eureka Stockade, 3.88, 7.6
Evans, Topsy, 7.15
evil, 1.40, 5.73
experience, peak, *see* enlightenment
faith,
    and frailty, 4.26
    and prayer, 3.10
Fell, Margaret, 3.50, 3.54, 7.16
Fellowship of Healing, and Friends Lodge, 7.16
Firkin, Patricia, 7.15
Fletcher, Percy, 7.12
Flinders Island, *see* Tasmania
forgiveness, 3.70, 3.75, 3.77, 6.22
Fox, George, 1.40, 1.71, 1.81, 1.83, 1.86, 1.87, 1.94, 2.19, 2.71, 2.72, 3.8, 3.72, 5.73, 7.1

Fox, George, song, 1.82
Fox, Mathew, 1.80, 4.60
freedom, 3.66
Fremantle, see Western Australia
Friends Service Council Australia (FSCA), 7.14
Friends World Conference, 5.54
Friends' Ambulance Unit, 7.12
friendship, 2.23, 3.36, 3.44, 3.66, 6.21
Fry, Elizabeth, 7.1, 7.10
Fryer, Charles Francis, 3.35
Gandhi, 1.76, 3.96
gatheredness, gathered meeting, 2.9, 2.13, 2.14, 2.22, 2.33, 2.35, 2.56, 2.62, 3.91, 4.59, 5.67, 6.8
General Meeting, Australia, 2.60, 2.64, 3.55, 3.90, 5.63, 5.65, 7.9, 7.10, 7.15
God,
  'that of God in everyone', 1.78, 1.94, 2.8, 3.20, 3.22, 3.40, 3.42, 3.87, 3.93, 4.21, 4.31, 5.2, 5.75, 6.17, 6.43
  dependence on, will of, 3.30, 2.53, 6.3
  experience of, 1.9, 1.89, 2.82, 4.47, 4.52
  guidance from, 2.56
  nature of, 1.4, 1.8, 1.14, 1.38, 1.41, 3.8, 3.45, 4.35, 5.61, 5.75
  paths to, 1.98
  presence of, 1.16, 1.88, 2.4, 2.28, 5.45, 6.26
  principles from, 3.45
  response to, 2.72, 3.4, 3.8, 4.39
  that which is not of God within, 3.71
  see also enlightenment
Godde, 4.47
Gower, Edward, 7.12
Greenham Common, 3.41, 3.114, 3.116, 5.69
grief, 4.9, 4.23, 4.30, 4.50, see also death
Groom, Donald, and Erica, 7.15
Haarhoff, Enid, 7.15
Haig, Ruth, 7.15
Ham Sok Hon, 5.60
Handbook of Practice and Procedure, 7.15
hate, righteous, 5.60
healing, 3.13, 3.14, 3.15, 4.51, 4.61
helping one another, 3.58, 3.59
Henry Freeling, 3.33, 7.3
Hirschfeld, Olive, 7.14
Hobart, see Tasmania
Hodgkin, David, 7.15

Hodgkin, Thomas, family, 2.70, 7.11, 7.15
home, 6.26
homosexuality, see sexuality
Hopkins family, 7.7
human,
  frailty, 3.71
  rights, 3.26
illness, 4.14, 4.32, 4.37, 4.41, 4.43, 4.46, 4.48, 4.50, 4.58
immortality, 4.31, 4.35, see also life, after death
inclusiveness, see equality
Indigenous Concerns Committee, 7.13
indigenous peoples, 3.18, 3.31, 5.22, 5.59, 5.73, see also Aboriginal
individual,
  smallness, 1.41
  uncertainty, insecurity, 4.57, 5.2
injustice, 3.16, 5.72, 6.33, see also oppression
inner promptings, 1.3, 1.7, 1.20, 1.76, 2.4, 2.16, 2.17, 2.50, see also leadings and light
inspiration, see enlightenment and spirit
integrity, see truth
internment, 3.37, 3.38, 7.12
Ireland, 1846 disaster, 2.39
Islam, 3.13
isolation, 1.92, 4.27, 5.38, 5.41, see also remoteness
Israel, 1.69, see also Jews, Judaism
Jesus,
  acknowledgement and centrality of, 1.75, 1.76, 1.77
  inspired and inspiring, 1.5, 1.10, 2.19, 6.2, 6.4
  love, 3.5
  prayer-life, 3.9
  teachings, offerings, actions, 1.3, 1.66, 1.67, 1.74, 3.3, 3.17, 3.63, 3.86, 5.6, 5.36, 5.62
Jews, Judaism, 1.67–69, 5.6, see also Israel and Middle East
Jones Peter, 7.12
Jones Rufus, 4.39
Jones, William, 7.12
journey, spiritual, 1.7, 1.87, 4.1, 5.44, see also seeking
justice, 3.21, 4.53, 5.11, 6.33
Keane, Sheila, 7.16

land, connection to, rights, 1.51, 1.54, 5.17, 5.20, 5.22, 5.43, 5.48, 5.59,
Lau Wai Har, 5.18
leadings, 1.32, 1.73, 2.17, 2.18, 2.52–55, 2.58, 3.16, 3.22, 3.60, 4.47, 6.1
League of Nations, 3.35, 3.89
learning, to live, *and* from others, 3.67, 6.5
life,
    adventure, 3.63, 6.27
    affirmation, 3.116
    after death, 4.32, *see also* immortality
    force, 1.42, 1.46
    inward, 5.4
    mystery, 1.35
light,
    dancing, 1.18
    for my path, 1.94
    held in the, 4.45
    inner, within, 1.5, 2.1, 2.17, 2.19, 3.46, 4.3, 6.5
    insightful, 2.54,
    international, 3.99
    inward in children, 5.3
    led by, 2.51
    living in the, 3.71
    universal, 1.82
    using the, 5.77
Lindsey, Robert, 7.6,
listening, 2.4, 2.16, 2.18, 2.25, 2.32, 2.34, 2.73, 3.64, 4.28
Littleboy, Wilfred, 7.11
London Yearly Meeting, 1.81, 2.60, 7.1, 7.6, 7.8–10, 7.12, 7.15
love,
    all embracing, 3.5, 5.49
    here and now, 5.1
    in service, 3.24, 3.25, 5.76
    mutual, 3.61
    of God, 3.4
    power of 3.86
    spoken, 3.57
    supportive, 4.42, 4.39
    to save the world, 5.67
Mackie, Frederick, 7.6
Margaret Fell Bookshop, 7.16
marriage, partnership, 4,12, 2.49, 4.19, 4.20, 6.23, *see also* singleness
Martin, Sieneke, 7.14
materialism, *see* consumerism

Mather family, 7.1, 7.2, 7.9, 7.10,
May, Joseph and Rachel, 7.4, 7.6
Meacham, Charlotte, 5.16, 5.17
meditation, 1.7, 1.27, 1.32, 3.12
Meeting for Discipline, 2.46, 7.2, 7.3, 7.6, 7.10,
Meeting for Learning, 7.16
Meeting for Sufferings, 2.64, 7.1, 7.11
meeting for worship for business, 1.2, 2.37–39, 2.43, 2.58 , 6.14, 6.15
meeting for worship,
    concerns about, 1.72, 2.61, 2.62
    essence of, 1.2, 2.3, 2.8, 2.9, 2.15, 2.19, 2.22–4, 2.29, 2.34, 4.26, 5.67, 6.8,
    essence of, 6.9, 6.10
    experience in, 2.21, 2.36, 2.68. 3.75, 4.47, 6.12
    in the open air, 1.43
    simplicity, 3.81
    see also ministry
Melbourne, *see* Victoria
membership, 2.44, 2.45, 2.48
men, masculinity, 3.51, 3.62, 4.11, 4.18
Meredith, Bronwyn and Richard, 7.14, 7.15
metaphor, myth, 1.37, 1.76
Middle East, 1.69, 3.97, 5.70
millenium, welcomed, 3.113
ministry, 2.9, 2.25–28, 2.31, 2.33, 2.34, 2.52, 6.13
money, 2.45, 2.55, 3.83, 6.20, 6.37, *see also* Aboriginal, paying the rent
Moreton Bay, *see* Queensland
mother, motherhood, 3.108, 4.14, 4.17, 4.20
Mount Barker, *see* South Australia
music, 1.30, *see also* creativity
mystery, 1.34–36, 2.52
mysticism, 1.22, 1.71, 3.1
nature,
    attachment to, 1.49, 4.60, 5.47
    caring for, 3.27, 3.28, 6.42
    cooperation with, 1.59
    inspiration from, 1.11, 1.50, 1.51, 5.44, 5.45
    knowledge of, 5.46
    learning from, 1.26, 3.27
    natural order, 1.59, 3.9
    solace from, 1.53, 1.56–58, 2.35, 4.62, 5.51
    song of the earth ,1.47
    the wonder in, 1.46, 1.48, 1.52, 1.55, 1.60

Neave, Joseph James, 2.55, 2.60, 5.13, 7.8
New South Wales, 7.1, 7.3, 7.6, 7.8, 7.10, 7.12, 7.14–16
New Zealand, 2.64, 2.70, 3.33, 4.30, 5.42, 5.54, 7.10, *see also* Asia Pacific region
Nichols, Valerie, 7.14
non violence, *see* violence, non
Norfolk Island, 7.1, 7.2
O'Shea, Janey, 2.71
oath, 3.55, 6.37
Oats, William, 7.9, 7.15
oneness, 1.16, 1.39, 1.41, 1.44, 1.52, 2.22, 3.1, 3.4, *see also* connectedness
oppression, 3.16, 3.17, 4.55, 5.11
outback, 1.61, 5.39, 2.65, 7.8, *see also* countryside, environment, remoteness, *and* isolation
Pabeny, Aziz, 3.82
pacifism, 3.91, 4.59
Parkinson, Sydney, 7.1
pastoral care, 2.65
peace,
    acting and working for, 3.96, 3.102, 3.103, 3.106, 3.109, 3.116, 5.54, 5.63, 7.12
    and the environment, 3.29
    community, 2.72
    dedication to, 4.53
    inner, 3.4, 3.72
    lasting , 5.65
    living it, 3.117
    Mothers and Others for, 3.108
    testament, 3.29, 5.53, 7.12
    universality of, 3.86, 3.105
peak experience, *see* enlightenment
Pembleton, Judith, 7.15
Penington, Isaac, 1.79
Penn Friends, 7.16
Penn, William, 3.80, 5.22
Pine Gap, 3.96
place, spirit, 1.43, 1.45, 1.58, *see also* land
plainness, 3.79, *see also* simplicity
Pollard, Eric, 7.15
Polzin, Beverley, 7.15
Port Macquarie, *see* New South Wales
power, 3.103
prayer,
    by children, 5.4
    effectiveness, 3.7, 3.9, 3.13, 3.15, 3.65, 6.10

forms, focus, 1.7, 1.14, 3.8, 3.11, 3.12
in faith 3.10
Presiding Clerk (AYM), 7.15
principle, godly, 3.45, 4.35
prison and prisoners, 3.42, 3.54, 3.96, 3.110–112
promptings, 1.9, 1.76, 2.4, 2.54, 3.59, *see also* leadings
Propsting, Dick, 2.55
Propsting, Henry, 7.2
Purnell, David, 7.12, 7.15
Quaker Service Australia (QSA), 3.95, 7.13, 7.14
Quaker Service Council Australia (QSCA), 7.14
Quakers for a Reconciled Australia, 7.13
Quaker United Nations Offices, 3.99, 7.12
Quakers and Quakerism,
    activities, 2.57, 3.23, 3.87; *see also* by State
    and aboriginal spirituality, 5.35
    and other faiths, 2.3, *see also* ecumenism, Islam *and* Jews, Judaism
    characteristics, 1.94, 1.95
    concerns, 2.3
    corporate experience, 1.96, *see also* gatherdness
    developments and activities in Australia, *see also* by State
    discipline, 2.47
    discovery, becoming one, 1.6, 1.88, 4.11
    faith, beliefs, teaching, ways, 1.65, 1.66, 1.70, 1.85–.87, 1.89, 1.90, 1.95, 1.96, , 2.8, 3.87,   4.16, 5.73
    history, pre-Australia, 1.81, 1.83, 1.95, 3.23, 3.87, 7.1
    history, in Australia, *see* Chapter 7 *and* by State
    limitations, 5.68
    organisation and methods, 1.90, 2.57
    shop, 7.14
    task, 1.84
    testimonies, *see* Our Testimonies in Chapter 3
    The Religious Society of Friends (Quakers) in Australia, incorporation, 7.15
    worship, *see* meeting for worship *and* meeting for worship for business
Queensland, 5.22, 5.24, 5.35, 7.1, 7.7, 7.8, 7.10, 7.12, 7.13, 7.15

racism, 4.17, 5.27, 5.29, 5.59, 5.72, 5.75, 7.13
Ransome, Edward R, 7.9
regeneration, 3.27, 3.28, 4.26
relationships, 3.5, 3.61, 3.68, 3.107, 6.25, 7.15
religion, 1.64, 1.66, 1.96, 1.97, 4.37
Religious Society of Friends, *see* Quakers
religious, heritage, 1.68
religious, truth, 1.78
remoteness, 2.61–63, 2.66, 7.8, *see also* isolation
rent, paying the, *see* Aboriginal, paying the rent
risk, 2.73, 3.60
ritual, 4.60
Roberts, Margaret, 2.65, 7.15
Robson, Walter, 5.13, 7.8
Rockhampton, *see* Queensland
Rowntree, John Wilhelm, 4.39
sacraments and sacredness, 1.45, 1.47, 1.92, 2.1
Sansom, Clive, 5.6
School, Adult (Sydney), 7.10
School, Friends (Melbourne, Hobart), 2.70, 7.6, 7.9, 7.11, 7.12
School, Ramallah Friends, 1.69
school, for Aborigines, 5.24, 5.26
science, 1.33, 1.36, 1.37, 1.40, 4.34, 4.54
searching, *see* journey
Secretary, 7.15
seed, 3.8, 3.46, 4.33
Seekers Open Letter, 7.16
seeking, 1.91–94, *see also* journey
self, self examination, self discovery, 1.42, 2.9, 2.14, 4.57, 6.11, 6.31, 6.32
selfishness, 4.12, 5.34
sensitivity, 2.32, 3.59
separation, division, 1.29, 4.18, 4.19, 4.21, 4.23, *see also* divorce
service, 3.20, 3.22, 3.24, 3.30, 5.76
sexuality, 3.52, 4.11, 4.13, 4.50, 4.55, 7.15
sharing, 2.66, 3.60, 3.92, 6.20
silence, 1.17, 1.42, 2.3, 2.5, 2.7, 2.9, 2.14, 2.27, 2.31
silence, deafening, 5.74
simplicity, 3.53, 3.79–82, 3.84, 3.85, 6.41
singleness, 4.12, *see also* marriage
Smith family, 7.7
song, 1.47, 3.43, 4.15, 5.50

sorry, 5.32, 5.33. *see also* Aboriginal, reconciliation
South Australia, 2.61, 3.34, 3.35, 7.1, 7.4, 7.6, 7.14, 7.15
Spirit, Holy, 1.5, 1.12, 1.75, 6.3, 6.9
spirit,
 affirmation, recognition, expression, 1.1, 1.73, 1.76, 4.36
 authority, 1.2
 God, divine, 1.4, 1.7, 2.7, 2.25
 guidance, 5.67
 healing, 3.13, 3.14
 life, 2.2, 3.60
 living in, 3.2
 place, 1.12, 1.43, 1.45, 1.58, 5.47
 strength of, 1.75
 truth, 1.6
 waiting on, 2.24, 2.71
 within, 1.16
spiritual benefit, goal, values, 1.28, 3.84
Standing Committee (AYM), 7.15
Stephenson, Marmaduke, 1.8
stillness, 2.5, 2.6, 2.10, 2.13, 2.20, 5.52, 6.3
stress, dealing with, 4.52, 4.56
suffering, 3.4, 4.43–45, 4.47
Sydney, *see* New South Wales
symbol, 3.98, 3.114, 5.69
Tasmania, 3.47, 7.1, 7.2, 7.6, 7.9, 7.10, 7.12, 7.14–16
Tawell, John, 7.3
terra nullius, of heart 5.52
testimonies, *see* Our Testimonies in Chapter 3
Thorp, J Eliott, 7.11
Thorp, J Herbert and family, 7.12
Thorsen, Victoria Frances, 7.16
threshing meeting, 2.41
tolerance, 3.19, 3.76, 4.41
Toowoomba, *see* Queensland
transcendence, *see* enlightenment
truth, 1.37, 1.78, 3.53, 3.56, 6.37, 6.38
United Nations, 3.99, 5.70, *see also* Quaker United Nations Offices
unity, 2.12, 2.40
Van Diemen's Land, *see* Tasmania
victims, 3.18
Victoria, 3.88, 7.1, 7.4, 7.6, 7.8, 7.9, 7.10, 7.12–15

Vidler, Alec, 1.81
violence,
  dealing with, 3.101, 5.69
  domestic, 3.107, 4.20, 4.21, 4.22
  in parenting, 4.15
  justification, 3.97
  long term effect, 3.87
  personal involvement, 3.101
violence, non,
  AVP (Alternatives to Violence Project), 3.110–112, 7.12
  displayed, 3.100
  faith in humanity, 3.104
  models of, 3.87, 3.97
  power, 3.41
  with respect, 3.43
virtues, 3.85
vows, 2.44
vulnerability, 4.4, 4.26, 4.57, 5.31
walk cheerfully over the earth, 5.75, 6.43
Walker, George Washington, 2.53, 3.32, 5.22, 7.1–4,
Wallis, Annette, 2.66
War Victims Relief, 3.35, 7.12
war,
  aftermath of, 3.98, 3.115
  and environment, 3.29
  anti, 3.87, 3.41, 5.63–65, 5.70, 5.74, 6.31, *see also* conscription
  challenge of, 5.55;
  devastation of, 5.57
  Friends in, 3.35, 7.12
  participation in, 3.97
  prevention of, 3.5, 3.90. 3.116
  toys, media, children, 3.108, 4.3, 5.57;
Watson, Len and Lilla, 5.17
Watson, Ruth, 7.15
Watts, 7.12
Weber, Simon, 7.12
wellbeing, societal, 2.42
Wendell–Smith, Colin, 7.15
Werona, 7.13, 7.16
Western Australia, 5.14, 7.1, 7.4–6, 7.10, 7.15
'What canst thou say', 1.2, 1.85, 1.87
Wheeler, Charles and Daniel, 3.33, 7.3
Wholeness, 7.16
Wider Quaker Fellowship Network, 7.16
Wilkinson, Nancy, 7.16

women, 3.49, 3.50, 3.116, 4.55, 5.69
Woolman, John, 2.75, 3.18, 4.43, 5.22, 5.53
words, power of, 3.57
world,
  distraction, 3.80
  making it better, 4.49
  worship, 3.14, 5.7, 5.62
Wright, Alfred, 7.8
Yearly Meeting, Australia, 2.57, 2.58, 2.66, 3.95, 5.20, 5.27, 5.33, 7.2, 7.8, 7.11, 7.15
youth and young friends, 2.46, 2.67, 2.68, 4.8, 4.10, 4.17, 5.2, 5.8, 5.66, 7.11, 7.16

Acknowledgments

We are grateful to all those who have shared their work for this publication and each of us regrets material we have not been able to include.

Extracts from Britain Yearly Meeting publications and Swarthmore Lectures are published by permission of Britain Yearly Meeting of the Religious Society of Friends.

The interview with Jo Vallentine from The Search for Meaning by Caroline Jones, published by the Australian Broadcasting Corporation is reproduced by permission of the ABC and Caroline Jones.

Frederick Mackie's pencil drawing of 'Fairfield' is used by permission of the National Library of Australia. Nan Kivell Collection (an 4769570).

Every effort has been made to source material and to find and approach owners of copyright. Any omissions will be rectified in later printings if current owners can be brought to our attention.

Australia Yearly Meeting Faith and Practice Committee members: Helen Bayes*, Susannah Brindle, Annabelle Cameron, Ronis Chapman, Valerie Clements, Jane Donnelly, Sabine Erika, Joon Garfit*, Adrian Glamorgan*, Heather Herbert*, Lister Hopkins*, Ruth Johnston, Tim Johnstone, Glynne Jones, Elizabeth Kwan*, Katherine Purnell*, Michael Richards, Justine Shelton, Roberta Turner*, Vidya (Lyndal Sutton)*, Nancy Wilkinson, Lloyd Williams*

Convenors:	1994–2001	Glynne Jones and Nancy Wilkinson
	2002	Elizabeth Kwan*
	2003	Heather Herbert*

Designer: Fiona Edge

Editors: Shona Verity and the committee

Historian: Lister Hopkins, with suggestions from Susannah Brindle, Sheila Given, Peter Jones, Kathy Rundle, Roger Sawkins, Charles Stevenson, Pam Wendell–Smith and Patricia Wood

Indexer: Malcolm Whyte

Preparers of text: Design Edge and Les Hartshorn

Regional correspondents: Susannah Brindle, Elizabeth Stevenson, Norman and Jean Talbot, Barbara True, Susan Wilson, Patricia Wood, Barbara Wright, Ann Zubrick

Reviewers: Helen Bayes, Susannah Brindle, Adrian Glamorgan

Visual ministry editors: Deborah Faeyrglenn, Peter Farrelly, Erica Fisher, Joon Garfit, Carol Guida, Lainie Shorthouse and Roberta Turner

* current member

Innumerable lives not named in this book have helped to form, and continue to sustain and inspire, Australian Quaker life, faith and thought.

James Backhouse Lectures

1964	*The Evolutionary Potential of Quakerism*, Kenneth Boulding
1965	*The Shaping Spirit*, Clive Sansom
1966	*Seeking in an Age of Imbalance*, Rudolf Lemberg
1967	*On Being Present Where you are*, Douglas Steere
1968	*In the Spirit of the Family*, William N. Oats
1969	*Toward a Multi-racial Society*, A. Barrie Pittock
1970	*Security for Australia*, Keith A. W. Crook
1972	*The Quaker Message*, L. Hugh Doncaster
1973	(Jan) *Friends and other Faiths*, Otto van der Sprenkel
1973	(Aug) *Pilgrimage Toward the Fountainhead*, Yukio Irie
1975	*A Time to Reap. A Time to Sow – Retirement*, W.A. McNaughton
1976	*Imperialism Without Invading Armies*, Charlotte and Stewart Meacham
1977	*Papua New Guinea: Third World on our Doorstep*, Mary Woodward
1978	*Wisdom: The Inward Teacher*, Margaret Wilkinson
1979	*Quakers in the Modern World*, J. Duncan Wood
1981	*What Jesus Means to Me: Jesus the Liberator*, Roger C. Wilson
1982	*Celebration: A Missing Element in Quaker Worship*, Ormerod Greenwood
1983	*An Adventure into Feminism with Friends*, Sabine Willis
1984	*Pilgrims for Justice and Peace*, Peter D. Jones
1985	*For All the Saints*, Gerald Priestland
1986	*Looking for Meanings of My A-Bomb Experience in Nagasaki*, Susumu Ishitani
1987	*The Vision that Connects – Building the Future We Choose*, Carol and Dougald McLean
1988	*Creative Conflict*, David Purnell
1989	*A New-born sense of Dignity and Freedom*, Erica Fisher
1990	*Quakers in Politics: Pragmatism or Principle?* Jo Vallentine and Peter D. Jones
1991	*Loving the Distances between: Racism, Culture and Spirituality*, David James and Jillian Wychel
1993	*Living the Way: Quaker Spirituality and Community*, Ursula Jane O'Shea
1994	*As the Mirror Burns: Making a Film About Vietnam*, Di Bretherton
1995	*Emerging Currents in the Asia-Pacific*, Donna Kyle Anderton and Barbara Baker Bird
1996	*Our Children, Our Partners – A New Vision for Social Action in the 21st Century*, Elise Boulding
1997	*Learning of One Another. The Quaker Encounter with Other Cultures and Religions*, Richard G. Meredith
1998	*Embraced by Other Selves. Enriching Personal Nature through Group Interaction*, Charles Stevenson
1999	*Myths and Stories, Truth and Lies*, Norman Talbot
2000	*To Learn a New Song. A Contribution to Real Reconciliation with the Earth and Its Peoples*, Susannah Kay Brindle
2001	*Reconciling Opposites: Reflections on Peacemaking in South Africa*, Hendrik W van der Merwe
2002	*To Do Justly, and to Love Mercy: Learning from Quaker Service*, Mark Deasey
2003	*Respecting the Rights of Children and Young People: A New Perspective on Quaker Faith and Practice*, Helen Bayes

Darwin

Guildford
Mt. Lawley
Fremantle

South Coast

Quakers in Australia

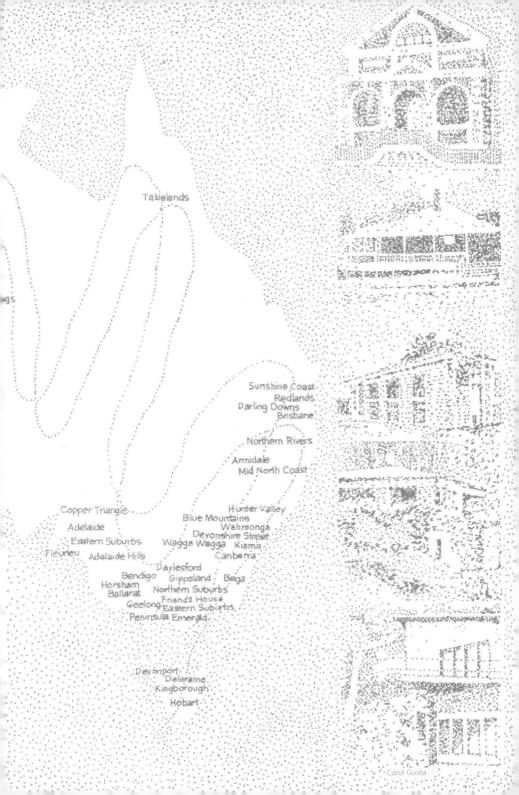